D0899133

Studies in Applied Regional Science

This series in applied regional, urban and environmental analysis aims to provide regional scientists with a set of adequate tools for empirical regional analysis and for practical regional planning problems. The major emphasis in this series will be upon the applicability of theories and methods in the field of regional science; these will be presented in a form which can be readily used by practitioners. Both new applications of existing knowledge and newly developed ideas will be published in the series.

STUDIES IN APPLIED
REGIONAL SCIENCE 16

ECONOMIES OF SCALE, TRANSPORT COSTS, AND LOCATION

GEORGE NORMAN
Department of Economics
University of Reading

Martinus Nijhoff Publishing
Boston / The Hague / London

For Denise

Distributors for North America:
Martinus Nijhoff Publishing
Kluwer Boston, Inc.
160 Old Derby Street
Hingham, Massachusetts 02043

Distributors outside North America:
Kluwer Academic Publishers Group
Distribution Centre
P.O. Box 322
3300 AH Dordrecht, The Netherlands

Library of Congress Cataloging in Publication Data

Norman, George, 1946–
    Economies of scale, transport costs, and location.

    (Studies in applied regional science ; v. 16)
    Based on the author's thesis, University of Cambridge.
    Bibliography: p.
    1. Cement industries – Great Britain – Case studies.
2. Industries, Location of – Great Britain – Case studies.
3. Economies of scale – Case studies. I. Title.
II. Series.
HD9622.G72N67   338.6'042   79–9545
ISBN 0–89838–017–0

Printed in the United States of America.

PREFACE

The presence of nonconvexities does severe damage to conventional theories of the firm and of the individual. The essential contribution of location theory, however, is in a world in which there are such nonconvexities. If resources are distributed evenly and the usual convexity assumptions made, then economic activity would be distributed evenly; there would be no concentration of production. Thus the statement that is usually made, that the standard results carry over to a world in which there is spatial choice, is too weak and fails to capture the essence of location theory.

Nevertheless, we must also concede that, while the introduction of the spatial dimension is interesting and fruitful when (perhaps only when) there are non-convexities, space should not be thought of as a panacea whereby problems— those associated with economies of scale, for example—can be made to disappear. There is no guarantee, for example, that production units will be operated in convex regions of their total cost curves, even if they are constrained to operate in a 'space economy'.

These considerations led to the conclusion that the role of spatial choice and the determinants of such choice would be best analysed by case study. This book is one such study. It is based on my doctoral dissertation at the University of Cambridge, financed by a grant from the Social Science Research Council.

Most of the research was completed over the period 1972–77, under the supervision of Mr. M.J. Farrell until his death in October 1975, and subsequently under the supervision of Professor D.G. Champernowne and Mr. G.B. Aneuryn Evans.

It is difficult to express the extent of my debt to Mr. Farrell. The work demands he imposed, and his continual advice and encouragement, were more than a research student had any right to expect. I also wish to express my sincere thanks to Professor Champernowne and Mr. Aneuryn Evans for the help they gave me in the closing stages of my research, and to my colleagues in the seminar group at the University of Reading for their helpful comments.

Finally, I would like to thank my wife for her constant help and encouragement.

CONTENTS

Preface   v

1 INTRODUCTION   1
   1.1 Introduction   1
   1.2 Least Cost Theory   2
   1.3 Central Place and Interdependence Theories   7
   1.4 Other Approaches   13
   1.5 Conclusion   13

2 OBJECTIVES OF THE STUDY   17
   2.1 Introduction   17
   2.2 Description of the Theoretical Model   19
   2.3 Comparison with Planning Models   21
   2.4 Objectives of the Study   22

**3 STATIC MODEL ASSUMING CONSTANT
RETURNS TO SCALE**   26
   3.1 Introduction   26

vii

3.2 Locational Framework, Production and
     Transport Activities   27
3.3 Disposal Activities   31
3.4 Constraints Imposed by Market Conditions   32
3.5 Costs   35
3.6 Specification of the Programming Problem   36

4 THE STATIC MODEL WITH INCREASING RETURNS   40
4.1 Introduction   40
4.2 Economies of Scale   41
4.3 Respecification of the Programming Problem:
     Part I   47
4.4 Quasi Production Activities   48
4.5 Total Production Costs for the Production Unit   49
4.6 Respecification of the Programming Problem:
     Part II   51
4.7 Combination of Production Activities   53
4.8 Computational Problems   56

5 CASE STUDY – THE CEMENT INDUSTRY   60
5.1 Introduction   60
5.2 Structure of the UK Industry   61
5.3 Cost Structure of the Industry   63
5.4 Spatial Characteristics of the Market Area   78

6 SOLUTION OF THE STATIC CEMENT STUDY   88
6.1 Introduction   88
6.2 The Calculated Optimum for the Static Study   88
6.3 Sensitivity Analysis   94
6.4 Comparison of Actual and Calculated Distributions   118
6.5 Conclusion   125

7 THE MULTIPERIOD VERSION OF THE MODEL   127
7.1 Introduction   127
7.2 Restatement of the Objective   129
7.3 Decision Variables   129
7.4 Cost Parameters   132
7.5 Edge Effects Associated with Capital Costs   139

7.6 The Multiperiod Programming Problem 142
7.7 Case Study: Introduction 144
7.8 Market Area 145
7.9 Cost Estimates 146
7.10 Solution of the Multiperiod Model 152

8 A COMPETITIVE MODEL ASSUMING FREE ENTRY 157
8.1 Introduction 157
8.2 The Model 158
8.3 Application to the Cement Study 160
8.4 Solution of the Model 162
8.5 The Model Assuming Elastic Demand 164
8.6 Solution Assuming Elastic Demand 166
8.7 Conclusions 170

9 CONCLUSIONS 171
9.1 Introduction 171
9.2 Programming Models and Planning 172
9.3 The Nature of Economies of Scale 173
9.4 Locational Influences: The Static Model 174
9.5 Locational Influences: The Multiperiod Model 176
9.6 The Competitive Model 176
9.7 The Importance of Transport Costs 177

APPENDICES
A Additional Notation for Chapter 3 178
B Summary of United Nations (1963) Study Data 180
C General Data for the U.K. and U.S. Cement Industries 182
D Regional and County Analysis of Cement Deliveries
(1965) 187
E Estimated Road Distances 189

Bibliography 190
Notes 195
Index 202

TITLES OF FIGURES

5.3 Total Capital Costs related to Capacity
5.4 Average Capital Costs related to Capacity
5.5 Elements of Capital Costs
5.6 Elements of Capital Costs
5.7 Coal Deposits in England and Wales
5.8 The Market Area

6.2 Calculated Optimum for Case 0
6.6 Calculated Optimum for Case 1
6.7 Calculated Optimum for Case 2
6.18 Calculated Optimum for Case 3
6.20 Comparison of Actual and Calculated Optimum Distributions

8.2 The Market Area
8.3 Solution of the Competitive Model
8.5 Solution of Competitive Model with Demand Curve 1
8.6 Solution of Competitive Model with Demand Curve 2

TITLES OF TABLES

5.1   UK Cement Manufacture 1966
5.2   Structure of the UK Cement Industry 1963
5.3   UK Imports and Exports of Cement and Clinker
      (th. tons)
5.4   Energy Consumption per tonne of Cement 1960–68
5.5   Mineral Consumption per tonne of Cement
5.6   Wage Rate in UK Cement Manufacture 1963
5.7   Relationship between Plant Capacity and Capital
      Costs: West German Cement Industry 1971
5.8   Relationship between Capital Costs and Plant
      Capacity: UK and West German Cement Manufacture
5.9   Total Production Costs: UK Cement Manufacture 1963
5.10 Quasi Production Activities for UK Cement Manufacture
      1963
5.11 Transport Costs (shillings per ton) 1966
5.12 Towns and Estimated Demand
5.13 Potential Production Sites

6.1   Calculated Optimum for Case 0
6.2   Calculated Optimum for Case 1
6.3   Calculated Optimum for Case 2
6.4   Indices of Cost Parameters
6.5   Calculated Optimum for Case 3
6.6   Cement Capacity (m. tonnes) England and Wales
6.7   Frequency Distribution of Plant Capacities
6.8   Comparison of Plant Size Distribution

7.1   Demand Estimates (m. tonnes p.a.)
7.2   Capital Cost Estimates UK Industry 1963 (£m.)
7.3   Linear Spline for Capital Costs
7.4   Minimum Efficient Scale
7.5   Index of Capital Costs (1963 = 100)
7.6   Adjusted Linear Spline for Capital Costs
7.7   Index of Labour Costs in UK Cement Production
       (1963 = 100)
7.8   Labour Costs UK Cement Production
7.9   Indices of Input Costs to Transport (1963 = 100)
7.10   Index of Transport Costs (1963 = 100)
7.11   Variable Costs (u_{kvt}) in Cement Production
7.12   Operating Costs on Pre-Existing Capacity
7.13   Calculated Optima for the Multiperiod Model

8.1   Transport Costs 1966
8.2   Solution of the Competitive Model
8.3   Solutions of the Competitive Model with
       Elastic Demand

Appendix B
B.1   Capacity, Capital Costs, Labour Requirements
B.2   Physical Inputs per ton of Cement related to Capacity

Appendix C
C.1   Size Distribution by Employment
C.2   Comparison of Establishments: excluding small
       establishments

Appendix D
Regional and County Analysis of Cement Deliveries

Appendix E
Estimated Road Distances

ECONOMIES OF SCALE, TRANSPORT COSTS, AND LOCATION

1 INTRODUCTION

1.1 INTRODUCTION

It has often been stated that the spatial aspect of economic behaviour is a relatively neglected area of economic analysis. A casual glance at many of the microeconomic theories of competition—perfect, monopolistic, or oligopolistic—gives the impression that economic activity is assumed to be conducted at a single point in space.[1] Nevertheless, the relative neglect of space is much less obvious now than it was even ten years ago. Indeed, it could reasonably be claimed that in recent years location theory and regional science have been two of the major growth areas of economic (and geographic) investigation.

There is little to be gained from a comprehensive survey of this rapidly growing body of literature, however; the more so since it is generally derivative of a few major works. We shall therefore concentrate upon drawing out the main elements of some of the most important and original contributions and indicating the directions in which they have been developed by later researchers.

Theories of location are generally concerned with answering one of two questions. On the one hand we might ask: given the locations of all other economic agents, how should a particular agent—perhaps a firm or industry—be located in order to minimise the cost of serving a known, fixed demand? Alternatively we

1

might ask: given that firms are in direct competition with each other, how will they locate and what market areas will they control, given knowledge of demand conditions (but not necessarily an inelastic demand)?

The first question lies at the heart of the 'least cost' approaches to location theory based generally upon the work of Weber, while the second question underlies the development, firstly, of the central place theories of Lösch and Christaller, and, secondly, of the interdependence theories of Hotelling and Smithies.

1.2 LEAST COST THEORY

1.2.1 Alfred Weber

By far the most influential of the least cost theories has been that developed by Weber. Weber was concerned with analysing the 'general factors of location which are applicable to a greater or lesser degree in every industry' (Weber 1929, p. 23). These factors were split into those which determined the interregional location of industry and those which influenced the intraregional location (the latter were termed *forces of agglomeration*).[2] Analysis was developed in three main stages on the basis of a number of simplifying assumptions as follows:

(i) The firm choosing a location is characterised by a fixed-coefficient, constant-returns-to-scale technology.
(ii) Inputs to production are available in unlimited supply at fixed prices independent of location.
(iii) These inputs are either ubiquitous, i.e. available everywhere in the market area, or strongly localised at a few known sources. (Note that assumption (ii) applies to localised and ubiquitous factors of production.)
(iv) Demand is concentrated at a number of known points and is fixed at each point.[3]
(v) Transport is feasible in any direction, and transport costs for each commodity are directly proportional to weight and distance transported.

The first stage of the analysis is to answer the question: Given assumptions (i) through (v), how should a firm locate to minimise the cost of serving a particular consumption site? This stage is concerned with interregional locational forces, in particular the role of transport costs. A visual analysis is probably simplest.

Assume a technology consuming two localised inputs a_1 and a_2 to produce one unit of output for final demand. The localised inputs are available at sources M_1 and M_2 respectively in Figure 1.1 and the consumption site is at C. Trans-

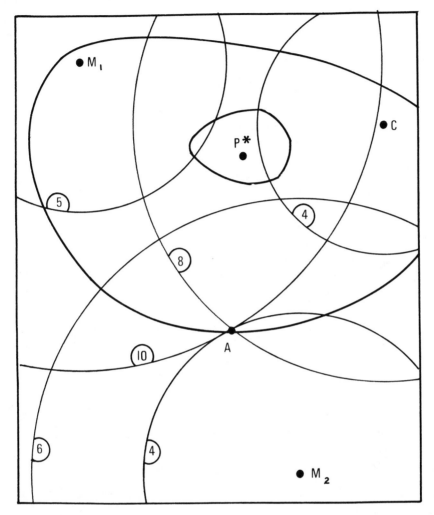

Figure 1.1.

port costs for each commodity are respectively t_1, t_2 and t_C. Find the least cost location P* from which to supply C.

We begin by constructing lines of equal assembly costs around M_1 and M_2 and equal delivery costs around C. These lines are termed isotims. (See Alonso, 1964.) Given assumption (v), each isotim is a circle centered on either M_1, M_2 or C, and any circle of radius r is associated with assembly or delivery costs of $t_i a_i r$ ($i = 1, 2, C$)—where $a_C = 1$. Total assembly and delivery (i.e. transport) costs associated with production at any point P in the market area are then obtained by summing the transport costs associated with the three isotims passing through P (e.g assembly and delivery costs at point A in Figure 1.1 are £22). We can join lines of equal transport costs to form isodapanes—the heavy curves in Figure 1.1. Thus, for example, all points on the isodapane through A are associated with transport costs of £22. Given the assumptions (i) through (v), these isodapanes will radiate from a unique, best, i.e. least cost, location P*.

Clearly, the position of P* is determined by the relative importance of the quantities t_1a_1, t_2a_2 and t_C. For example, if $t_1a_1 > t_2a_2 + t_C$ then the least cost location would be at M_1. In other words, the least cost location is determined by transport costs and the production technology, i.e. by what Weber terms the 'materials index'.[4]

The essential features of the analysis are given in Figure 1.1. The next stage is to consider the effects of a source of cheap labour.[5] Assume that such a source is located at the point L in Figure 1.2 and would give rise to a reduction of £26 in production costs per unit of output. Assume further that unit costs of production (and transport) at P* are £19. We construct the isodapane associated with transport costs of £45 (£(26 + 19))—termed the critical isodapane. If L lies inside (outside) this isodapane, then the least cost location is L (P*). Clearly, labour orientation is more likely when labour costs in production are more imtant relative to other costs. In addition, the possibility of labour orientation to point L would be increased if L were close to an alternative source of localised input 1—source M_1' in Figure 1.2.

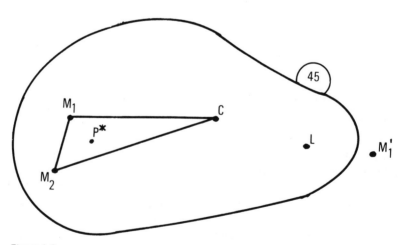

Figure 1.2.

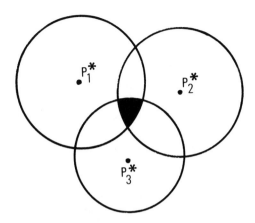

Figure 1.3.

The third and final stage is to modify assumption (i). We maintain the fixed co-efficient technology, but now assume that there are economies of agglomeration.

'An agglomerative factor . . . is an "advantage" or cheapening of production or marketing which results from the fact that production is carried on to some considerable extent at *one* place.' (Weber, p. 126)

Agglomerative factors arise at two stages in production. Firstly, there may be economies from 'simple *enlargement of plant*'.[6] Secondly, there may be advantages from 'close local association of *several* plants.' (Weber, pp. 127, 128)

Consider a situation in which transport orientation with respect to three de-mand sites gives the locations P^*_1, P^*_2, and P^*_3 in Figure 1.3. Now assume that agglomeration economies are such that, if total demand at the three consumption locations is supplied from a single production site, unit production costs would be reduced by £25. Then if the critical isodapanes — those isodapanes which involve an increase in transport costs of £25 per unit of production for each production site — around each of the points P^*_1 intersect, agglomeration will reduce total costs.[7] Thus in Figure 1.3 the least cost location to supply total demand at the three consumption sites lies in the shaded area, i.e. agglomeration would reduce total production costs.

1.2.2 Extensions of the Weberian Model

Weber considered many variations on the basic themes outlined above and also formulated (in Chapter 7) one of the first general theories of industrial location.

His analysis suffered, however, from the lack of any strong mathematical programming techniques which are necessary if the more restrictive assumptions are to be relaxed and the full set of locational interdependencies are to be considered.

The assumption that has come in for most criticism has been the linearity of transport costs with distance. So long as we use a geometric approach this is not really a problem. We merely change the spacing of the isotims around each source M_i and consumption site C. Attempts to generalise lead to more severe difficulties. Within the geometric framework Isard (1956) and Alonso (1964) have analysed the effects of alternative transport cost functions on the simple Weberian diagram. Alonso, for example, indicates that the introduction of loading/unloading charges increases the possibility of least cost locations occurring at one of the vertices of the locational triangle.

As was stated above, once we move beyond the geometric approach nonlinear transport costs introduce more severe complications. One possibility would be to impose a lattice on the market area and introduce the constraints that all materials sites, points of consumption, and production locations occur at vertices of the lattice. We can then identify the transport cost from any vertex i to any other vertex j, t_{ij}, no matter the relationship between transport cost and distance, and use standard programming techniques to identify the least cost production locations. Alternatively we can characterise the market area as a graph or network—see, for example, Lea (1973). Production locations must be chosen from nodes in the graph and the lengths of the branches of the graph are expressed as costs by application of the appropriate transport cost function.

Whichever of these approaches is adopted, subsequent analysis owes a great deal to the conceptual framework developed by Weber. The intellectual debt owed to Weber is clear also in much of the empirical work on industrial location. Some of the earliest such work in English was produced by Hoover (1937, 1948) in classic studies of the shoe and leather industries. In addition, Isard (1956) acknowledges the importance of Weberian analysis to his studies of the iron and steel industry, while studies of the optimal location of hospitals and warehouses[8] have a strong Weberian flavour.

The analysis of the role of economies of scale in industrial location has also tended to proceed by case study and again the Weberian influence is strong—see, for example, the recent work by Scherer (1975) and Beckenstein (1975) on the location and plant size decisions of a number of selected industries. This work extends into analysis of the multiplant firm in general and the multinational enterprise (MNE) in particular. Thus, for example, the study of Buckley and Casson (1976) has its foundations in an essentially Weberian model, although it is subsequently extended in terms of explicit consideration of the effects of market imperfections of various types.

1.3 CENTRAL PLACE AND INTERDEPENDENCE THEORIES

1.3.1 Central Place Theory

Probably the most important contributions in this field come from Lösch (1938, 1954). Whereas Weberian theory is conducted in terms of a heterogeneous market area with consumption fixed and concentrated at distinct points, Lösch considers location on an unbounded, homogeneous plain over which consumers are evenly distributed. The demand side of the analysis is explicitly introduced in that each consumer is assumed to have a downward-sloping demand curve for whatever is being produced.

The important assumptions (Lösch 1954, pp. 94-97) are:[9]

(i) The location for an individual (entrepreneur) must be as advantageous as possible, i.e. must be a maximum profit location.
(ii) Locations must be so numerous that the entire space is occupied.
(iii) In all activities that are open to everyone, abnormal profits must disappear.
(iv) The areas of supply, production, and sales must be as small as possible.
(v) Consumers at the boundaries of economic areas must be indifferent as to which of the neighbouring locations they belong.

Lösch begins by assuming a homogeneous plain which contains 'nothing but self sufficient farms that are regularly distributed'. (1954, p. 105) Assume now that one farmer wishes to produce and sell beer, and that each consumer has the same demand curve d (as in Figure 1.4(a)). Then for any brewery price OP individual demand will be PQ. When transport costs PR are added, individual demand falls to RS. Finally, at F individual demand falls to zero.[10] Total sales for the brewer equal the volume of the cone formed by rotating PQF around PQ as axis, multiplied by consumer density. Clearly, total sales will vary with the brewery price OP. Thus the same calculation must be carried out for all possible brewery prices, leading to the demand curve Δ in Figure 1.4(b). If we now introduce the planning curve Π that indicates the minimum average cost at which a given output could be produced in a new factory built for that purpose, then brewing will be profitable if Δ and Π intersect.

This analysis will give rise to a circular market area as in Figure 1.5(a), and either surplus profits or an extensive market area for the brewer. Other producers will enter — assumptions (iii) and (iv) above — and compete away demand, i.e. move the demand curve Δ to the left until only normal profits remain — the point N' in Figure 1.5(b). Assumption (iii) is then such that the shape of the individual market areas is also modified: Lösch gives an intuitive proof that a system of hexagonal markets will emerge as in Figure 1.5(c) and (d). This has been formalised by Bollobas and Stern (1972).

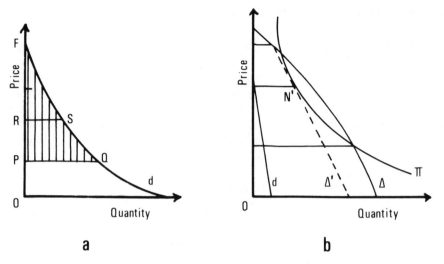

Figure 1.4.

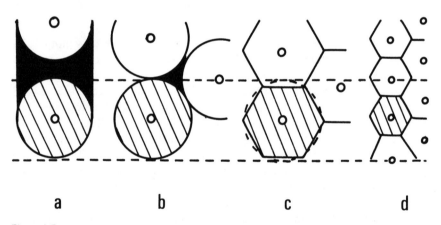

Figure 1.5.

Obviously, the size of the individual hexagons for a particular industry is determined by the relationship between production and demand conditions. Thus different industries will give rise to different sizes of hexagons, and for each industry we can derive a net of hexagons covering the market area.

If now nets of hexagons of different sizes are superposed in an ordered manner—see Lösch 1954, p. 124 ff.—a hierarchy of production centres will emerge as in Figure 1.6(a):

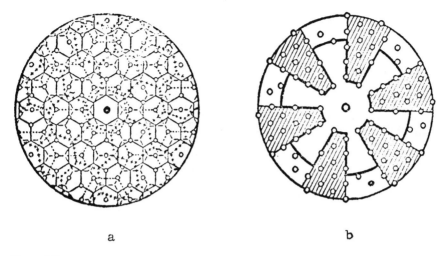

a   b

Figure 1.6.

'we suddenly have crowds of economic areas on a plain which we deprived of all spatial inequalities at the outset.' (Lösch 1938, p. 75)

The important point Lösch wanted to make in this connection was that the sectoral arrangement of economic activity derived by superposing systems of hexagons would give rise to city-rich and city-poor sectors as in Figure 1.6(b).

Despite this seeming empirical aim, Lösch was not concerned with explaining reality.

'The real duty of the economist is not to explain our sorry reality, but to improve it. The question of the best location is far more dignified than determination of the action one.' (Lösch 1954, p. 4)

Thus while Lösch completes his investigation with the analysis of a number of examples of actual distributions of towns, shapes of market areas, etc., his intention is not to verify or refute his theory, but to indicate to what extent actual location is rational. In his 1938 article, for example, Lösch compared his theoretical distribution of activity with the area within 100 miles of Indianapolis, while in his book he made the same comparison with the area surrounding Toledo. Figure 1.7 illustrates these 'actual' landscapes.

It is worth mentioning in concluding this section that there is a high degree of uniformity between Lösch's analysis of market area and that presented by Christaller (1966). Differences do exist, both in the formal presentations of the two models and in their conclusions. Christaller, for example, requires that any central place that contains a function of order m also contains functions of all

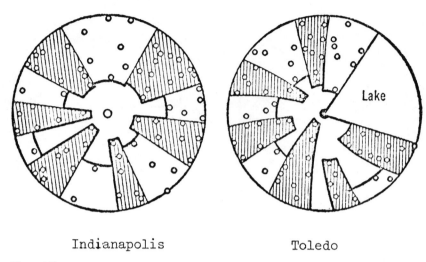

Indianapolis   Toledo

Figure 1.7.

lower orders. In the Lösch system this constraint need not be operative.[11] But in most important respects the models are alike.

1.3.2 Extensions

While Weber can be accused of ignoring the demand factor in his locational analysis, Lösch goes to the other extreme and ignores all spatial variation in cost conditions. It has been shown, however, that with a heterogeneous economic space a hierarchy of central places will emerge – see Berry and Garrison 1958.

A great deal of research has also been devoted to an examination of the exhibited distribution of economic activity. In general, the results do not support the hypothesis that the distribution of a particular economic function will be regular – see, for example, Getis 1963. In view of Lösch's professed intentions, however, these findings need not be taken to constitute a major attack on central place theory.

More fundamentally, Lösch ignores the economic linkages between different industrial sectors. As a result, his system cannot be used to analyse the location of an industry that produces or consumes an intermediate product. In other words, we must assume that all industries are producing for final demand since in any other situation the hexagonal arrangement for particular industries may be significantly distorted.

It has also been suggested that, even if there are no intermediate products, the emergence of central places will lead to an uneven distribution of demand and so to distortion of the hexagonal arrangement of productive activity.

Some attempts have been made to build on the basic Löschian framework to derive general 'rules' that characterise optimal location in a general equilibrium system. The main obstacles facing this type of investigation are the nonconvexities that enter when economies of scale are introduced on the production side. Starrett (1974), however, has formulated such a system and derived certain necessary conditions relating in particular to the degree of increasing returns and the demand for transport.

But we are still left with a relatively abstract framework that is of limited usefulness in the analysis of industrial location behaviour.

1.3.3 Interdependence Theories

The Löschian system recognises that the location of one economic agent involved in a particular activity will affect and be affected by the locations of other economic agents involved in the same activity. Central place theory is concerned, however, with cases in which there are many agents. Interdependence theories, on the other hand, are rather more concerned with situations in which there are few agents. In other words, while central place theory is concerned with the spatial implications of imperfect competition, interdependence theories are generally concerned with the spatial implications of non-collusive oligopoly.

The largest amount of early work in spatial oligopoly was carried out in terms of duopolists competing within a well-defined, bounded market. The seminal work in this field was that of Hotelling (1929); it was later extended and summarised by Smithies (1941).

Hotelling was concerned with the pattern of location of two sellers of a homogeneous product when buyers are evenly distributed on a linear market. Each buyer is assumed to consume one unit of output and bear all transport costs, i.e. the demand side is essentially ignored. A simple illustration is perhaps useful; the best known is the analysis of the location of two ice-cream salesmen on a bounded, linear beach when each consumer is assumed to purchase one ice-cream and to purchase it from the nearest salesman.

Hotelling's analysis then indicates that if the salesmen start, for example, at the points A and B in Figure 1.8 (a), and if we assume that the seller at A is fixed, then the seller at B will maximise his sales by locating adjacent to A, on the side nearer to the centre of the beach. But if B is now fixed in this new location, A would benefit by leapfrogging over B, and this leapfrogging will continue until the salesmen are back to back in the centre of the beach.

The tendency to agglomerate that characterises the one stable outcome of the

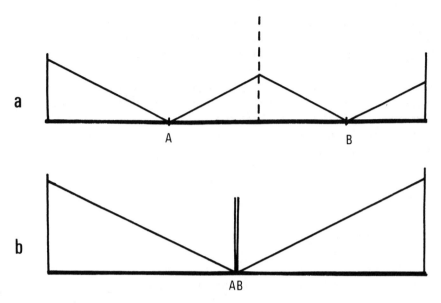

Figure 1.8.

Hotelling model has been questioned by most subsequent researchers. Smithies (1941), for example, indicates that with a non-zero elasticity of demand and non-zero transport costs the two competitors will separate. If the market is drawn as a closed curve – a beach around an island, perhaps – then, no matter the locations of the two sellers, each serves half the market. Location side by side is only one of an infinity of equally profitable location strategies.

Finally, Eaton and Lipsey (1975) and Rothschild (1976) have shown that if we allow for more than two sellers in the market, these sellers will tend to disperse rather than agglomerate.

While the various modifications of Hotelling's original work mentioned above have contributed to our understanding of spatial competitive oligopoly, they suffer from the basic limitations which characterise competitive oligopoly in general: the outcome of the competitive process is crucially dependent upon the assumptions we make about the behaviour of the oligopolists.

This realisation has led to an increasing concentration in traditional oligopoly on the analysis of the behaviour of oligopolists if they collude, e.g. in the price setting and market sharing decisions. The analogous situation in spatial oligopoly would be to assume that the oligopolist has little discretion over his pricing policy but has knowledge of the market share he is likely to capture. If we can also assume that expected market share is related more to the way in which the new oligopolist differentiates his product than to where he produces it, attempts to maximise profits through a locational strategy will lead to an analysis very like a least cost approach. Thus, while it is difficult to see the relevance of theories of spatial oligopoly to the analysis of industrial location, if we allow for collusion we may be able to appeal to least cost theories.

1.4 OTHER APPROACHES

By concentrating on these seminal works we have omitted a great deal of useful and important analysis. Of particular importance are the major contributions of Greenhut (1956) in drawing together least cost and interdependence theories to derive an integrated theory of location. Similarly, Isard (1956, 1960) has combined the Weber and Lösch traditions into a general theory of location. In doing so, he introduces several modifications to the Weberian analysis, one of the most important of which is to replace the Leontief-type production function by a neoclassical production function. Isard then shows that the choice of factor mix in production will not, in general, be independent of location.

We have to accept, however, that many of the elements of the work of Greenhut and Isard have to be sacrificed once we move to an 'applied' approach – if for no other reason than the lack of reasonable data.

1.5 CONCLUSION

The discussion in the previous sections indicates that if we are concerned with both theoretical and empirical analysis of industrial location we shall probably have to work within an essentially Weberian, least cost tradition.

The model to be developed in the following chapters is in this tradition. As will be indicated in more detail in Chapter 2, it is a least cost model in which we take the distribution of demand as given, explicitly allow for the existence of economies of scale to the production unit, and analyse the interplay of demand distribution, production costs, and transport costs as determinants of the allocation of production.

There are, however, several departures from the original Weberian formulation. Our major departure is that we formulate the locational model as a mathematical programming problem. We can then take into account simultaneously all of the effects – cheap labour locations, economies of agglomeration, etc. – that Weber analysed separately. In addition we shall be able to identify the market area controlled by each plant that is operated in a calculated optimal solution.

Secondly, we do not assume that all consumption sites are of the same size.

Demand is concentrated at a number of discrete locations, but these can, and in general will, be of varying sizes. We shall find in the discussion of our results (Chapters 6 and 7) that this aspect of our model has strong implications for locational behaviour.

Thirdly, we adopt an activity analysis approach to the production side. There is, therefore, the possibility of substitution between production activities under the influence of space, i.e. the factor mix in production may vary with location. Activity analysis can be considered to be the intermediate case between the two extremes of zero substitutability (Leontief production function) in Weber, and perfect substitutability in Isard.

Fourthly, we consider location on a network. Thus we can allow for a completely general specification of transport costs with respect to distance,[12] and can introduce loading and unloading costs.

Finally, we shall be concerned in much of our analysis with the role of economies of scale in the locational decision. As a result we explicitly introduce such economies to production costs associated with each production unit. Economies of scale have been considered by other researchers. Vietorisz and Manne (1963), for example, constrain production costs to the form in Figure 1.9, and other authors have constrained total production costs to be strictly concave. Our approach is to allow production costs to take a perfectly general form, as illustrated by the smooth curve in Figure 1.10. We then approximate to this curve by a linear spline as indicated. There is no presumption that the spline will be concave; indeed, our expectation would be quite to the contrary.

On the negative side, our model contains limited economies external to the production unit. Some such economies will, of course, be available, e.g. through the reduction of transport costs on intermediate products if production and consumption sites are near to each other. But no specific 'firm-type' economies, e.g. development of a pool of skilled labour, management expertise etc., are introduced. We do not feel that this is a severe handicap; recent work by Scherer et al. (1975) would appear to indicate that these agglomeration economies may not be major determinants of the plant size and location decisions.

The basic model is developed in its static form in Chapters 3 and 4. It is then applied in a case study of the United Kingdom cement industry. This industry was selected partly for reasons of convenience and data availability, but also because it is an industry in which the interplay between the distribution of demand, economies of scale to production, and transport costs is of interest. The industry has been considered by other writers. The Organisation for Economic Cooperation and Development (OECD 1972), for example, considers a very simple example in which two alternative sites for a cement plant in India are compared, and Manne (1967) uses the cement industry as one case study in an analysis mainly concerned with the timing of facility expansions.

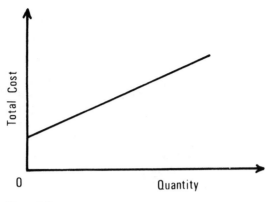

Figure 1.9.

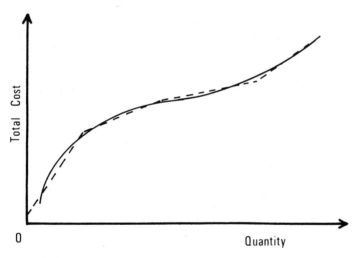

Figure 1.10.

Estimates of production costs, transport costs, demand, etc., for the UK cement industry are given in Chapter 5, and the solution to the case study is discussed in Chapter 6. Our interests are essentially normative, i.e. we are concerned with what the configuration of the industry should be, and with how sensitive this configuration is to changes in various market conditions. We also introduce some positive elements in that we compare actual and calculated optimal locational patterns in an attempt to identify to what extent the industry reflects, or does not reflect, our calculated optimum.

This comparison leads to a recognition that time may be important in the industrial location decision. We therefore present a multiperiod version of the model in Chapter 7 and discuss the calculated optimum for this model when it is applied to a part of the whole UK market. The point is that time introduces both an additional dimension of scale, and a diseconomy to industrial concentration. We examine the trade-off between these conflicting influences.

The application of the Weberian model implies either perfect monopoly or perfect collusion in the industry under investigation. As a result, the impacts of competition for 'good' locations and of interactions between competitive plants are eliminated. The solution of a Weberian model may, therefore, imply the existence of rather larger scale plants than would be generated by a competitive model.

As was indicated in section 1.3.3, the development and application of competitive models is fraught with difficulties, particularly with respect to the behavioural rules to be attributed to the competitors and the assumptions made about demand. One such model has been developed by Gee (1976) which has the important merit of being easily adapted to our uses. This model is presented in Chapter 8, and some solutions generated for the cement study. These solutions are compared with those in Chapters 6 and 7.

Our final chapter—Chapter 9—draws together the main conclusions and indicates their general relevance, rather than their specific application to a particular industry.

2 OBJECTIVES OF THE STUDY

2.1 INTRODUCTION

In the construction of any economic model, a statement has to be made about which variables are to be treated as exogenous, or given, and which as endogenous, or simultaneously determined in the solution of the model.

We can conceive of a spectrum of possible models classified by the amount of information taken as exogenous. At one end of the spectrum we might attempt to treat all economic variables as endogenous and test various hypotheses about the ways in which they interact. But while such models would be very fruitful in extending our knowledge of particular economic systems, the associated case studies are generally impossible to formulate or solve. At the other end of the spectrum would lie those models in which only one variable is endogenous. In such cases the models are easily solved, but they contribute a limited amount to our knowledge of any economic system.

Between these extremes a multitude of possible partial equilibrium models are open to us, depending upon the information we take as given and the hypotheses we are interested in testing.

We might, for example, be interested in how the consumption of various commodities changes with changes in disposable income. In this case disposable income is treated as exogenous, and the spending of this income in various ways as endogenous. Alternatively, we could go one stage further back and treat disposable income as endogenous. We might then ask how it is affected by investment, etc.

In location theory, the discussion in Chapter 1 indicated that the questions to be asked could be relatively simple, such as how a particular activity would locate given the locations of all other activities. Alternatively, we might ask a much more complex question, such as how a number of industries would locate in relation to each other given the distribution of certain raw materials and final demands for particular commodities.

No matter how complex the question we ask, however, once more than one variable is treated as endogenous the important questions to which we seek answers can be reduced to:

(i) how do the endogenous variables interact with each other, and
(ii) how are they influenced by changes in the exogenous variables.

The actual choice of endogenous variables is influenced by the interactions we feel to be important, i.e. by the hypotheses we are interested in testing. Chisholm and O'Sullivan (1973), for example, take as exogenous:

(i) the spatial distribution of production of a number of commodities,
(ii) the spatial distribution of consumption of these same commodities,
(iii) the cost of transporting each commodity from each region to every other region; taken as proportional to the linear distance between the centroids of the various regions.

They treat as endogenous the flows of the various commodities between the various regions and attempt to test the hypotheses:

(i) the greater the potential accessibility of an area, the larger the volume of freight per resident or per worker, and
(ii) the greater the potential accessibility of an area, the shorter the mean haul on freight traffic.

Our own approach is very different in emphasis. We confine our attention to a particular industry in our case study, taking as exogenous the location of all other industries. The view is then taken that industrial location decisions are affected by the spatial distribution of primary inputs and final demands, and by the available transport network. We attempt to estimate:

(i) the degree of response of industrial location decisions to changes in particular economic stimuli, and
(ii) the rate of response of industrial location to changes in overall economic conditions.

It is clear that this view is by no means the only relevant one. For example, we could argue that final demand is influenced in its spatial distribution by the growth of industrial complexes. Similarly, the transport network could be treated as endogenous—changes resulting from the pressure on particular branches as a result of the growth of industrial and urban conurbations at particular points. We feel that the approach we adopt is informative and important in that it allows us to focus on particular factors influencing the industrial location decision and to examine ways in which these factors react with each other and with changes in certain of the exogenous factors.

2.2 DESCRIPTION OF THE THEORETICAL MODEL

The theoretical model is formulated as an activity analysis production-transportation model in which we define production activities and transportation activities, and is defined as a programming problem. We develop the model in various stages, starting with a simple one-period, constant-returns-to-scale version. Our case study concentrates, however, on those versions in which production activities exhibit economies of scale to capital and other components of production costs. The objective is then to find that pattern of production which will minimise the cost of meeting total demand in our locational framework, subject to constraints imposed by the availability of resources and the transport network.

Attention will be confined in Chapters 3 through 6 to an essentially static model. In introducing capital costs to such a model, therefore, we assume:

(i) that the market conditions existing in the period to which the data refer will remain unaltered over the life of the plant, thus effectively reducing the demand side of the analysis to a single period,

(ii) that the industry with which we are concerned is adjusted to the technology, and that the technology will not change significantly over the life of the plant. Thus the industry will employ the latest techniques and will have available the full range of capacities, and

(iii) that there is no inherited capital, i.e. that the market consists of a series of green-field sites.

One consequence of these assumptions is that great care has to be exercised in the choice of the base date for the static model, quite apart from considerations relating to data availability. In particular, we would hope to choose a technology at a time when the industry has adjusted closely to this technology.

Some such assumptions are necessary, since the inclusion of a capital cost element introduces a time element into the static model. We shall state that a given capital cost creates a given capacity and has associated a given activity vector. What is also clear, however, is that the capital equipment—machinery, etc.—that is created has a finite life rather longer than any reasonable definition of a single period. Further, a given technology relevant to the time period is implicit in the production activities chosen. Technology is not a static phenomenon, however, and is liable to develop over the lifetime of a particular plant with consequent implications for production and location decisions.

Within these limitations the static model can be looked upon as the equivalent of a snapshot of a particular industry taken at some specified time. For our purposes, the most important characteristic of this 'snapshot' is that it is a picture of the optimal location of the industry at the chosen base date. But then, the greater the changes in technology and other parameters of the model over the lifetime of the plant, the less accurate the snapshot is likely to be.

The multiperiod version of the model takes more account of history and of the changes over time in certain of the parameters. It is applied to a finite time horizon, however, and therefore it abstracts from the full set of factors that influence the development of a particular industry. This model also produces a snapshot of the industry.

We have indicated that we treat as exogenous the transport network and the spatial distribution of primary inputs and final demand. We then define the market area in the form of a graph made up of a set of nodes joined by a given network of branches.

The network is a representation of the transport facilities, e.g. trunk roads, motorways, etc., existing in the market. It is assumed to be such that a path exists from any node to any other node, but this path need not consist of only one branch; there is not necessarily a direct road link, for example, from any node to every other node. The length of a branch is defined to be the cost of moving one unit of a commodity along that branch; as such, 'length' is dependent not only upon geographic distance but also upon the types of commodity being moved.

The nodes that are defined fall into three types, not mutually exclusive:

(i) towns at which the output is demanded,
(ii) sites at which the input materials are available, and
(iii) sites at which the output can be produced.

Problems will arise in defining the set of nodes, since by doing so we implicitly assume that labour, raw material deposits, demand, etc., are localised at a set of distinct points, although these factors are, by their nature, dispersed unevenly throughout the economy. For example, we confine mineral availability to particular points in the market although we know that mineral deposits tend to occur in sometimes extensive bands.

Finally, we have stated that our study employs an activity analysis approach to production and transportation. As a result the relevant activities are considered in detail. Our data requirements will be difficult to satisfy and some awkward estimating problems will arise.

2.3 COMPARISON WITH PLANNING MODELS

It might be expected from the discussion in the previous section that the various versions of our model will shed light on planning problems, but they are not meant to have direct planning implications. For them to do so we would need to construct a truly dynamic model, whereas our own work is more an exercise in comparative statics. We shall not attempt to give an exhaustive description of the properties and aims of planning models, but a brief summary will give some indication of the differences between such models and our own work.[1]

In general, the planning problem can be presented as an exercise in constrained optimisation, and is usually framed in terms of a command economy. When this type of economy exists, it is sensible to talk of 'the state of the economy': a state in which every economically important variable is enumerated. Each state of the economy can then be represented by a vector s whose components are, e.g. amounts of different forms of consumption, inputs, and outputs associated with each firm, etc. The components of each vector s will be constrained by resource availabilities, technology restrictions, etc., and we may define from these constraints a feasible set S. The problem facing the planning authority is to choose some s in S to maximise an objective function u(s).

Just how u(s) is formulated depends upon the aims of the planning model, and in particular whether we are concerned with long-run or short-run plans. The division of plans into short-run and long-run is obviously subject to some degree of arbitrariness, but does indicate a fundamental property of planning models – they are concerned with dynamic problems.

Short-run plans are generally 'concerned with detailed plans – plans that give a complete description of production and distribution.' (Heal 1973, p.63) As such, a short-run plan 'controls in detail the day-to-day allocation of resources' (p.64), taking as given some constraints on overall aggregates within the economy, e.g. the amount of fixed capital equipment.

Long-run plans on the other hand are 'concerned not with the detailed allocation of resources within the economy, but with the direction in which the economy's capital stock and productive potential evolves.' (p.239) In this case the components of each vector s are economic aggregates such as consumption, investment, stocks, etc., differentiated by the time period to which they refer. A typical objective would be to maximise 'welfare' up to some specified time T subject not only to initial constraints from the available technology, capital stock, etc., but also to the constraint that some of the economic aggregates should have specified values in time T. The plan then consists of target quantities for each of the economic aggregates for each of the time periods from the initial period to time T.

Our analysis does not fit into the framework of either short-run or long-run planning. But the differences between our model and planning models, while great, are not so great that we cannot hope to produce results which are useful in a planning context.

2.4 OBJECTIVES OF THE STUDY

The problems with which we have been concerned above only acquire significance if we attempt to compare the results of a case study with situations actually existing in a particular industry. Although the discussion so far has concentrated upon the limitations of the models to be developed in the following chapters, the central aim of this chapter is to outline the various ways in which comparisons can be drawn with conditions actually existing in the industry being studied. The existence of the limitations must be recognised, but this is not to say that they need restrict the conclusions we draw from our analysis.

We have described the results of the solutions to both single and multiperiod models as snapshots of the optimal location of a particular industry over a particular period. The first and most obvious way in which any such snapshot may be used is then clear. It can be compared with the actual configuration of the industry over the same period. The extent to which the two pictures differ gives us a qualified measure of the degree to which the industry is nonoptimally located.

Consideration of the ways in which this measure is qualified leads us to a more informative method of comparison of optimal and actual locational patterns. For the static model, the most important qualification lies in the assumption that the industry has no history. Industrial distribution at any point in time is affected, on occasions significantly, by decisions made in previous periods. These historical effects, which we have assumed away, will be partly responsible for the degree to which the actual location diverges from our calculated optimal distribution, even if the inherited decisions were correct given the then known set of parameters.

In addition, given an inherited capital stock, it is clear that adjustment of the actual location cannot be assumed to be either costless or timeless, and differences between the optimal and actual locations at the base date may well be due to lags in the adjustment process.

As a result, rather more information about the degree of optimality (or nonoptimality) of the actual industrial location and about the ways in which the industry has (or has not) adjusted will be obtained from examination of the actual locational pattern of the industry over a number of periods preceding and subsequent to the base date of the static model. We should expect to find some tendency towards our calculated optimal location, since old capital will be written off and new capacity installed on the basis of data relevant to periods closer to our base date.

Variations between actual and optimal locations will still exist, of course, arising firstly from the effects of inherited decisions and adjustment lags on the actual location, and secondly from the strong simplifying assumptions which result in our models giving only an approximation to the optimal location towards which the industry should be moving. But a strong basis for comparison will be obtained and the results of this comparison will allow us to make some statements about the nature of the adjustment lags. From these statements it is a short step to an estimate of the *rate of response* of industrial location to changes in the overall market situation – one of the two factors in which we are particularly interested.

The analysis can be extended to embrace other factors in which we might be interested. For example, comparison of actual and optimal location patterns in the manner suggested above will allow us to analyse the effects of the competitive structure of the industry on its location decisions.

Both single and multiperiod versions of the model reflect an optimum subject to some simplifying assumptions and given certain parameters. This optimum could conceivably be produced by a perfectly competitive industry or by a state monopoly. It will be such that, if transport costs are low relative to other costs and economies of scale are important, we would expect optimal location to consist of a small number of large-scale plants, each serving a large area. In general, however, we would expect any industry studied, certainly within a UK context, to show some oligopolistic features with consequent implications for the optimal spatial structure. We are liable to find either (i) smaller-scale production more widely spread over the market, leading to lower average capacity and higher average production costs, or (ii) a greater amount of transshipment, leading to higher transport costs, since each producer would probably prefer to be represented in each of the spatially distinct markets. Any degree of brand loyalty will strengthen either of these two tendencies. Similar comments would apply to other forms of competitive structure.

All in all, we would expect to find higher average production cost and lower concentration of production of final and intermediate commodities and/or higher transport costs than would characterise the perfectly competitive industry or state monopoly. This expectation is tested to at least some extent by the 'competitive' model presented in Chapter 8.

In our discussion above, the limitations of the models have been mentioned several times, but no attempt has been made to suggest ways in which the importance of these limitations might be assessed. Sensitivity analysis is especially useful in this respect, because it gives us some indication of the extent to which the calculated optimal location is dependent upon our estimates of transport costs, production costs, etc. All our problems, of course, cannot be resolved by this form of analysis. Sensitivity analysis is multidimensional, and we cannot hope to perform a comprehensive analysis of all the relevant variables. We can only perform a limited number of experiments and draw inferences from the results of these experiments with regard to the experiments we do not conduct. In particular, our results will be strongly dependent upon our choice of nodes — which, as we have indicated, are themselves influenced by and influence our choice of transport network. But we cannot hope to check directly on the strength of the dependence; we shall have to rely on the results of other experiments giving an indirect check.

Whether or not the industry proves sensitive to particular parameters, we may expect to achieve a net gain by our analysis of the industry. If the optimal location of the industry is not sensitive to changes in some or all of the various parameters, then we can reside more confidence in the conclusions drawn from the comparisons discussed above. In any case, we shall learn something of the relative importance of the various factors that affect the optimal and actual locations, and shall therefore learn something about the nature of the industry.

In short, sensitivity analysis should not be thought to be useful merely as a check on the effects of our assumptions. This form of analysis is also useful as a policy tool. It introduces to our analysis an exercise in comparative statics; by holding fixed certain of the parameters influencing the calculated optimal location other determinants of this location can be isolated and studied.

For example, sensitivity analysis will give us an indication of the change in the calculated optimal location consequent upon a change in transport costs. One result of the sharp increases in the prices of oil, coal, and electricity during the 1970s has been a change in transport costs. It is interesting to examine the ways in which the 'new' calculated optimum, based on altered transport costs, varies from our original calculated optimum.

The usefulness of the results is, of course, restricted by our simplifying assumptions, but we shall obtain some measure of the required restructuring of the industry or the cost of maintaining the previous structure unaltered.

Our interest here is in the second of the two factors we consider important — the *degree of response* of industrial location to changes in particular economic variables. That is, the degree to which industrial location is sensitive to changes in particular parameters, all other parameters 'remaining equal'.

In analysing the rate and degree of response of industrial location to various parameters, we shall also shed light on two other factors. Firstly, since we are explicitly assuming economies of scale to characterise the production process, we shall have to produce a clear statement of what is meant by economies of scale, and indicate to what extent such economies are important in our case study. The case study for the static model is then an analysis of the trade-off between economies of scale in production and diseconomies of scale through increased transportation.

Secondly, our discussion in this section has concentrated upon the static model. As we have indicated, sensitivity analysis applied to this version of the model is an exercise in comparative statics. No matter how many experiments we conduct, therefore, we shall obtain only limited knowledge of the effects of *time* on the industrial location decision. The multiperiod model can then be considered as a form of sensitivity analysis in which we consider the ways in which the calculated optimal location predicted by the static model will be changed by the introduction of time. A more important consideration, however, is that in the same way as there is a trade-off between production and transportation costs, so also there is a trade-off in a growing market between economies of scale and the timing of capacity expansion. A simple expression of this trade-off is that the industry can either instal large-scale units at widely spaced intervals and carry spare capacity for a number of periods, or instal small-scale units and sacrifice economies of scale for full capacity utilisation. The case study for the multiperiod model (Chapter 7) indicates how this trade-off is resolved for one particular industry and the factors important in its resolution.

3 STATIC MODEL ASSUMING CONSTANT RETURNS TO SCALE

3.1 INTRODUCTION

In the previous chapter we introduced without definition the theoretical model and much of the terminology used in our analysis. Many of the terms we used, e.g. commodity, activity, node, etc., are clear at an intuitive level, but we now give a rigorous interpretation of the way in which we use them. The first part of this chapter is devoted to these definitions.

We then present a formal derivation of the static model, assuming constant returns to scale; economies of scale are introduced in Chapter 4. While we shall in general be dealing with production processes characterised by economies of scale, we feel that the approach we have taken is advisable; it is better to start with an initial framework—the linear version of the model—and build on this frame.

The model will be constructed on the assumption that there are no constraints upon either data availability or computer capacity. Clearly these constraints will 'bite' when we undertake particular industry studies, and certain of the factors introduced in the following sections, particularly capacity constraints on the transport network and the disposal of waste products, may have to be dropped from the analysis. But we feel that it is preferable to give a complete description of the model at this stage, even if it is not set up in its entirety in our empirical work.

An initial statement of the objective is to find the distribution of productive capacity over our locational framework that will minimise the total cost of supplying all demand subject to restrictions imposed by the availability of inputs to the production process and capacity of the transport network.

The crucial assumption is that a perfectly inelastic demand must be satisfied. Total revenue is then $R = \Sigma_n \Sigma_v (f_{nv} p_{nv})$ say, where f_{nv} is demand for final product n at node v and p_{nv} is selling price (given) of final product n at v. Given the f's and the p's, R is a constant and profit maximisation, where profit = R - Z (Z = total cost), becomes cost minimisation. If the assumption that demand is perfectly price-inelastic is dropped, then final demand would perhaps be some function of delivered price, and price would be some function of output and transport costs. For example, if the demand functions are of the form $f_{nv} = a_v + b_v p_{nv}$, the objective function would contain quadratic terms in output, i.e. we would be involved in some variant of quadratic programming.

3.2 LOCATIONAL FRAMEWORK, PRODUCTION AND TRANSPORT ACTIVITIES

3.2.1 Locational Framework

The locational framework is represented by a graph, and is illustrated diagrammatically in Figure 3.1. The points in the graph are called *nodes* or vertices and the lines are called *branches.*[1]

The branches of the graph represent the transport facilities available in the market. Each branch is taken to represent only one transport mode. Thus, if there is a road and rail link between nodes 1 and 2, two branches will be defined, one for each transport mode. We can then talk of the movement of commodities *between* nodes by any particular transport mode. Complications will arise when

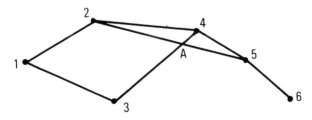

Figure 3.1.

we try to deal with situations in which the movement of a commodity to a particular node is only part of the commodity's total journey through the market. What we have to allow for in these cases is the movement of commodities *through* a node, when the commodity is moved to the node on one transport mode and leaves on the same or a different mode.

Such intranodal movements are handled by introducing transshipment activities by which the commodities may be unloaded from an incoming branch to a node and loaded onto an outgoing branch. These transshipment activities will incur nonnegative costs whenever they are performed, and the usual concept of a node has to be altered to incorporate this feature.

The method for doing so is illustrated in Figure 3.2. Assume that the initial graph is denoted G' and that a particular node v' in G' is the source and destination of branches in two transport modes: see Figure 3.2(a). We now define a new graph G as follows. Disaggregate the node v' in G' into three nodes v_1, v_2 and v_0 in G such that:

(i) v_i is the source/destination of branches in the ith. transport mode (i = 1, 2),
(ii) if v' is a node at which final products are demanded, or at which labour or a primary factor is available, then v_0 is the corresponding node in G, otherwise v_0 is not defined,
(iii) there is a single branch from v_0 to v_1 and from v_0 to v_2,
(iv) there is a branch from v_1 to v_2.

Transport costs on the branch between v_1 (and v_2) and v_0 are loading/unloading costs, and between v_1 and v_2 are transshipment costs involved in changing the transport mode at v'.

Note that this procedure relies on the assumption that transshipment is costless if the transport mode is unaltered. For example, if a commodity is moved to a node v' in G' by road and from v' by road, no transshipment, i.e. loading, un-

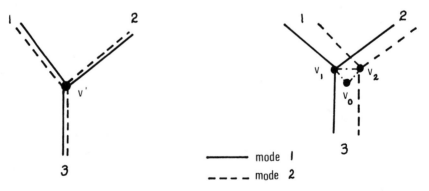

Figure 3.2.

loading, charges are incurred. If, on the other hand, the commodity is moved to v' by road and from v' by rail, a charge is incurred. We assume further that this charge is independent of the origin of the incoming branch to v' and the termination of the outgoing branch from v'.

We assume that there are V nodes in G and denote the set of nodes v_0 by the set G^S. We need no longer distinguish between transport and transshipment branches or activities; these are grouped under the common heading of transport branches and activities. The set of transport branches in G will be denoted G^B. A particular branch between node v and node u will be denoted (v, u).

3.2.2 Production and Transport Activities

A commodity in G is defined by two characteristics in our one-period world — type and location. As a result, all variables and parameters referring to commodities are subscripted

$$nv \quad (n = 0 \ldots N; v = 1 \ldots V), \qquad (3.2.1)$$

where n defines the type of commodity and v the node at which it is located.[2] There will be occasions below when we shall wish to classify commodities by type but not by location. In these cases we shall refer to the *nth. good,* by which we shall mean those commodities mv such that $m = n$ and $v = 1 \ldots V$. Four types of commodity can be distinguished at any location:

Primary Factors of Production. Primary factors are those commodities entering into production, the initial exogenous endowments of which are negative.[3] Further, there are no production activities from which a primary factor is net output.

Final Products. Final products are those commodities that enter into the consumption constraints. We define a *town* as a node at which there is nonzero demand for at least one final product.

Waste Products. A waste product is a final product that is net output from at least one production activity and the demand for which is zero. Further analysis of the place of waste products in the model will be left until we have developed the concept of an activity.

Intermediate Commodities. All other commodities are defined to be intermediate commodities. Intermediate commodities can be thought of as a residual. Eliminate primary factors, final products, and waste products, and the remainder are intermediate commodities. Since there are no initial endowments of intermediate commodities, their net output at every node must be nonnegative; no more can be consumed at or moved from a node than is produced at or moved to that node.

We assume that there are NV commodities of the above four types. There is, in addition, the commodity labour, which will be subscripted 0v ($v = 1 \ldots V$). The assumptions we shall make about the labour input are detailed in paragraph 3.4.1.

All commodities (including labour) are assumed to be infinitely divisible.

An activity in G is defined in terms of the commodities that are input to and output from that activity. Three types of activity can be distinguished:

Production Activity. Each production activity is represented by a production activity vector:

$$\mathbf{a}_{kv} = \begin{bmatrix} a_{0kv} \\ \cdot \\ \cdot \\ a_{Nkv} \end{bmatrix} \qquad (v \in G^S; k = 1 \ldots K) \qquad (3.2.2)$$

such that a_{nkv} indicates the quantity of the commodity nv involved in unit amount of the kth. production activity at node v. As we have seen, the subscript nv makes the necessary differentiation of commodities by place and type and so allows for possible variation of the a_{nkv} between nodes. Negative a_{nkv} indicates that the commodity nv is used up in the kth. production activity at node v, positive a_{nkv} that the commodity is produced by the kth. production activity at node v, and zero a_{nkv} that the commodity is not involved in activity k at node v.

We assume that there are K production activities at each node v in G^S. There is no presumption, however, that the kth. production activity at node v involves the same goods in the same ratios as the kth. production activity at node u.

Two further assumptions are made about production activities:

(i) Each activity is capable of continuous proportionate expansion, i.e. we ignore indivisibilities. We may therefore define scalars:

$$x_{kv} \geq 0 \qquad (k = 1 \ldots K; v \in G^S) \qquad (3.2.3)$$

describing the *level* of the production activity kv; the activity vector is independent of the activity level x_{kv}.

(ii) Production activities may be combined at any location without alteration of the technical ratios by which each activity vector is defined.

Provided that the constraints specified below (paragraph 3.4) upon the availability of commodities do not 'bite' the existence of the x_{kv} implies constant returns to scale to each production activity.

Transport Activity. A transport activity can be looked upon as an activity by which one unit of a particular good may be moved between two nodes that are directly connected. Combining transport activities then allows us to move goods between any two nodes. The quantity of the nth. good transported from node v to node u ((v, u) in G^B) is represented by the set of coefficients:

$$w_{nvu} \geq 0 \quad (n = 1 \ldots N; (v, u) \epsilon G^B) \tag{3.2.4}$$

Disposal Activities. Disposal activities at a node v dispose of the waste products from production activities at v. They have as inputs waste products at v plus non-positive[4] amounts of primary factors, labour, and intermediate commodities, and produce no output.

A common feature of production and disposal activities is that they can be represented by a set of coefficients a_{kv} (where k is now assumed to include the disposal activities).[5] Disposal activities are discussed more fully in the next section.

3.3 DISPOSAL ACTIVITIES

Production activities will have as net output not only final products and intermediate commodities but also produce waste products; disposal activities are required to destroy these waste products.[6] To say 'destroy' is somewhat misleading, since confusion may arise between destruction of a waste product in the eyes of the producer and in the eyes of society. For a producer, a waste product might be considered to be destroyed once it has been burned, say; but to society, all that may have happened is that one form of waste has been substituted for another. It is not possible to remove completely the conflict of interest implied by these considerations. We therefore define the set of disposal activities as those that the legal system declares to be legally available.[7] Clearly, the producer will choose the cheapest of these, and we leave the legal system to decide whether this should remain an acceptable form of waste disposal.

In saying 'cheapest,' we have made some judgment about the cost of operating the disposal activities. We could, of course, assume that disposal is costless to the producer in money and resources. This would imply that disposal consumes resources not commanded by or available to the producer,[8] i.e. is performed by some outside agency. As such the assumption appears to be too general. Even ignoring pollution control regulations to which many production activities are subject, it is easy to envisage cases in which resources employed by a producer will have to be diverted by him to waste disposal and so incur direct and indirect costs; moving waste from a factory to a slag heap uses up man and machine time which are not then available for use in other activities.

Given that waste disposal cannot be ignored by making it costless, Koopmans (1951) has suggested that a separate set of disposal activities be defined with activity vectors:

$$a_{kv} \quad (k = (K+1) \ldots K') \tag{3.3.1}$$

whose properties are the same as those of the a_{kv} defined by equation (3.2.2). In particular, disposal activity levels x_{kv} may be defined.

The values taken by the coefficients of the activity vectors (3.3.1) are slightly different from those of the production activity vectors in that for all disposal activities (3.3.1):

$$a_{nkv} \quad = 0 \text{ if nv is a nonwaste final product,} \tag{3.3.2}$$

$$\leq 0 \text{ if nv is a waste product and}$$

$$< 0 \text{ for at least one nv a waste product,}$$

$$\leq 0 \text{ otherwise and}$$

$$< 0 \text{ for at least one such commodity nv.}$$

The vectors (3.2.2) and (3.3.1) may be adjoined to form Technology Matrices[9] :

$$T^v = \|a_{nkv}\| \quad (v \in G^S) \tag{3.3.3}$$

where: $K'-K$ is the number of disposal activities at v.

We then define net output to be net output from production and disposal.

3.4 CONSTRAINTS IMPOSED BY MARKET CONDITIONS

3.4.1 Supply and Demand Constraints

3.4.1.1 Labour.   Labour is assumed to be

(i) a nonzero input to all production and disposal activities:

$$a_{0kv} < 0 \quad (k = 1 \ldots K'; v \in G^S) \tag{3.4.1}$$

(ii) available solely at nodes in G^S and in quantities $\ell_v \leq 0$ (since labour is a net input).

Assumption (ii) implies that any labour used in operating the transport activities in G is labour of a different type from that employable by the producer and can be assumed to be independent of that available to him. In addition, we do not rule out the possibility that there may be nodes t such that t is a town but such that $\ell_t = 0$.

(iii) immobile between nodes. We therefore assume:

$$w_{0vu} = 0 \quad ((v, u) \in G^B) \quad\quad\quad (3.4.2)$$

Assumptions (i) through (iii) give the first set of constraints: No more labour can be used in the technology matrix at any node in G^S than is available at that node.

3.4.1.2 Primary Factors of Production. No primary factor can be net output from any technology matrix. The supply limitations upon the primary factors are then given by scalars

$$p_{nv} \leq 0 \quad \text{(commodity nv a primary factor)} \quad\quad (3.4.3)$$

with equality if node v is not a source of primary factor nv, and the second set of constraints are:
Net input at node v of any commodity nv that is a primary factor of production, plus net export of that factor from node v, must be within the supply limitations (3.4.3) on primary factor nv at v.

3.4.1.3 Intermediate Commodities. As we indicated above, in a static world no more of any intermediate commodity can be consumed at or moved from a node than is produced at or moved to that node.

3.4.1.4 Final Products. We assume that the producer is constrained to meet all demand in G, that demand for final products is nonzero only at towns in G, and that demand for final product nv at town v is a given exogenous amount.[10] We can then denote demand for final products by the scalars

$$f_{nv} \geq 0 \quad \text{(nv a final product; v = 1 ... V)} \quad\quad (3.4.4)$$

with equality if node v is not a town.
    The fourth set of constraints is then:
The net output of final product nv at node v plus net imports of that final product to v must at least satisfy the demand for nv at v.

3.4.1.5 Waste Products. We have defined waste products as final products the demand for which is zero. The constraints applicable to these products are then given by $f_{nv} = 0$. It should be noted that this set of constraints will ensure that no more of a waste product is disposed of than is produced.

3.4.1.6 Summary. The demand and supply constraints specified above are of the same form and may be combined to give general constraints for all commodities in G, the signs of the inequalities coming from our conventions regarding the signs of the a_{nkv}.

Constraints 1:

$$\sum_{k=1}^{K'} a_{nkv}x_{kv} + \sum_{G^B} w_{nuv} - \sum_{G^B} w_{nvu} \geq \lambda_{nv} \qquad (n = 0 \ldots N; \quad v = 1 \ldots V)$$

such that $x_{kv}, w_{nvu} \geq 0$ all n,k,v,u and such that for all $v = 1 \ldots V$:

$$\lambda_{nv} = \begin{cases} \ell_v & \text{if } n = 0, \\ p_{nv} & \text{if nv is a primary factor,} \\ 0 & \text{if nv is an intermediate commodity,} \\ f_{nv} & \text{if nv is a final product.} \end{cases}$$

The L.H.S. of Constraints 1 defines the net output from production, disposal, import and export of commodity nv, and the R.H.S. the net availability of or requirement for commodity nv.

3.4.2 Transport Constraints.

All branches (v,u) defined in G^B are assumed to have capacity limitations[11] :

$$d_{vu} \geq 0 \qquad \text{(all } (v,u) \in G^B\text{).} \tag{3.4.5}$$

For simplicity we assume that unit flow of all commodities requires the same amount of transport capacity. The transport activity levels w_{nvu} must then satisfy the constraints:

Constraints 2:

$$\sum_{n=1}^{N} w_{nvu} \leq d_{vu} \qquad \text{(all } (v,u) \in G^B\text{)}$$

   In optimisation over a graph with capacity restrictions upon the branches of the graph, we usually require further constraints to ensure that no more is moved from a node than is available at or moved to that node, and to prevent stocks being built up at that node. The general Constraints 1 meet the first requirement and we have seen that the cost-minimising objective will result in Constraints 1 meeting the second.

3.5 COSTS

3.5.1 Commodity Costs

Commodities are assumed to be available to the producer at uniform prices c_n at all nodes that are sources of these commodities or at which the commodities are produced.[12] If the objective were that profit be maximised, then the selling prices of the final products would also appear in the objective function. But the objective is to minimise cost subject to the constraint that all demand be satisfied, and given that the producer is a price taker. As has been indicated (paragraph 3.1) we may then drop 'revenue' from the formal statement of the objective function leading to the following cost structure:

$$c_n \geq 0 \text{ if nv is a primary factor or labour,}$$
$$c_n = 0 \text{ otherwise.} \tag{3.5.1}$$

While equation (3.5.1) states that the cost to the producer in purchasing the nth. good is zero when this good is produced by a production activity under his control, this is not to say that these goods are costless to him. The production activities by which they are produced consume primary factors and labour which are available at nonzero cost (of purchase and transportation); in this sense direct costs are incurred. Indirect (opportunity) costs may also be incurred since the movement of commodities consumes transport capacity and production consumes scarce resources, both of which could be used to satisfy demand for other commodities.

3.5.2 Transport Costs

Nonnegative costs are associated with the transport activities in G and are assumed to vary in direct proportion to the quantity of the commodity involved in the activity. We make no assumptions regarding the relationship between transport costs and distance transported.

The length of a transport branch is expressed as a cost by applying the transport cost function for unit amount of any particular good to the geographic length of the branch. Thus the 'length' of a branch will vary with the good transported along the branch.

Two further points should be noted about transport costs:

(i) It need not be the case that $t_{nvu} = t_{nuv}$ where t_{nvu} is the cost of transporting unit amount of the nth. good from node v to node u along the branch (v,u), and (ii) t_{nvu} is defined only if the branch (v,u) is defined.

3.6 SPECIFICATION OF THE PROGRAMMING PROBLEM

From the 'shape' of the Constraints 1 and 2, it is possible to construct a more concise formulation of the programming problem. The notation we use and some of the derivation are given in Appendix A. (The full derivation is not given since this is simple but tedious.)

Some comments should be made about the vectors and matrices defined in Appendix A. The vector λ is the vector of availabilities and requirements of all commodities at all nodes, while y is the vector of net outputs of each commodity at each node in G. The cost vector is c (recall the comments in paragraph 3.5.1). Production and disposal activity levels are given by the vector x and the transport activity levels by the vector w. Thus (x,w) is the vector[13] of all activity levels in G.

The matrix T can be considered to be the general technology matrix in G — the matrix of production and disposal activities in G — while W is the matrix representation of the transport network in G.

The vector t is the vector of transport costs and d the vector of transport capacities; the matrix D serves to sum the elements of w over n (see Constraints 2).

We can now restate the constraints on activity levels in G:

Constraints 1(A):   The activity levels (x, w) must be such that

$$(T, W)\begin{bmatrix} x \\ w \end{bmatrix} \geq \lambda; \quad (x, w) \geq 0$$

Constraints 2(A):   The vector of transport activity levels must be such that

$$Dw \leq d; \quad w \geq 0.$$

Total purchase costs are given by,

$$-cTx = v \cdot x, \tag{3.6.1}$$

the negative sign appearing since $\Sigma_{k=1}^{K'} a_{nkv} x_{kv} \leq 0$ when nv is a primary factor, or labour.

Transport costs are

$$t \cdot w \tag{3.6.2}$$

It is now possible to state the model in standard linear programming form. As we indicated in paragraph 3.1, the objective is to find the distribution of productive capacity in G which will meet the demand for final products in G at least cost, subject to constraints upon the availability of primary factors and labour, and subject to capacity limitations upon the transport network. This can be expressed as a linear programme as follows:

The Linear Programme (LP): Find activity levels $(x^*, w^*) \geq 0$ which minimise total cost

$$Z^* = v \cdot x^* + t \cdot w^*$$

subject to the constraints:

(i) $\qquad\qquad\qquad\qquad Tx^* + Ww^* \geq \lambda$

(ii) $\qquad\qquad\qquad\qquad Dw^* \leq d$

(iii) $\qquad\qquad\qquad\qquad x^*, w^* \geq 0.$

The solution for (x^*, w^*) will give the optimal distribution of productive capacity over G together with the optimal quantities of each of the commodities moved between the nodes of G, all subject to the supply, demand and capacity constraints.

The linear programme is well documented, and efficient solution techniques have been developed which will handle most sizes of problem.[14] We do not feel, therefore, that we need say very much about the nature of the linear programming problem we have developed in this chapter. But some simple properties of the solution are worth stating. For simplicity we ignore the restrictions on the transport network.

We introduce imputed values (shadow prices) β with typical element β_{nv} $(n = 0 \ldots N; v = 1 \ldots V)$ and specify the Lagrangian

$$L(x,w,\beta) = v \cdot x + t \cdot w + \beta(\lambda - Tx - Ww). \qquad (3.6.3)$$

According to the Kuhn-Tucker theorem – Kuhn and Tucker 1951, Intriligator 1971 – (x^*, w^*) is a solution to the LP if there exists a vector β^* such that the following conditions hold:

(i)
$$\begin{cases} \dfrac{\partial L}{\partial x}(x^*) = v - \beta^* T \geq 0 \\[2em] \dfrac{\partial L}{\partial x}(x^*) \cdot x^* = (v - \beta^* T) \cdot x^* = 0; \quad x^* \geq 0 \end{cases}$$

(ii)
$$\begin{cases} \dfrac{\partial L}{\partial w}(w^*) = t - \beta^* W \geq 0 \\[2em] \dfrac{\partial L}{\partial w}(w^*) \cdot w^* = (t - \beta^* W) \cdot w^* = 0; \quad w^* \geq 0 \end{cases}$$

(iii)
$$
\begin{cases}
\dfrac{\partial L}{\partial \beta}(\beta^*) = (\lambda - Tx^* - Ww^*) \leq 0 \\[2em]
\beta^* \cdot \dfrac{\partial L}{\partial \beta}(\beta^*) = \beta^*(\lambda - Tx^* - Ww^*) = 0; \quad \beta^* \geq 0.
\end{cases}
$$

The interpretation of these conditions is standard in the literature. Taking conditions (iii) first, these conditions state that the imputed value of a commodity nv that is in excess supply in an optimal solution is zero—it is a free good. In other words, we can state that a commodity will have a nonzero imputed value if and only if Constraints 1(A) are satisfied as equalities. Conditions (i) then state that the imputed values are such that no production activity will make a profit, and only those activities that break even will be operated at nonzero activity levels. Conditions (ii) are best examined by considering typical elements of the vector $t - \beta^*W$ and scalar $(t - \beta^*W)w^*$. These are:

$$t_{nvu} - (\beta^*_{nu} - \beta^*_{nv}) \geq 0 \tag{3.6.4}$$

$$(t_{nvu} - (\beta^*_{nu} - \beta^*_{nv}))w^*_{nvu} = 0. \tag{3.6.5}$$

Reorganising (3.6.4), we have

$$\beta^*_{nu} \leq t_{nvu} + \beta^*_{nv}. \tag{3.6.6}$$

The imputed values must be such that the value of a commodity nu is no greater than the value of commodity nv plus the transport cost involved in moving the good n from node v to node u along the transport branch (v,u). Clearly this relation is transitive and we can state the rather more general condition that the imputed value of a commodity nu must be no greater than the imputed value of commodity nv plus the transport cost of moving good n from node v to node u along the least cost path from v to u. Equation (3.6.5) then indicates that a transport activity will be operated at a nonzero level only if the increase in imputed value of the good as a result of the move is sufficient to cover the transport cost.

Comparing imputed values gives us an indication, therefore, of the relative locational advantage of particular nodes for each good. For example, comparing β^*_{nu} with β^*_{nv} ($v \neq u$) indicates the comparative advantage of node v over node u for good n.

As we indicated, each of these conditions is standard in the literature. What is peculiar to our study is that the imputed values must satisfy all three conditions at once. In other words, when the β^*_{nv} are partitioned by good, they must satisfy the transportation conditions; and when they are partitioned by location, they must satisfy the production conditions.

A final point should be made in closing this chapter. Our analysis in this section has shown that an optimal solution could be maintained by a decentralised pricing system. The introduction of transport costs does not bring with it the complications discovered by Koopmans and Beckmann (1957). The reason for this is clear. Koopmans and Beckmann were concerned with the integral assignment of plants to locations. Our analysis of the linear model does not involve this indivisibility condition and so does not induce the failure of decentralised decision making.

4 THE STATIC THEORETICAL MODEL WITH INCREASING RETURNS

4.1 INTRODUCTION

A theoretical model such as that specified in the previous chapter may be used to 'explain' location decisions of two broad types. Firstly, we may assume that the market area contains no pre-existing productive capacity for the industry being studied. The decision-maker is presented with a known demand, known supply sources, and a number of green-field sites. He has to decide what productive capacity to put at each site to satisfy total demand at least cost. Since there is no pre-existing capacity, there are no constraints upon the type or quantity of productive capacity that may be located at any site, other than constraints which may arise from commodity availability and the current technology. The industry can, therefore, be assumed to be adjusted to the technology.

The second type of decision is taken in a market in which some productive capacity already exists. In this case, considerations additional to those mentioned above are introduced, affecting the type and distribution of new productive capacity. The industry is not fully adjusted to the technology since these considerations affect the range of techniques which may be used at any site.

We shall confine our attention to the former class of decisions. But then a significant limitation of the model as it stands is the assumption of constant

40

returns to scale. The model attempts to explain the location of new productive capacity, but the linearity assumptions are too simple for us to make valid statements about the ways in which industry concentrates in space. The influence of transport costs is to encourage spatial dispersal of productive capacity. As long as we maintain the assumption of constant returns in production, this influence will be overstated for any industry characterised by increasing returns. For example, if we consider the market to be homogeneous with all commodities available at every location, then in the optimal solution there would be no transportation. Each source of demand for final products would supply itself and no-one else. If we allow for varying factor endowments at the various nodes, then we may see some spatial concentration emerging; but, again, this will be through the effects of transport costs alone and not from the properties of the production process.

In the following paragraphs we shall investigate the form that returns to scale should take in our model, the form of the resulting cost curves, and the computational problems involved in their introduction to a linear programme.

4.2 ECONOMIES OF SCALE

The existence, nature, and measurement of economies of scale have been the subject of debate at least since the writings of Adam Smith. The existence debate has long been resolved, but there remains an ongoing discussion regarding the nature of economies of scale and how they are best measured.

4.2.1 Definition of the Production Unit

Any empirical or theoretical contribution to the debate mentioned above must first pose the question: what is meant by the blanket term 'economies of scale'? This question, in turn, can only be answered given a definition of the production unit with respect to the scale of which economies of scale are to be measured. In other words, we have to indicate whether we are considering economies of scale with respect to the plant, the establishment—which may be made up of a group of contiguous plants—or the firm—which can be looked upon in the majority of cases as an organisational unit containing a number of establishments.

Although the sources of economies of scale and their absolute and relative importance will vary with the choice of production unit, there should be no presumption that any one choice of production unit is any 'better' or 'more relevant' than any other. What should be recognised, however, is that no matter whether it is a plant, establishment, or firm, the production unit will generally consist of a number of separate production activities that are more or less integrated. The degree of integration and its direction — vertical or horizontal — are important. For example, we should ask whether the pattern of horizontal or vertical integration is fixed. Is there any economic reason why all plants at a particular stage of the production process should contain the same activities in the same relationship to each other? Do firms in an industry organise plants at the various stages of production along the same lines? Clearly, the more variable is the possible intraplant or intrafirm organisation in an industry, the more ambiguous will be any empirical investigation of economies of scale for that industry for any choice of production unit other than the individual production activity.

Finally, we must define what we mean by the 'scale' of the production unit. Silberston (1972) has indicated that scale is a multidimensional concept; it refers not only to the rate of output per unit period, but also to the total quantity produced over the life of the production unit, the range of goods produced, etc. Obviously, the more complex the choice of production unit, the more difficult it will be to find an unambiguous measure of scale, e.g. in any industry the scale of a plant will be easier to define than the scale of a firm.

No attempt will be made at this stage to answer the various questions raised above, for the simple reason that they do not admit of general answers. They can only be resolved in the light of knowledge of the particular industry under investigation.

4.2.2 The Definition of Economies of Scale

We propose the following series of assumptions on the basis of which a definition of economies of scale can be formulated for a particular choice of production unit:

Assumption 1: We can identify an unambiguous measure of the scale of the production unit.

Sufficient conditions for this assumption to be satisfied are either that the production unit produces a single output, or that joint products are produced in fixed proportions.

Assumption 2: Inputs and outputs are homogeneous.
Assumption 3: The production unit is utilised for a constant proportion of each 'week' or 'year'.
Assumption 4: Production is in a steady state and the sole determinant of scale is the rate of output per unit period.

The first part of assumption 4 implies that there is no stockbuilding of work in progress. A sufficient condition for the second part would be that deposits of nonreplaceable inputs do not impose any constraints upon the scale of the production unit. A necessary condition is that the expected life of the production unit is independent of its rate of output per unit period.

We shall concentrate on a static definition of economies of scale and so add the further assumption:

Assumption 5: There is a given state of technical knowledge and managerial skill.

We now define economies of scale for a production unit in terms of the magnitude of the elasticity of the cost function for that unit. The elasticity of a function f with respect to some decision variable x is defined as:

$$e_x^f = \frac{d\log(f)}{d\log(x)} \, . \tag{4.2.1}$$

The function f is easily defined for our purposes as being the cost function, but the elasticity of f cannot be defined without first defining 'x', the variable with respect to which the elasticity is to be measured. The various alternatives are perhaps best illustrated by reference to the following classificatory scheme:

Table 4.1

	Elasticity with respect to:	
	Single Input	*All Inputs*
Elasticity of Cost Function	I	II

Elasticities I will vary depending upon the assumptions we make regarding the behaviour of the other inputs. On the one hand, we might assume that other inputs are fixed. The elasticity of $f(x_1, x_2, \ldots x_n)$ with respect to x_i is then:

$$e_{x_i}^{\prime f} = \frac{\partial f}{\partial x_i} \cdot \frac{x_i}{f} \tag{4.2.2}$$

Alternatively we might assume that other inputs vary to maintain an optimal input mix, in which case the elasticity of f with respect to x_i is:

$$e_{x_i}^{\prime\prime f} = \frac{df}{dx_i} \cdot \frac{x_i}{f} = \frac{\sum_j \frac{\partial f}{\partial x_j} dx_j}{dx_i} \cdot \frac{x_i}{f} \, . \tag{4.2.3}$$

We rule out of consideration elasticities (4.2.2). Such elasticities relate to the returns to a variable factor used in combination with other factors which are indivisible in the short run, and have no direct relevance to estimates of economies of scale for the production unit.

There are then two main types of elasticity:

(i) cost elasticity of scale for a particular factor input:

For each relative factor price regime we can determine for a given output the cost minimising expenditure on each input.[1] We then allocate to I the elasticity of expenditure on each input with respect to scale given by:

$$e_q^{C_i} = \frac{d\log(C_i^*(q))}{d\log(q)} \quad (i = 1 \ldots n) \tag{4.2.4}$$

where: $C_i^*(q)$ = cost minimising expenditure on factor i under the particular factor price regime,

q = output (scale).

(ii) total cost elasticity of scale:

The total cost function is given by:

$$TC^*(q) = \sum_i C_i^*(q) \tag{4.2.5}$$

and we allocate to II the elasticity:

$$e_q^{TC} = \frac{d\log(TC^*(q))}{d\log(q)}. \tag{4.2.6}$$

It should be emphasised that the elasticities I and II are defined with reference to a particular set of relative factor prices. In other words, we might expect different relative factor price regimes to give rise to different elasticities. One corollary of this is that, no matter which elasticity is considered, this elasticity will not in general be independent of location.

It should be noted that the elasticity II is identical to the 'scale factor' referred to by Silberston (1972) and is the inverse of the degree of homogeneity of the production function.

We can now define what we mean by economies of scale with respect to our choice of production unit. Economies of scale are said to exist with respect to a particular input, or to all inputs, when the appropriate elasticity of the cost function evaluated at constant relative factor prices and incorporating a given technology is less than unity over some or all of the range of attainable scales.[2]

This definition makes no presumption that the elasticity of the cost function will be constant with scale. Indeed, the work of Griliches and Ringstad (1971) would lead us to expect some variation in elasticity, i.e. in the degree of economies of scale available to some or all inputs, over the range of attainable scales.

The definition is static since a date has been put on the cost function. Extensions of the definition to include economies of scale deriving from those factors which work to change the position or form of the function should be obvious but will not be considered in this study.

4.2.3 The Sources of Economies of Scale

This subsection is of necessity brief and no attempt will be made to survey the large body of literature which exists. A number of the more important and seminal references are given in footnote 3.

We can identify four major sources of economies of scale within our static definition:

(i) the topological properties of production. For example, capacity may be related to volume (oil tankers, rotary kilns, etc.) while materials used (and so their cost) may be related to surface area.

(ii) indivisibilities. It may be necessary to employ certain factors in indivisible 'lumps' independent of the scale of the production unit for at least some ranges of scale.

(iii) organisational economies. Unit costs may be reduced by changing the degree of vertical or horizontal integration, e.g. by internalising an imperfect intermediate product market, by reducing the uncertainty of information flows, etc.

(iv) financial economies. Expansion of the production unit may lead to some internalisation of the short term capital market, give rise to monopsony powers in the factor markets, etc.

As has been indicated, the relative importance of these four sources will vary with the choice of production unit. Thus (i) and (ii) are liable to be the dominant sources for the individual production activity, while (iii) may accrue to the plant or establishment and (iv) to the firm.

Little further progress can be made unless we make explicit our choice of production unit. We therefore anticipate the discussion in Chapter 5 and take the cement plant as our production unit. Such a plant consists of three separate production processes whose degree and direction of integration are to all intents and purposes fixed. They may therefore be treated as a single production activity. No great violence is done to empirical realities if we further assume that the materials, fuel, and energy inputs to the plant and the output from the plant are homogeneous. Scale of the production unit is then its rated annual cement-making capacity.

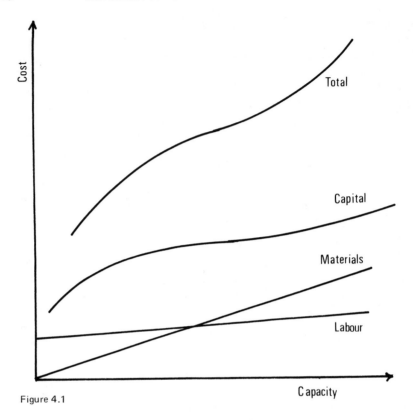

Figure 4.1

Economies of scale to the production unit derive mainly from sources (i) and (ii) above. There is no reason in principle why we should not include economies from (iii), perhaps by defining a coordinating activity to which other activities are input. Data limitations preclude any such attempt, however.

Our approach is then to define the total production cost (TPC) function associated with the production activity **kv**. This function is of the form[4]:

$$TPC_{kv} = T_k \ (x_{kv}) \tag{4.2.7}$$

where: x_{kv} = capacity of the kth. production unit at node v.

It is assumed to consist of three cost elements:

(i) a capital cost element associated with machinery, etc., inputs which can be expected to vary other than proportionally with scale. Economies of scale to this element accrue mainly from source (i).

(ii) a labour cost element, part of which is fixed—management, clerical, and other overheads—and part of which varies linearly with scale. Economies of scale to this element of costs accrue from spreading the fixed labour costs over greater plant scales, i.e. source (ii).

(iii) a variable cost element associated with fuel, energy, mineral and other materials costs which can be expected to vary linearly with capacity. Figure 4.1 illustrates a typical cost function $T_k (\ )$.

Given these assumptions, the production activity vector associated with the production unit has as inputs the variable labour component and the commodities that enter into cost element (iii), and has as output, units of cement.[5] The total costs of operating the production unit consist of an element related to the capital and fixed labour inputs (which do not enter into the production activity vector) plus an element linear in the activity level.

4.3 RESPECIFICATION OF THE PROGRAMMING PROBLEM: PART I

Given a cost function of the form $T(x)$, the most important question is how this cost function can be incorporated in the model developed in Chapter 3. With $T(x)$ a smooth, continuous function, the short answer is that, as it stands, it cannot.[8] We therefore replace $T(x)$ by a function which captures the essential features of $T(x)$ but which is more amenable to inclusion in the model.

The most convenient form for our purposes is a linear spline, i.e. a piece-wise linear, continuous function. In other words, we replace the smooth function $T(x)$ by a piece-wise linear function which we shall denote $TT(x)$, and which approximates $T(x)$ to some desired degree of accuracy; a typical estimate is illustrated in Figure 4.2. The method we have adopted for estimating $TT(x)$ is discussed in Chapter 5.[9]

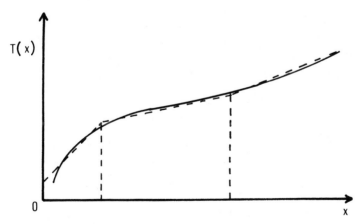

Figure 4.2

4.4 QUASI PRODUCTION ACTIVITIES

For technical reasons we would like to associate some form of production activity with each of the linear segments of the linear spline for production unit kv. The first point to note in this respect is that the assumptions made in paragraph 4.2 in defining the cost function $T_k(x_{kv})$ are such that we can identify an activity vector a_{kv}^i for each of the $I(k)$ segments of the linear spline for production unit kv. Secondly, the activity vectors identified for a particular spline are identical.[10] Thirdly, from the construction of Figure 4.2, we note that the ith. linear segment of the spline for production unit kv is defined for a range of capacities $(\hat{x}_{kv}^{i-1}, \hat{x}_{kv}^i]$ and has equation:

$$TT(x_{kv}^i) = m_{kv}^i + v_{kv}^i x_{kv}^i \quad \text{if } x_{kv}^i \in (\hat{x}_{kv}^{i-1}, \hat{x}_{kv}^i] \tag{4.4.1}$$

$$= 0 \text{ otherwise} \quad (i = 1 \ldots I(k); k = 1 \ldots K; v \in G^S).$$

We now assume that the segments of the spline for production unit kv are numbered from left to right and define

$$\hat{x}_{kv}^o = 0 \quad \text{all } k,v. \tag{4.4.2}$$

A quasi production activity is then defined as follows:

Quasi Production Activity: A quasi production activity $k^i v$ of production unit kv is defined by the ordered quadruple $(m_{kv}^i, v_{kv}^i, a_{kv}^i, x_{kv}^i)$ $(i = 1 \ldots I(k); k = 1 \ldots K; v \in G^S)$ where:

m_{kv}^i, v_{kv}^i are the cost components of quasi production activity $k^i v$,
a_{kv}^i is the activity vector for quasi production activity $k^i v$ such
that $a_{kv}^i = a_{kv}$ for all i,
x_{kv}^i is the activity level of the quasi production activity $k^i v$.
The activity vector is as defined in Chapter 3. The activity level
x_{kv}^i is such that $x_{kv}^i = 0$ or $\hat{x}_{kv}^{i-1} < x_{kv}^i \leq \hat{x}_{kv}^i$. Total production cost
of operating quasi production activity $k^i v$ is
$TT(x_{kv}^i) = 0$ if $x_{kv}^i = 0$ and $= m_{kv}^i + v_{kv}^i x_{kv}^i$ if $\hat{x}_{kv}^{i-1} < x_{kv}^i \leq \hat{x}_{kv}^i$.

Quasi production activities are defined solely at nodes in G^S.

Several points should be noted from this definition. Firstly, the cost component v_{kv}^i should not be considered to be a variable cost component, since it will generally include some element of capital costs. Secondly, if the quasi production activity is operated at all it must be operated *at least* at activity level $\hat{x}_{kv}^{i-1}$. Finally, with the exception of total operating costs $TT(x_{kv}^i)$ and the restrictions on activity levels x_{kv}^i, quasi production activities are identical with production activities as defined in Chapter 3.

4.5 TOTAL PRODUCTION COSTS FOR THE PRODUCTION UNIT

The definition of a quasi production activity is such that unit production costs for the activity are monotonic decreasing (increasing) if $m_{kv}^i > (<) 0$. We are more interested, however, in the behaviour of unit production costs for the production unit as a whole. The case study in the following chapters refers to one of the process industries, and we have already noted that these industries are generally characterised by economies of scale. In other words, if we define average production costs for quasi production activity $k^i v$ as

$$AA(x_{kv}^i) = TT(x_{kv}^i)/x_{kv}^i \quad \text{if } x_{kv}^i \in (\hat{x}_{kv}^{i-1}, \hat{x}_{kv}^i] \qquad (4.5.1)$$

then in general:

(i)
$$\left. \begin{array}{l} \dfrac{dAA}{dx_{kv}^i} < 0 \\[4mm] AA(x_{kv}^i) > AA(x_{kv}^{i+1}) \end{array} \right\} \quad \text{all } i,k,v. \qquad (4.5.2)$$

(ii)

In Figure 4.3 the shaded area is the attainable point set for production costs of operating production unit kv, while the boundary ABCD is the efficient point set. The quasi production activity $k^i v$ then represents the least cost method of operating the production unit at activity levels in the range $(\hat{x}_{kv}^{i-1}, \hat{x}_{kv}^i]$. In addition, given that (4.5.2) holds, corresponding to each activity level of the production unit up to some maximum activity level $\hat{x}_{kv}^{I(k)}$ there is a single quasi production activity that produces the associated output at least cost.

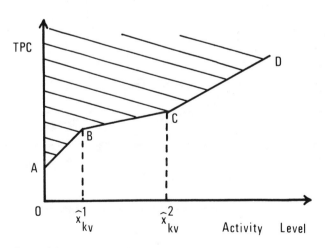

Figure 4.3

Let us examine the implications of postulating the existence of such a maximum activity level. If the output associated with this activity level is less than total market demand, then an absolute limit is defined on economies of scale available to the production unit. More important, however, is the further implication that production in excess of $\hat{x}_{kv}^{I(k)}$ will lead to an increase in unit production costs from the need to replicate production unit kv. In Figure 4.4, unit production costs for production unit kv are minimised (at A*) at activity level $\hat{x}_{kv}^3$ and at integer multiples of this activity level. For all other activity levels, however, unit production costs are greater than A*.

The empirical studies to which we refer in footnote 3 indicate that in certain of the process industries economies of scale are exhausted at some finite activity level. They also indicate, however, that there is little justification for the proposition that decreasing returns then set in. We shall assume, therefore, that each production unit is characterised by constant returns for output in excess of some limit. In other words, the I(k)th. quasi activity for the production unit **kv** is assumed to have the total production cost function:

$$TT(x_{kv}^{I(k)}) = v_{kv}^{I(k)} \cdot x_{kv}^{I(k)} \qquad \text{all } k,v \qquad (4.5.3)$$

and is such that

$$x_{kv}^{I(k)} = 0 \text{ or} > \hat{x}_{kv}^{I(k)-1}. \qquad (4.5.4)$$

No upper limits are imposed on the activity levels of the quasi production activities defined by (4.5.3) and (4.5.4) other than those imposed by resource

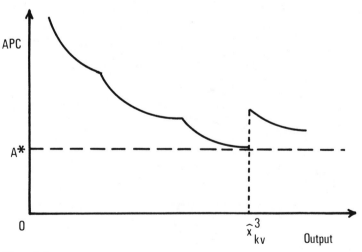

Figure 4.4

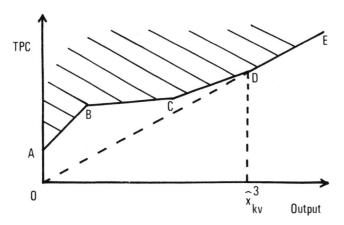

Figure 4.5

constraints, etc. The total production cost function for a production unit kv is then as illustrated in Figure 4.5.

It should be noted that this approach is necessary, and indeed justifiable, only if we have no information about the behaviour of TPC at 'very large' plant capacities. If data are available which indicate the presence of diseconomies of scale the assumption of constant returns is clearly untenable. We may then find that replication as in Figure 4.4 will prove to be the optimal strategy. Alternatively, given that, for example, we have observations on TPC up to plant capacities of $\hat{x}_{kv}^{J(k)-1}$, it appears unreasonable to extrapolate directly on the basis of these observations since such extrapolation may well overstate the available economies of scale. The assumption of constant returns to scale for plant capacities in excess of $\hat{x}_{kv}^{J(k)-1}$ can therefore be looked upon as a compromise forced by lack of data.

4.6 RESPECIFICATION OF THE PROGRAMMING PROBLEM: PART II

We recall the form of total production costs for a quasi production activity:

$$TT(x_{kv}^i) = m_{kv}^i + v_{kv}^i x_{kv}^i \qquad \text{if } x_{kv}^i \neq 0 \qquad (4.6.1)$$

$$= 0 \qquad \text{if } x_{kv}^i = 0,$$

subject to the constraints:

$$\hat{x}_{kv}^{i-1} < x_{kv}^i \leq \hat{x}_{kv}^i \text{ or } x_{kv}^i = 0 \qquad (4.6.2)$$

where $\hat{x}_{kv}^{J(k)}$ is some arbitrarily large number and $m_{kv}^{J(k)} = \hat{x}_{kv}^0 = 0$.

As can be seen the constraints define an 'either/or' situation. A neater way to present this system is to define variables γ^i_{kv} for each production unit such that:

$$\gamma^i_{kv} = 0 \text{ if } x^i_{kv} = 0 \qquad\qquad (4.6.3)$$
$$= 1 \text{ if } x^i_{kv} > 0 \qquad (\text{all } k,i,v)$$

The system (4.6.1), (4.6.2) then becomes:

$$TT(x^i_{kv}) = \gamma^i_{kv} m^i_{kv} + v^i_{kv} x^i_{kv} \qquad\qquad (4.6.4)$$

subject to

$$x^i_{kv} \geq \gamma^i_{kv} \hat{x}^{i-1}_{kv} \qquad\qquad (4.6.5)$$
$$x^i_{kv} \leq \gamma^i_{kv} \hat{x}^i_{kv} \qquad (\text{all } i,k,v). \qquad\qquad (4.6.6)$$
$$\gamma^i_{kv} = 0 \text{ or } 1 \qquad\qquad (4.6.7)$$

It is easy to show that this system is identical with that in (4.6.1) and (4.6.2):

(i) $\gamma^i_{kv} = 0$: From (4.6.6) we have $x^i_{kv} \leq 0$ and from (4.6.5) $x^i_{kv} \geq 0$, hence $x^i_{kv} = 0$ and $TT(x^i_{kv}) = 0$ from (4.6.4).

(ii) $\gamma^i_{kv} = 1$: From (4.6.5) and (4.6.6) we have $\hat{x}^{i-1}_{kv} < x^i_{kv} < \hat{x}^i_{kv}$ and from (4.6.4) $TT(x^i_{kv}) = m^i_{kv} + v^i_{kv} x^i_{kv}$.

Total production costs for the production unit kv are given by

$$TT(x_{kv}) = \sum_i (\gamma^i_{kv} m^i_{kv} + v^i_{kv} x^i_{kv}) \qquad (\text{all } k,v) \qquad\qquad (4.6.8)$$

where each element of the sum satisfies (4.6.5)–(4.6.7)
and $x_{kv} = \sum_i x^i_{kv}$.

It should be noted that the analysis above relies on the discussion in paragraph 4.5, i.e. on the assumption that returns to scale to the production unit are at worst constant. As a result, in an optimal production plan at most one of the γ^i_{kv} in (4.6.8) will be nonzero for any production unit kv. If the assumption of constant returns to scale is not acceptable in a particular industry, i.e. if decreasing returns set in at some plant scale, our formulation needs but little amendment. All that is required is that the restrictions on the γ^i_{kv} be relaxed to allow them to take any nonnegative integer values. The system is then totally general in that a producer can choose between having only one quasi production activity at a particular node, or replicating quasi production activities at that node.

The variables γ^i_{kv} can be regarded as activity levels defining which quasi production activities are to be operated, and the programming problem can be respecified to take account of equations (4.6.1) through (4.6.8). We define the vectors γ, m with typical elements γ_{kv}^i and m_{kv}^i and redefine the vector x with typical element x_{kv}^i as we did for the vector x in Chapter 3. The programming problem is then:

The Mixed Integer Programme (MIP). Find activity levels $(\gamma^*, x^*, w^*) \geq 0$ which minimise total cost

$$Z^* = m \cdot \gamma^* + v \cdot x^* + t \cdot w^*$$

subject to the constraints:

(i) $$Tx^* + Ww^* \geq \lambda$$

(ii) $$Dw^* \leq d$$

(iii) $$x_{kv}^i - \gamma_{kv}^i \hat{x}_{kv}^{i-1} \geq 0$$

(iv) $$x_{kv}^i - \gamma_{kv}^i \hat{x}_{kv}^i \leq 0$$

(v) $$\gamma_{kv}^i = 0 \text{ or } 1$$

(vi) $$\gamma^*, x^*, w^* \geq 0.$$

The constraints (i) and (ii) are as in Chapter 3 and the constraints (iii) through (v) are as discussed above.

As indicated, the programming problem is a mixed integer programme (MIP) in which some of the decision variables can take nonnegative real values and others are constrained to take only non negative integer values.[11] The solution of such a problem is far from straightforward since an MIP exhibits few of the 'nice' properties of linear programmes. In particular, concepts such as imputed values are rather awkward to interpret and we can say little about the general nature of the optimal solution. Gomory and Baumol (1960) have developed a concept of dual prices for problems in which all decision variables are constrained to be integer, but their techniques do not carry over to the mixed integer case.

4.7 COMBINATION OF PRODUCTION ACTIVITIES

Our analysis has associated with each production unit kv a set of quasi production activities $k^i v$ $(i = 1 \ldots I(k))$ and a unique activity vector a_{kv}. One consequence of this approach is that quasi production activities from different production units can be combined at any potential production site in G^S only if the full capital and fixed labour costs associated with *each* quasi production activity are incurred. The underlying assumption is that the machinery, etc., represented by the capital cost element of $TT(x_{kv}^i)$ can be used in only one way.

So long as the production unit produces a single output, or is one in which joint products are produced in fixed proportions, this assumption is not particularly restrictive. There are cases, however, in which significant changes in the commodity output mix produced by a particular production unit can be achieved solely by changing the commodity input mix. In these circumstances we should perhaps identify some *set* of activity vectors operable by the production unit, convex combinations of which will define all possible input/output commodity mixes attainable on the unit. Operating costs of the production unit would then be related to its joint production activity level.

Assume that we can define such a set of activity vectors a_{kv}^j, $j = 1 \ldots J(k)$ operable on the production unit kv. The costs of operating the production unit then consist of two components. Firstly, we have variable costs linear in the activity level x_{kv}^j of the particular activity vector:

$$v_{kv}^j = - \sum_{n=0}^{N} a_{nkv}^j c_n \qquad (j = 1 \ldots J(k); \text{ all } k, v). \qquad (4.7.1)$$

This component will include variable labour costs—assumed linear in the activity level—but will exclude fixed labour costs and capital costs. We assume that the latter costs are dependent solely on the capacity of the production unit, i.e. are independent of which activity vectors are actually operated on the production unit. Secondly, there are capital and fixed labour costs associated with the production unit. These will have a form similar to that illustrated in Figure 4.2, and we approximate to this form by a linear spline as in paragraph 4.3 to produce a cost function similar to (4.6.4). Assume that the capacity of the production unit kv is denoted by z_{kv}.[12] Then the cost function associated with capital and fixed labour costs is:

$$TT(z_{kv}^i) = \delta_{kv}^i \mu_{kv}^i + \nu_{kv}^i z_{kv}^i \qquad (4.7.2)$$

where μ_{kv}^i = fixed cost element of segment i of the spline,

$\quad\quad \nu_{kv}^i$ = variable cost element of segment i of the spline,

$$z_{kv} = \sum_i z_{kv}^i \, ,$$

subject to the constraints:

$$z_{kv}^i \geq \delta_{kv}^i \hat{z}_{kv}^{i-1} \qquad (4.7.3)$$

$$z_{kv}^i \leq \delta_{kv}^i \hat{z}_{kv}^i \qquad (4.7.4)$$

$$\delta_{kv}^i = 0 \text{ or } 1. \qquad (4.7.5)$$

We now assume firstly that the 'scale of operation' of the production unit is given by the sum of the activity levels x^j_{kv} and, secondly, that 'scale' and 'capacity' are identical. Thus we need a further constraint – the scale of operation cannot exceed installed capacity:

$$\sum_{i=1}^{I(k)} z^i_{kv} - \sum_{j=1}^{J(k)} x^j_{kv} \geq 0 \quad \text{all } k,v. \tag{4.7.6}$$

We can now respecify the MIP. In the objective function we replace the cost element $\mathbf{m}\cdot\gamma + \mathbf{v}\cdot\mathbf{x}$ by the element $\mu\cdot\delta + \upsilon\cdot\mathbf{z} + \mathbf{v}\cdot\mathbf{x}$ (where $\mathbf{x}$ now has typical element x^j_{kv} rather than x^i_{kv}). The technology matrix is amended to contain the activity vectors $\mathbf{a}^j_{kv}$. The revised MIP is then:

Revised Mixed Integer Programme. Find $(\delta^*,z^*,x^*,w^*) \geq 0$ to minimise total cost

$$Z^* = \mu\cdot\delta^* + \upsilon\cdot z^* + \mathbf{v}\cdot x^* + \mathbf{t}\cdot w^*$$

subject to the constraints:

(i) $\qquad\qquad\qquad Tx^* + Ww^* \geq \lambda$

(ii) $\qquad\qquad\qquad Dw^* \leq \mathbf{d}$

(iii) $\qquad\qquad\qquad z^i_{kv} - \delta^i_{kv}\hat{z}^{i-1}_{kv} \geq 0$

(iv) $\qquad\qquad\qquad z^i_{kv} - \delta^i_{kv}\hat{z}^i_{kv} \leq 0$

(v) $\qquad\qquad\qquad \sum_i z^i_{kv} - \sum_j x^j_{kv} \geq 0$

(vi) $\qquad\qquad\qquad \delta^i_{kv} = 0 \text{ or } 1$

(vii) $\qquad\qquad\qquad \delta^*, z^*, x^*, w^* \geq 0.$

It should be noted that in this revised version of the MIP, combination of production activities in *different production units* will still incur all capital and fixed labour costs associated with each activity. In other words, the only economy to agglomeration of production *units* comes from the reduction in transport costs associated with intermediate products output by one production unit and input to another at the same location.

Comparison of the two versions of the MIP indicates that they have very similar structures, but also indicates that the revised version contains rather more decision variables. As a result, if we can assume that each production unit has associated only one activity vector we would be better to use the version presented in paragraph 4.6. That is, if we can assume that the output from each production unit is homogeneous (or appears in fixed proportions), we can use the original formulation. We shall find that the homogeneity assumption is satisfied in our case study and shall therefore confine our attention below to the original version of the MIP.

4.8 COMPUTATIONAL PROBLEMS

The general problems to be faced when economies of scale are introduced have been illustrated by Farrell (1957).[13]

> 'The difference between the two cases (of increasing and decreasing returns) is illustrated in (Figure 4.6) for the simple case of one input and one output. Whereas under diseconomies of scale, the efficient production function S is convex, so that the average of two points on S is attainable . . . in the case of economies of scale this is not so. This is a serious matter, as the whole method is based on convexity.' (Farrell 1957, p. 258)

In a later article, Farrell and Fieldhouse (1962) suggest that one method of getting over the difficulties that increasing returns introduce is to transform the nonconvex attainable point set into a space in which this set is convex. Such a transformation cannot be defined for the MIP, however, since this type of problem involves discontinuity as well as nonconvexity of the iso-cost lines. Figure 4.7 gives a simple example.

Assume that there are two activities a_k ($k = 1,2$), which combine inputs of commodity 1 and commodity 2 in the ratios indicated to produce a single output. Points a_1' and a_2' define the activity levels x_k' ($k = 1,2$) that produce unit output, and the constraints are assumed to define the convex boundary ABCD. For simplicity, the minimum activity level x_k for each activity is assumed to be zero.

Total production costs are given by:

$$Z = \gamma_1 m_1 + \gamma_2 m_2 + v_1 x_1 + v_2 x_2 \qquad (4.8.1)$$

where: v_k = unit operating cost of activity k,

m_k = overhead cost of activity k,

$\gamma_k = 0$ if $x_k = 0$

$= 1$ if $x_k > 0$.

On Z_1 B is the only feasible point and cost at B equals

$$Z_1 = m_1 + v_1 x_1. \qquad (4.8.2)$$

Similarly at C cost is

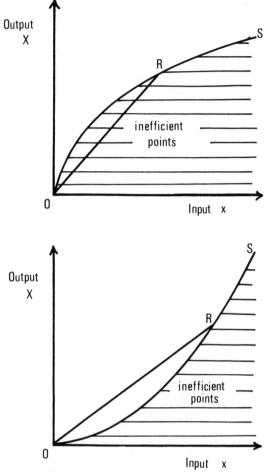

Figure 4.6

$$Z_2 = m_2 + v_2 x_2. \qquad (4.8.3)$$

By construction, Z_1 and Z_2 are parallel, and so:

$$v_1 x_1 < v_2 x_2 \qquad (4.8.4)$$

(these costs are made up of linear combinations of the costs of the two commodities).

If the model were strictly linear then B would be the optimal (minimum cost) solution. But if

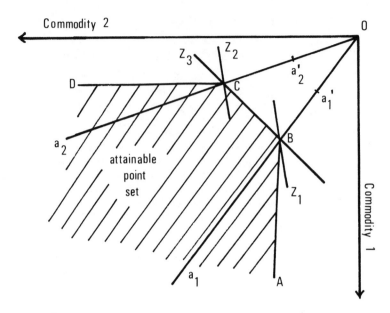

Figure 4.7

$$m_1 - m_2 > v_2 x_2 - v_1 x_1 \qquad (4.8.5)$$

then C will be the minimum cost solution. Any point between B and C can be ignored since at any relatively interior point on the line BC cost is

$$Z_3 = m_1 + m_2 + \alpha v_1 x_1 + (1 - \alpha) v_2 x_2 > Z_1 \text{ and/or } Z_2 \quad (0 < \alpha < 1). \quad (4.8.6)$$

The nonconvexity and discontinuity in Z which this simple example illustrates leads to a breakdown of the simplex method when it is applied to a problem in which a subset of the decision variables are constrained to be integer. Roughly, the simplex method starts by choosing an arbitrary, basic, feasible solution which is a vertex of the convex space defined by the constraints. Cost is computed at this vertex (in a minimising problem) and at the adjacent vertices. The next choice of basic, feasible solution is the adjacent vertex with the lowest cost. This process continues until a vertex is reached at which no adjacent vertex has lower cost; only a fraction of the basic, feasible vertices will have been searched.

The crucial property upon which the simplex method is based is that there will be no local optima of the objective function which are not global optima. But we have shown that as a result of the nonconvexities which characterise programming problems formulated as MIPs, the MIP may well contain vertices which are local optima but which need not be global optima: B in Figure 4.7 is a local minimum, but if (4.8.5), holds B is not the global minimum. There is then no guarantee that the simplex method will lead to the global optimum. If there are additional vertices which are basic and feasible $-V_1$ and V_2, say $-$ such that V_1 is adjacent to B but not to C and V_2 is adjacent to C but not to B, and such that cost satisfies

$$C < B < V_1 < V_2 \qquad (4.8.7)$$

then B will be the resultant local minimum if the system starts at B or V_1 while C would be the local minimum reached if the system starts at V_2 or C.

A great deal of work has been put into developing algorithms for solving programming problems with integer constraints $-$ see Balinski (1970) for a review of some of this work. The common feature of many of these algorithms is that they have been developed to deal with problems of specific types, but the underlying techniques can be applied to any MIP once the appropriate amendments have been made.

One of the most general algorithms is 'branch and bound' $-$ see Land and Doig (1960). Detailed discussion of some variants of this algorithm and some indication of its success are given in Agin (1966), Beale and Small (1965) and White (1970).

Branch and bound is a finite, general purpose technique. The basic idea is to formulate the MIP as an LP by ignoring the integer constraints. The convex feasible region of the resulting LP is then partitioned into convex subsets and a lower bound found for each subset in the partition. If a solution satisfying the integer constraints can be found which has an objective function value no greater (in a minimising problem) than the lower bound on all the subsets, it is the optimum solution.

The procedure relies on the property that adding a constraint to a minimising LP will either increase the value of the objective function, or at best leave it unchanged. As a result, only a fraction of the possible combinations of integer constrained variables need be searched to give an optimal solution, and the search procedure guarantees convergence on the global optimum in a finite number of steps.

We have been fortunate in that a programming package MPCODE developed by A. Land and S. Powell (1973) has been made available to us. The general solution procedure employed in MPCODE is a variant on the original branch and bound algorithm and is described in some detail by Land and Powell. They report that their algorithm obtains the optimal feasible solution to a wide class of problems with significant savings in computer time over other methods.

5 CASE STUDY– THE CEMENT INDUSTRY

5.1 INTRODUCTION

The cement industry has been chosen as our case study for several reasons. Firstly, we shall see below that the production process is relatively straightforward: there is a small number of homogeneous inputs that are combined to produce a homogeneous output. As a result the industry is easy to model.

Secondly, while the bulk of cement output is consumed by only two industrial sectors, this output constitutes a negligible proportion of the consuming sectors' costs. Thus we can assume that the location of cement production will have little effect upon the location of those industries which consume cement.

Finally, the inputs to and outputs from the cement production process are bulky and expensive to transport. As a result transport costs are high relative to value added. But there are significant increasing returns to scale in production. Thus, on the one hand transport costs encourage a spatially dispersed pattern of production, and on the other, production costs encourage a spatially concentrated pattern. The industry provides an interesting example of the trade-off between these two forces.

Portland cement is the product obtained by finely pulverising clinker. The clinker is produced by roasting at high temperature an intimate and properly

60

proportioned mixture of clay and limestone materials, with no additions subsequent to roasting except water and gypsum.

There are three distinct operations in cement manufacture. The first process involves assembling, preparing, grinding, and amalgamating the raw materials in the appropriate proportions. The resulting mixture will be either a liquid slurry or a dry rough powder, depending upon whether the wet or dry process is used at the next stage; the choice of process will usually be determined by the water content of the raw materials.

In the second process, the mixture produced by the first process is roasted at high temperature to form cement clinker. This is accomplished using rotary kilns that are inclined at a pitch of about 3/4 inch per foot and rotate slowly. The fuel most commonly used to fire the kilns is pulverised coal which is fed in at the discharge (lower) end of the kiln.

The hot clinker, after it drops out of the kiln, is conveyed to rotary or stationary coolers prior to the third process, in which the clinker together with a small amount of retarding agent (gypsum) is ground to the fine powder known as cement.

It is clear from this summary that the cement production process is capital intensive in the sense of employing several large units of capital equipment. We would expect to find significant economies to capital costs as scale increases since capacity of many of the units will probably be related to volume, while cost will be more closely related to surface area. In addition, there should be labour economies since labour performs a basically supervisory role.

5.2 STRUCTURE OF THE UK INDUSTRY

After an early history of pricing wars, a cartel was formed in 1934 when a gentlemen's agreement was made providing for price fixing and for regulating output on a quota basis. This price agreement survived, basically unaltered, into the 1960s, by which time amalgamation had reduced the number of firms in the industry to seven. Of these, Associated Portland Cement Manufacturers (APCM) maintained the dominant position built up in the early part of the century, as can be seen from Table 5.1. For a discussion of the effects of mergers in the industry, see Cook (1958).

Table 5.1 and Table 5.2 further indicate that the UK industry is highly concentrated, exclusive, and specialised. We can state therefore that the cement industry produces a homogeneous product and that an insignificant proportion of this product is produced by establishments classified to other industries, features which are desirable in terms of our theoretical model.

We can also treat the industry as being closed to the UK for the present study.

Table 5.1. UK Cement Manufacture 1966

Manufacturer	Output (th. tons)	Per Cent
APCM	9961	61
Tunnel	2224	14
Rugby	2046	12
Aberthaw (26% owned by APCM)	617	4
Ribblesdale (50/50 Tunnel and Ketton)	521	3
Ketton	519	3
ICI	427	3
	16315	100

Source: National Board for Prices and Incomes (NBPI) Report No. 38; Portland Cement Prices – 1967.

Table 5.2. Structure of the UK Cement Industry 1963

Degree of Specialisation[a]	85.5%
Degree of Exclusiveness[b]	98.2%
Degree of Concentration[c]	87.0%

Source: Census of Production 1963; Table 5.1.

Notes: (a) Percentage of total sales of goods produced and work done (by value) which is Portland Cement.

(b) Percentage of principal products (by value) of the cement industry sold by establishments classified to the industry.

(c) Percentage of output (by weight) of Portland Cement produced by the three largest firms in the industry. Derived from 1966 data.

Table 5.3. UK Imports and Exports of Cement and Clinker (th. tons)

	Clinker		Cement		
Year	Home Production	Imports*	Home Production	Imports*	Exports
1945	3733	–	4051	–	77
1950	9151	21	9752	91	1835
1955	11662	75	12513	43	1843
1960	12026	341	13288	117	1014
1961	12576	415	14149	215	678
1962	13052	275	14028	108	307
1963	13235	136	13837	100	261
1964	14010	269	16698	146	242
1965	14706	913	16704	194	179
1966	15861	246	16523	159	127

Source: NBPI op. cit.

*Includes imports from the Irish Republic.

The data in Table 5.3 indicate that by 1961 both imports and exports were a negligible proportion of total output. The same applies, with the exception of 1965, to imports of clinker; the sharp rise in clinker imports in 1965 was a result of a 'substantial increase in demand' (NBPI 1967) which could not be met from existing capacity.

5.3 COST STRUCTURE OF THE INDUSTRY

The discussions in paragraphs 5.1 and 5.2 lead us to choose the cement plant as the production unit—see Chapter 4, paragraph 4.2. We have seen that inputs to and output from a cement plant are relatively homogeneous. Further, while the production process consists of three distinct activities, these must be performed in strict temporal sequence. Finally, while there is no reason, in principle, for these activities to be performed at the same location, i.e. for each plant to contain all three activities, there is fairly strong justification for the assumption that this will in fact be the case. There are a few examples of plants that merely grind cement clinker imported from other plants, but these are very much the exception to the general rule that the quarrying, rotary kiln, and clinker grinders are located within the same plant.

We now go on to estimate for the UK industry:

(i) production activities for the industry, and
(ii) regional distribution of demand for and inputs to cement production.

In view of the comments above, the base date we have chosen for the estimates of parameters in the static model is 1963. By this time the industry was well adjusted to the rotary kiln technology first introduced in the early 1900s, and the move to replace exports by production abroad was well established. Inevitably, some of the data reported below refer to years other than the base date, but the majority of the data are taken from the period 1958-68, and as such can be assumed to approximate conditions facing the industry in 1963. Where cost data are taken from years other than 1963, an appropriate deflator is applied.

5.3.1 The Production Process

The basic data sources for the estimates in this section refer to the cement industries in West Germany and the United States, and are therefore not directly applicable to the United Kingdom. Some adjustment will have to be made to the data to allow estimation of the UK production process, and while this adjust-

Table 5.4.   Energy Consumption per tonne of Cement 1960-68

Commodity	Consumption per Tonne of Cement	Price per Unit of Commodity, 1963
Coal and Coke	0.161 tonnes	£4.32 per tonne
Electricity	107 Kwh	£0.00429 per Kwh
Petroleum and Creosote/Pitch	0.061 tonnes	£6.69 per tonne

Source: Ministry of Power, Digest of Energy Statistics, 1969, Table 9; Census of Production 1963.

ment is relatively easy for some items, it is rather awkward for others. We shall consider the more straightforward items – power and mineral consumption – first, then consider the labour and capital components of production in which more severe estimating problems arise.

5.3.1.1 Power Consumption. A United Nations team studied a sample of new cement plants built in the United States in the period 1956-60 (United Nations, 1963); the results are summarised in Appendix B. The data on power consumption in Appendix B are not in a form that can be used in our study, since the various commodities are aggregrated to give consumption in BTU and we would prefer disaggregated figures by commodity. As a result, fuel and energy consumption were estimated from data reported in the *Digest of Energy Statistics.* The data for the period 1960-68 were averaged to give the estimates in Table 5.4: there was little variation in consumption per tonne of cement year by year. Cost data refer to 1963 and were estimated from the *Digest of Energy Statistics* and the *Census of Production 1963.*

As a result of the findings of the United Nations study, consumption of fuel and energy can be taken to be directly proportional to output:

'In the view of a number of experts in this field, there appears to be no significant variation in unit fuel requirements with changes in scale of operation.' (p.9)

'There appears to be little change in electric power consumption with changes in scale of operations.' (p.10)

Consequently, we take fuel and energy costs in production to vary proportionally with output. The data in Table 5.4 give these costs as £1.56 per tonne of cement produced, in 1963 prices.

5.3.1.2 Mineral Consumption. Consumption of minerals per tonne of cement output was taken from the United Nations study on the assumptions:

(i) that the proportions of the various chemicals required to produce cement are the same in the US and UK, and

(ii) that the chemical content of the various raw materials is the same in the two countries.

Cost data refer to the UK in 1963; they have been estimated from the *Census of Production 1963*. The results are summarised in Table 5.5. It should be noted that no prices are given for limestone/chalk or slate/clay. In general these commodities are mined in quarries operated by the cement producers, and an allowance is made in labour and capital cost components for costs incurred in mining and quarrying. In adopting this approach we assume that limestone, chalk, etc., are free goods in their unmined state. As was indicated in Chapter 3, this abstracts from the question of exhaustible resources[1] since it is clear that any particular deposit is finite — and therefore exhaustible — and not replaceable.

Although the input data in Table 5.5 refer to conditions in the US industry in the period 1956-60, there is no reason to suppose that they would have changed significantly by 1963.

Examination of the UN data on mineral consumption indicates that there is no variation in the quantity of each mineral consumed per tonne of cement as scale expands. Thus mineral quantities and costs in production are taken to vary proportionally with output, and costs are estimated to be £0.05 per tonne of cement in 1963 prices. Variable costs of fuel, energy, and minerals thus amount to £1.61 per tonne of cement produced.

There is, in addition, miscellaneous expenditure on packaging materials that should be included as part of variable costs. We assume these materials to be ubiquitous, unlimited in supply, and to exhibit constant returns to scale. From the *Census of Production 1963,* expenditure on packaging materials was £3.785 m. for firms 'employing 25 or more persons'. Total domestic cement production was 13.588 m. tonnes, giving an estimate for packaging costs of £0.28 per tonne of cement. Fuel, energy, mineral and packaging costs, referred to below as variable costs, thus amount to £1.89 per tonne of cement produced.

Table 5.5. Mineral Consumption per tonne of Cement

Mineral	Consumption per Tonne of Cement	Price per Tonne of Mineral, 1963
Limestone/Chalk[a]	1.60 tonnes	—
Slate/Clay[a]	0.30 tonnes	—
Gypsum	0.04 tonnes	£1.22

Source: United Nations, 1963; Census of Production, 1963.
Notes: (a) These minerals are assumed to be one-for-one substitutes by weight.

5.3.1.3 Labour Input

The data at Appendix B indicate, as we expected, that there are economies of scale to the labour input. These data refer to the US industry, however, and are not directly applicable to the UK. Obtaining corresponding estimates for the UK industry is a more complex undertaking than for power or mineral consumption.

We use as a starting point a data series obtained from the *European Cement Association* (1972). These data relate to eighty-three plants in operation in the US in 1970. Employment and plant capacity are reported for each of these plants, and plant output is given for all but four of them.

Our hypothesis is that employment is determined by plant capacity and that there is a fixed relationship between capacity and plant output. In other words, the employment, capacity, output relationships will be estimated from the system:

$$\begin{cases} E = \alpha + \beta C + \epsilon \\ X = \gamma C + \mu \end{cases} \qquad (5.3.1)$$

where E = employment (no.)

X = reported plant output (th. tonnes p.a.)

C = capacity (th. tonnes p.a.)

ϵ, μ = error terms.

Figures 5.1. and 5.2 illustrate the scatter diagrams of employment against capacity, and output against capacity, respectively. It should be noted that the United Nations observations reported in Appendix B exhibit a high degree of agreement with those illustrated in Figure 5.1.

The estimates of (5.3.1) are:

$$E = 59.76 + 0.2309\ C \qquad (R^2 = 0.57;\ 81\ \text{d.f.}) \qquad (5.3.2)$$
$$(12.49)\ (0.0224)$$

and

$$X = 0.8276\ C \qquad (R^2 = 0.91;\ 78\ \text{d.f.}) \qquad (5.3.3)$$
$$(0.0147)$$

All coefficients are significant at the 1% level of significance.

In using the estimates (5.3.2) and (5.3.3) as a basis for estimates of the labour input to UK cement production, we begin with the assumption that the scale elasticity of employment is the same in the two countries.[2] As a result, employment in establishments with the same capacities in the two countries will be in constant proportion at each capacity level, and we may write:

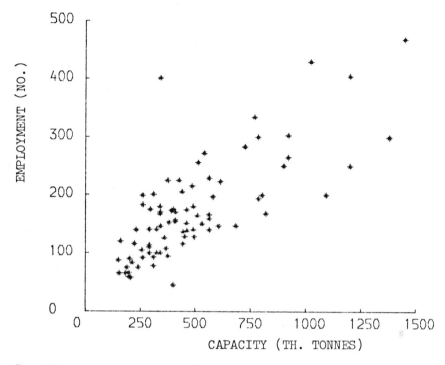

Figure 5.1.

$$E_{UK}(C) = \lambda E_{US}(C) \qquad \text{for all C.} \qquad (5.3.4)$$

What is required is an estimate of λ. The data used to estimate λ and the method of estimation are detailed in Appendix C. We estimate $\lambda = 1.548$, and the estimated equation for the labour input to UK cement production is then:

$$E = 92.51 + 0.3574 \, C. \qquad (5.3.5)$$

It should be noted that the labour input includes an allowance for workers employed in quarrying the basic raw materials (limestone/chalk and slate/clay).

The labour estimates are expressed in numbers per tonne of cement capacity. To convert these numbers to costs per tonne of cement, we estimate the wage rate from the *Census of Production 1963*. The results are summarised in Table 5.6.

By using the simple average reported in Table 5.6, we ignore the possibility that the composition of the labour force in a cement plant may vary with the capacity of the plant. For example, the UN data at Appendix B indicate that 'indirect' labour is, to all intents and purposes, independent of scale. We might

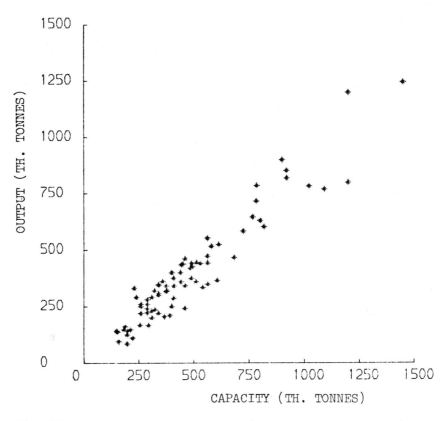

Figure 5.2.

Table 5.6. Wage Rate in UK Cement Manufacture 1963

Total Labour (th.)	14.2
Total Wage (£m.)	14.1
Wage Rate (£)	993.0

Source: Census of Production 1963.

expect the same relationship to carry over to the UK. The distinction in this case would be between 'operatives' and 'others', the respective average wage rates of which were £931 and £1183 in 1963. Attempts to make this distinction, however, indicated that our estimates of labour costs were changed by less than 5% from the simple average method reported above. We decided, therefore, to maintain the estimates in equations (5.3.5) and Table 5.6.

5.3.1.4 Capital costs. The problems that arise in estimating capital costs in UK cement manufacture are similar in many ways to those discussed above for the labour input. In particular, the data relating capital costs and plant capacities refer to the West German and United States industries. We estimate the UK relationship in a manner similar to that adopted in estimating the labour input.

Table 5.7 summarises the data which were made available to us by a firm that designs cement plants. These data are engineering estimates of the relationship between plant scale and 1971 capital costs for cement plants designed and constructed in West Germany.

The characteristics of the data are better seen from Figures 5.3–5.6. Figures 5.3 and 5.4 illustrate the relationship between total and average capital costs and capacity. Despite the convexity of total capital costs for plant capacities in excess of approximately 1.2 m. tonnes per annum, Figure 5.4 indicates that unit capital costs are monotonic decreasing, i.e. there are economies of scale to capital costs throughout the range of plant capacities. While there is a sharp fall in unit capital costs up to plant capacities of about 1.0 m. tonnes p.a. however, the reduction in unit capital costs for greater plant capacities is much less pronounced; there is a less than 6% reduction in unit capital costs when capacity is increased from 2.0 to 3.3 m. tonnes p.a. These data would appear to lend strong support to Pratten's estimate (Pratten, 1971) of a minimum efficient scale of 2.0 m. tonnes p.a. Support is also given to the Griliches and Ringstad finding (see Chapter 4) that the elasticity of scale can be expected to decline with scale. (The elasticity of scale is, on certain assumptions, the inverse of the *cost* elasticity of scale, and the elasticity of capital costs with respect to scale is given by the slope of the total capital cost curve in Figure 5.5.)

It is useful to examine the breakdown of total capital costs to see whether the various components behave differently. Again, a diagrammatic exposition is clearest and we use Figures 5.5 and 5.6. These diagrams are drawn on log-log axes to illustrate the extent to which economies of scale are present. With this type of graph, any curve with a slope less (greater) than the 45° line exhibits economies (diseconomies) of scale to the particular cost component. The slope of the cost curve at any point is the elasticity of the appropriate cost component with respect to scale; the lower the elasticity, the greater the degree of scale economies to that cost component.

Taking total capital costs first, we see that the cost elasticity of scale decreases quite sharply for plant capacities in excess of 250 th. tonnes p.a. and continues to decrease up to plant capacities of about 1.0 m. tonnes p.a. The elasticity then increases gradually but remains less than unity, i.e. unit capital costs continue to fall but at a slower rate for plant capacities in excess of 1.0 m. tonnes p.a.

Mechanical and electrical costs form the greater part of total capital costs. It is not surprising, therefore, that the two series exhibit roughly the same pattern. What *is* perhaps surprising is that economies of scale to mechanical and

Table 5.7. Relationship between Plant Capacity and Capital Costs: West German Cement Industry 1971

Capacity (th. tonnes p.a.)	Total Capital Costs* (DMx10⁶)	Average Capital Costs (DM/tonne)	Mech'l & Elec'l Costs (DMx10⁶)	Civil Eng'g Costs (DMx10⁶)	Machine Erection Costs (DMx10⁶)	Quarry Equip't Costs (DMx10⁶)
82.5	19.8	240	6.5	9.9	1.6	1.0
99.0	23.3	235	8.0	11.4	2.0	1.1
132.0	30.1	228	10.5	14.5	2.4	1.5
166.0	36.6	222	13.1	17.2	3.0	1.8
247.5	52.1	210	20.0	22.9	4.5	2.5
330.0	65.7	199	26.4	27.6	5.8	3.2
412.5	77.6	188	33.2	30.3	7.0	3.8
495.0	88.6	179	38.8	33.7	8.0	4.4
577.5	97.6	169	43.8	36.1	8.9	4.8
660.0	105.6	160	48.5	38.0	9.5	5.2
742.5	112.1	151	52.6	39.2	10.1	5.5
825.0	118.8	144	56.8	40.4	10.7	5.9
907.5	124.3	137	61.1	41.0	11.4	6.2
990.0	129.7	131	63.6	42.8	11.6	6.3
1155.0	142.0	123	70.1	46.9	12.3	6.9
1320.0	154.4	117	77.8	49.4	13.4	7.5
1485.0	167.8	113	85.2	53.7	14.3	7.9
1650.0	183.2	111	94.8	56.8	15.5	8.6
1980.0	213.0	108	111.7	66.3	17.6	9.6
2310.0	242.6	105	129.7	72.7	19.8	10.7
2640.0	272.0	103	146.4	81.6	21.7	11.4
2970.0	303.0	102	167.0	87.9	24.1	12.0
3300.0	330.0	100	185.6	92.4	26.0	13.0

Source: A designer in the industry.
*Includes an allowance for Spares not separately detailed.

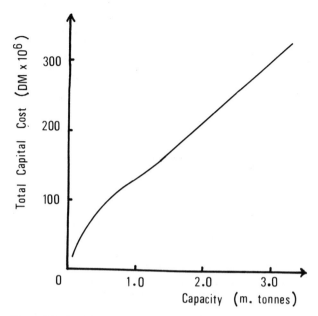

Figure 5.3. Total Capital Costs Related to Capacity.

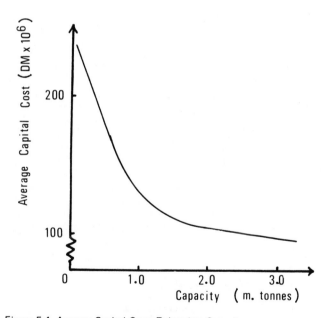

Figure 5.4. Average Capital Costs Related to Capacity.

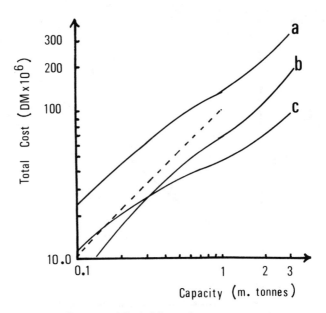

Figure 5.5. Elements of Capital Costs.

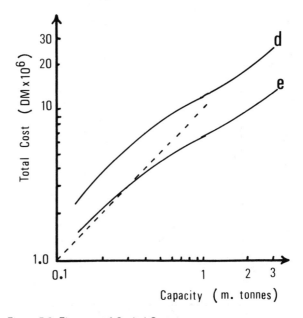

Figure 5.6. Elements of Capital Costs.

Notes: (a) total capital costs; (b) mechanical and electrical costs; (c) civil engineering costs; (d) machine erection costs; (e) quarry equipment costs.

electrical costs are not more pronounced at lower plant scales. The basic items of machinery to which these costs refer are rotary kilns, crushers, grinders, etc. On a priori grounds we might expect the '2/3 rule' to apply, at least approximately, with capacity being related to volume and cost to area. On the other hand, while kilns, etc., are basically tubes, the capacities of which are related to their volumes, they must be supported and driven. At low scales the costs of peripheral equipment can be expected to form a significant proportion of total costs of the equipment and might be expected to increase in direct proportion with scale. In addition, as scale increases, advantage can be taken of various refinements of the basic technology (such as changing the shape of the rotary kiln) that increase the output obtainable from a kiln of a given volume. Beyond some scale, however, the costs of supporting and driving ever larger kilns may well increase more than in proportion to the increase in kiln capacity—so offsetting any savings in the materials used to make the kiln. The gauge of metal used in constructing the kiln will also have to increase to maintain its strength, so introducing a 'volume' element to mechanical costs.

Somewhat the same pattern emerges with respect to the other components of total capital costs. It should be noted that there are quite sharp economies of scale to civil engineering costs (site clearance, foundations, etc.) and to the costs of quarry equipment. These items form a small proportion of total capital costs, with the result that they have little effect on the overall shape of the latter. They do, however, give rise to some degree of economies of scale at low plant capacities despite the near constancy of mechanical and electrical costs.

As with the labour estimates, the data in Table 5.7 cannot be applied directly to the UK industry. To obtain an estimate of UK capital costs, we assume that the elasticity of scale at each plant capacity will be the same in the UK as in West Germany, an assumption which is rather more justifiable than the similar assumption made with respect to the labour input.[3] We assume therefore that:

$$K_{UK}(C) = \mu K_{WG}(C) \quad \text{for all C.} \tag{5.3.6}$$

where: $K_{UK}(C)$ = capital costs in the UK industry (£m.)
                         for plant of capacity C,

$K_{WG}(C)$ = capital costs in the WG industry (DM m.)
                         for plant of capacity C.

To estimate μ we use data reported by Pratten (1971) as 'up to date estimates for new "green-field" cement plants in the UK' (p. 90): see Table 5.8. These data exclude costs of equipment, etc., used in quarrying the raw materials and column (3) of Table 5.8 was obtained by assuming that the ratio of quarry equipment costs : total capital costs is the same in the two countries.

Table 5.8. Relationship between Capital Costs and Plant Capacity: UK and West German Cement Manufacture

Plant Capacity (th. tonnes) p.a.) (1)	UK Capital Costs (1968) (£m) (2)	UK Adjusted Capital Costs (1968) (£m) (3)	West Germany Capital Costs (1971) (DMx10^6) (4)
100	3.0	3.33	23.54
300	7.5	8.20	60.84
600	12.5	13.56	99.83
1200	22.0	23.68	145.38

Source: see text.
Notes: column (4) estimated by interpolation from Table 5.7.

Several methods are available for estimating μ from the data in columns (3) and (4). The approach we have adopted is to choose μ to minimise the total squared deviation given by:

$$TD(\mu) = \sum_{i=1}^{4} (K_{UK}^i - \mu K_{WG}^i)^2 \qquad (5.3.7)$$

This gives an estimate for μ of 0.152. The data reported by Pratten refer to 1968, however, and we should deflate the UK estimates to 1963 prices. To do so we apply the index of capital costs published in the *National Institute Economic Review* (NIER) 5/74, that refers to 'plant, vehicles etc.'. The index is 1.14, giving a revised estimate for μ^4 of:

$$\mu = 0.152/1.14 = 0.133. \qquad (5.3.8)$$

It should be noted that our estimates assume that the 1971 technology was available in 1963. We have already seen that the elasticity of capital costs with respect to scale for plant capacities up to 1.0 m. tonnes p.a. had not changed much over the period 1960–71. This is not to say, however, that the technology existed by 1963 to build plants of capacities up to 3.3 m. tonnes p.a. exhibiting the cost characteristics of Table 5.7. Further consideration of this aspect of the capital cost estimates will be left to the next section.

This completes our estimates of the capital and labour inputs to UK cement production. These estimates rely on some rather heroic assumptions, but it is difficult to see how we could obtain better estimates given the nature of the available data.

5.3.2 Total Production Costs

The data reported in paragraph 5.3.1 are drawn from a mixture of actual and hypothetical plants. Any attempt to bring the various series together to estimate total production costs is therefore based on two assumptions about efficiency:

(i) the estimates derived from observations of actual plants are estimates of the most efficient use of factors, and
(ii) manufacturers in choosing from hypothetical plants will only choose efficient techniques.

Given these assumptions, we use the results of paragraph 5.3.1 to estimate total production costs (TPC) for UK cement manufacture. In doing so, one further complication should be noted. In 5.3.1 labour and other variable costs have been estimated as functional forms, but capital costs have been presented as a series of disjoint observations. TPC will be estimated initially, therefore, as a series of observations.

No matter how we estimate TPC we have to take account of the fact that our estimates of capital costs give the *total* capital costs of opening a cement plant, while the estimates of labour and other variable costs refer to costs per annum in producing cement. It is necessary either to express capital costs as an annual charge or to calculate the total (discounted) variable costs over the expected life of the plant. We have adopted the former approach, and convert capital costs to the equivalent uniform annual payments series assuming an expected plant life of 40 years and an interest rate of 10%.[5] We then obtain the estimates in Table 5.9.

The next stage is to fit a linear spline to the data in Table 5.9. Before doing so, however, we should return to the question of whether the technology implicit in this table was actually available in 1963. Our discussions with the designers confirmed that in 1963 the technology existed to construct plants with capacities of at least 2.5 m. tonnes p.a. and with the cost characteristics of Table 5.7. We feel, therefore, that we should take a capacity of 2.5 m. tonnes p.a. as the limiting capacity at which economies of scale run out, i.e. as our estimate of $\hat{x}_{kv}^{I(k)}$ in Chapter 4. Returns to scale are assumed to be constant for capacities in excess of this limit.

A linear spline is, therefore, fitted to the data in Table 5.9 for plant capacities less than 2.5 m. tonnes p.a. Given the number of knots in the spline, the parameters in the spline are the locations of the knots and the slopes and intercepts of the various linear segments; there are $2I$ parameters for a spline with I linear segments, i.e. $(I-1)$ knots. We used a full-information maximum likelihood programme developed by Deaton (1974) to estimate these parameters.

What we have to decide is how few knots to have in the spline. A spline with

Table 5.9. Total Production Costs: UK Cement Manufacture 1963

Capacity (th. tonnes p.a.)	Capital Cost (£m)	Labour Cost (£m)	Variable Cost (£m)	Total Cost (£m)	Average Cost (£)
82.5	0.269	0.121	0.156	0.546	6.62
99.0	0.317	0.127	0.187	0.631	6.37
132.0	0.409	0.139	0.249	0.797	6.04
166.0	0.498	0.151	0.314	0.963	5.80
247.5	0.709	0.180	0.468	1.357	5.48
330.0	0.894	0.209	0.624	1.727	5.23
412.5	1.055	0.238	0.780	2.073	5.03
495.0	1.205	0.268	0.936	2.409	4.87
577.5	1.327	0.297	1.091	2.715	4.70
660.0	1.436	0.326	1.247	3.009	4.56
742.5	1.525	0.355	1.403	3.283	4.42
825.0	1.616	0.385	1.559	3.560	4.32
907.5	1.691	0.414	1.715	3.820	4.21
990.0	1.764	0.443	1.871	4.078	4.12
1155.0	1.931	0.502	2.183	4.616	4.00
1320.0	2.100	0.560	2.495	5.155	3.91
1485.0	2.282	0.619	2.807	5.708	3.84
1650.0	2.492	0.677	3.119	6.288	3.81
1980.0	2.897	0.795	3.742	7.434	3.75
2310.0	3.299	0.912	4.366	8.577	3.71
2640.0	3.699	1.029	4.990	9.718	3.68
2970.0	4.121	1.146	5.613	10.880	3.66
3300.0	4.488	1.263	6.237	11.988	3.63

Source: see text
Notes: Capital Cost – see text.
Labour Cost – $(92.51 + 0.3574 C) \times 0.993/1000$.
Variable Cost – $1.89 C/1000$.

one knot does not perform particularly well in the middle range of capacity levels, but the introduction of an additional knot produces a spline that we feel to be a sufficiently good approximation. The addition of a third knot would improve the approximation, of course, but would also introduce at least ten additional integer-constrained variables. This would increase the size of the programming problem by several orders of magnitude, and we do not feel that the improvement in the approximation justifies the increase in computer capacity needed to solve the problem.

We decided, therefore, that we should define three quasi production activities

Table 5.10. Quasi Production Activities for UK Cement Manufacture 1963

| | Cost Components (£m) | | | |
Activity Number (i)	m^i_{kv}	v^i_{kv}	Minimum Activity Level (m.t.p.a.)	Maximum Activity Level (m.t.p.a.)
1	0.221	4.492	0.0	0.5
2	0.810	3.315	0.5	1.6
3	0.566	3.694	1.6	2.5
4	0.0	3.917	2.5	—

Source: see text.

in the spline, with the maximum output of the highest level quasi activity being 2.5 m. tonnes p.a. In view of our assumption of constant returns to scale for capacities in excess of 2.5 m. tonnes p.a., we then define a fourth quasi production activity. The production costs for this quasi activity are represented by a ray through the origin intersecting the cost curve for the third quasi activity at a capacity of 2.5 m. tonnes p.a. The operating costs and other parameters of the various quasi activities are given in Table 5.10.

We now reiterate the points made in Chapter 4 regarding the nature of these quasi production activities. The cost of operating the ith quasi production as defined by Table 5.10 represents the minimum cost of operating the production unit[6] at a given activity level x^i_{kv} in the interval $[\hat{x}^{i-1}_{kv}, \hat{x}^i_{kv}]$. This quasi activity can be operated at *no other* nonzero activity levels. In other words, points below the linear spline are *not* attainable.

In addition, we have indicated that the quasi production activities defined above need not correspond to any actual production activities. Our assumptions about the activity vector associated with a quasi production activity are such, however, that the mineral, fuel, energy, and variable labour inputs estimated in paragraph 5.3.1 give the components of the activity vector. No element has been defined in the vector for packaging materials, since these are assumed to be ubiquitous and not limited in supply.

5.3.3 Transport Costs

Transport costs are estimated from 1966 data collected by Deakin and Seward (1969) for their study of productivity in transport and kindly made available to

Table 5.11. Transport Costs (shillings per ton) 1966

Good	No. of Obs'ns	a_i	b_i	R^2
Cement	32	12.543	0.142	0.75
Coal and Coke	40	8.973	0.223	0.63
Crude Minerals other than Ore	48	2.891	0.259	0.77

Source: Deakin and Seward (1969)

us. These data are used to estimate transport cost functions of the form:

$$t_i = a_i + b_i x \qquad (5.3.9)$$

where: t_i = transport charge in shillings per ton
for good i,

x = average length of haul in miles.

Thus a_i constitutes a loading/unloading charge and b_i a mileage charge for good i. We assume that a_i and b_i are linear in the tonnage transported, giving a total transport cost function of the form:

$$T_i = w_i(a_i + b_i x) \qquad (5.3.10)$$

where: w_i = tonnage of good i transported.

The estimates of (5.3.9) are given in Table 5.11.[7]

As can be seen, these estimates refer to 1966. No clear indication is available of the inflation in transport costs 1963–66, but the discussion below in Chapter 6, paragraph 6.3.2, and Chapter 7, paragraph 7.9.3, would imply that the transport cost for index for 1966 is 109 with 1963 = 100. We shall use this estimate to deflate the estimates in Table 5.11 when we come to apply these to estimates of geographic distance between nodes.

The estimates in Table 5.11 and the input coefficients estimated in paragraph 5.3.1 indicate that the choice of production sites will be strongly influenced by the raw material sites. We shall find below that limestone and slate or chalk and clay tend to occur together, making this influence all the stronger, but consideration of the actual extent to which location decisions will be dominated by the transport costs of the input raw materials is best left to paragraph 5.4.

5.4 SPATIAL CHARACTERISTICS OF THE MARKET AREA

As we have indicated in previous chapters, the market area is represented as a graph. We shall be concerned in the following paragraphs with defining the graph for the cement study, i.e. with indicating how we define the nodes and branches that make up the graph.

While we treat the derivation of the transport network—the set of branches—and the raw material, consumption, and production sites—the set of nodes—separately in the analysis below, this is for expository convenience alone rather than from any belief that the two are independent. In fact, the choice of nodes is affected by the choice of transport network, while the branches assumed to exist in the network are related to the choice of nodes.

Exposition is eased if we anticipate the results of this section and refer at various stages in the discussion to Figure 5.8 and Table 5.13 in which we present the final graph representation of the market area.[8] This is putting the cart before the horse to some extent, but the degree of interdependence between nodes and branches and the subjective judgement involved in the discussion are such that we feel this to be a legitimate procedure.

5.4.1 Transport Network

The transport network is related to the network of major roads reported in the 1966 report on *Roads in England.*

Thus we assume that there is only one transport mode and convert the resulting road distances to costs by applying the results of paragraph 5.3.3. The final choice of roads to include was not made until we had made the choice of nodes, but an element of suboptimising was introduced in that we eliminated relatively inefficient transport links in defining the network. That is, we eliminated all duplication of branches between nodes, leaving only the minimum cost branch. While, as we indicate, this introduces an element of suboptimising, it also reduces the study to one of manageable size.[9]

5.4.2 Towns—Sources of Demand for Cement

We confine our attention to England and Wales and assume that this is a closed market; a small quantity of cement is shipped from England to Scotland, but the amounts involved are negligible. In addition we have seen that imports and exports account for less than 3% of total output.

We start from data supplied by the Cement Makers' Federation (CMF) that give cement deliveries by county for 1965—see Appendix D. From these data a number of dominant counties can be identified. Problems arise with East Anglia in which no county dominates, and in this case two regions are defined containing nodes 18 and 19. The demand in each of the regions so defined is then taken to be the sum of deliveries in those counties to which the particular region is geographically nearest. Total demand is taken as the average of cement deliveries over the period 1968–74, i.e. 17.0 m. tonnes.[10]

The dominant regions so defined are of quite significant spatial extent and the process of concentration has to be carried farther. We therefore define centroids in each region and assume that all demand allocated to the region by the process above is exercised at the centroid. The choice of centroid is made by taking the major city or cities in the region. Thus, for Northumberland and Durham we define Newcastle as the centroid, while for the East and West Ridings we define two centroids, Hull and Leeds. Similarly, for Staffordshire and Warwickshire we choose three centroids—Stoke, Birmingham and Coventry—and for Lancashire we choose Manchester and Liverpool. Table 5.12 indicates the towns defined and the estimated demand at each; their geographic distribution is illustrated in Figure 5.8.

Table 5.12.   Towns and Estimated Demand

| Town | | Demand |
Number	Name	*(m.t.p.a.)*
1	London (GLC)	5.032
7	Nottingham	0.835
9	Hull	0.284
10	Leeds	0.598
14	Southampton	1.268
15	Plymouth	0.491
16	Bristol	0.802
17	Cardiff	0.898
18	Norwich	0.418
19	Peterborough	0.360
20	Leicester	0.452
21	Coventry	0.451
22	Birmingham	1.013
23	Stoke	0.510
24	Sheffield	0.400
25	Manchester	1.392
26	Liverpool	0.746
27	Teesside	0.469
28	Newcastle	0.581
	Total	17.000

Source: see text.

In adopting this approach we have taken somewhat the same line as Dunford (1969) and produce a similar list of nodes. But as we indicated in Chapter 2, the framework of our analysis and the factors we are interested in testing are very different.

5.4.3 Sources of Input Commodities

The basic goods consumed in cement manufacture are (i) limestone and slate or shale, (ii) chalk and clay, (iii) coal, (iv) gypsum, (v) electricity and liquid fuel, and (vi) packaging materials. We assume that (v) and (vi) are ubiquitous, but this cannot be assumed for the other goods. These latter goods tend to occur in bands rather than at discrete points, but they are by no means evenly distributed, as the map of coal deposits—Figure 5.7—indicates.

This map and further data from the *Digest of Energy Statistics* are used to estimate the geographic extent of the various coal deposits.

The Cement and Concrete Association give some indication of the distribution of other mineral deposits relevant to cement production:

> 'Chalk occurs mainly in South-East, Midland and Northern England and Wales. Clay suitable for cement manufacture is found in most parts of the country.' (Cement and Concrete Association, 1951)

Further, deposits of clay or slate tend to occur in the same areas as those of chalk or limestone, a point that will be important below.

The geographic distribution of these deposits and of the deposits of gypsum were estimated rather more closely from geological studies of England and Wales, and the mineral bands so produced reduced to distinct nodes, taking account of our previous decisions regarding the locations of towns. As a first step, where a town lies within a mineral band, the town is considered to be a source of the mineral. The next step is to define nodes to represent those mineral bands that do not contain towns. Some of these nodes are simple to choose, e.g. node 5 coincides with the mineral deposits near Cambridge, and node 13 with the coal deposits in Kent. To choose other nodes—in particular, nodes 4,6,8 and 11— requires a degree of subjective judgement in that the main considerations in their locations are that they be near to the towns we have defined, and that they lie on the transport network.

Production sites have still to be defined, but the nodes derived in this section, plus the towns defined in 5.4.2, complete the set of nodes—28 in all. It should be noted that these are nodes as defined with respect to the graph G', i.e. before the nodes are disaggregated to allow for transshipment. The distances between them can be obtained by referring to Appendix E, which gives the

SOURCE: Digest of Energy Statistics

Figure 5.7. Coal Deposits: England and Wales.

estimated road distances between those nodes that are directly connected. These distances are converted to costs by applying to them the transport costs reported in paragraph 5.3.3.

The full set of nodes and their nature is given in Table 5.13 and illustrated in Figure 5.8. We have associated a place name with each node. The sole reason for doing so is a belief that the subsequent analysis in this and the following chapters will be clearer if we refer to 'Coventry' say rather than 'node 21'. No inference should be drawn to the effect that the place names refer to other than the regions in which they are located.

Table 5.13. Description of the Nodes in the Graph

Node	Place Name	Town	Mineral Input	Coal	Gypsum
1	London (GLC)	X	X		
2	Shoreham		X		
3	Redhill				X
4	Swindon		X		
5	Cambridge		X		
6	Monmouth		X		
7	Nottingham	X		X	X
8	High Peak		X	X	X
9	Hull	X	X		
10	Leeds	X		X	
11	Preston		X		
12	Carlisle		X		X
13	Canterbury			X	
14	Southampton	X			
15	Plymouth	X	X		
16	Bristol	X	X	X	
17	Cardiff	X	X	X	
18	Norwich	X	X		
19	Peterborough	X	X		
20	Leicester	X		X	
21	Coventry	X	X	X	X
22	Birmingham	X		X	
23	Stoke	X	X	X	
24	Sheffield	X		X	
25	Manchester	X	X	X	
26	Liverpool	X		X	
27	Teesside	X	X		
28	Newcastle	X		X	X

Notes: 'X' indicates non-zero availability of primary factor or demand for final product.

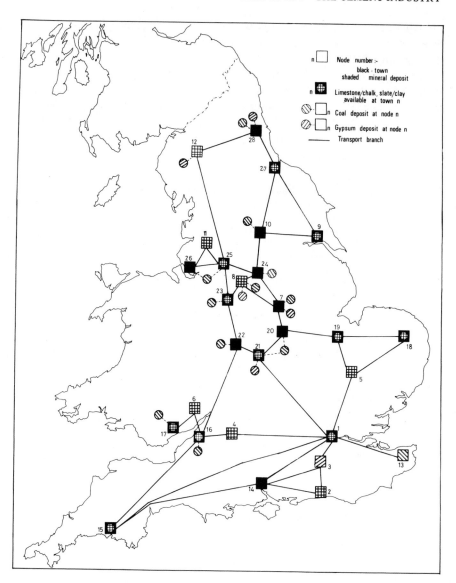

Figure 5.8. The Market Area.

5.4.4 Production Sites

In our initial development of the model we assumed that labour was immobile, and available only at some subset of the nodes in G. But our estimates of labour requirements indicate that cement plants do not require particularly large labour forces. It can be argued, therefore, that a cement works will draw its labour from a relatively small catchment area no matter where it is located. Of course, if labour is obtained in this way, then we should include an element of transport costs in labour costs: given that these costs would be met by the producer they could be treated as an increase in wage costs per worker. But the TPC function is not sensitive to increases in wage costs—a 10% increase would raise TPC by about 2% at low capacities falling to about 1% for capacities above 800 th. tonnes p.a. We propose, therefore, to assume that labour is available to every node in sufficient supply to permit any desired level of operation.

As a result, all of the twenty-eight nodes we have defined are potential production sites. The programming problem which results from this approach is far too large for us to solve, however; we must reduce the number of potential production sites. We begin by using the estimates in Tables 5.4, 5.5 and 5.11 to reformulate transport costs as costs per ton of cement produced. In doing so we treat limestone/slate and chalk/clay as a single input good—'mineral input'—a simplification that can be made as a result of our finding that they tend to occur together. The results are given in Table 5.14.

We now proceed to make a series of comparisons between nodes to identify those at which production would be uneconomic, i.e. those nodes which, on a minimum-cost criterion, are dominated by other more favourably located nodes, and at which, therefore, production should be zero. While this approach is lacking in rigour, we feel that it is justified since it reduces the effective size of the problem and enables us to handle a study that is larger overall.

Consider a pair of nodes such that one is a town and the other a mineral input

Table 5.14. Transport Costs per ton of Cement (shillings) 1963

Good	Transport Cost per ton of Cement	
	a_i	b_i
Mineral Input	5.039	0.451
Coal and Coke	1.326	0.033
Gypsum	0.106	0.009
Cement	11.507	0.130

Source: see text.

Table 5.15.   Potential Production Sites

Node	Name	Node	Name
1	London*	17	Cardiff*
2	Shoreham	18	Norwich*
5	Cambridge	19	Peterborough*
6	Monmouth	21	Coventry*
8	High Peak	23	Stoke-on-Trent*
9	Hull*	25	Manchester*
15	Plymouth*	27	Teesside*
16	Bristol*		

Source: see text.
*This node is also a town.

source. They are otherwise similar with respect to the commodities available at them, and are such that the mineral input source is the nearest such source (in cost terms) to the town, e.g. Southampton and Shoreham. Then if the mineral input source is more than $(11.507 - 5.039)/(0.451 - 0.130) = 20$ miles from the town, it is cheaper to produce cement at the mineral input source and transport it to the town than to transport mineral input to the town and produce cement there.

Using such a criterion we can eliminate Redhill, Nottingham, Leeds, Canterbury, Southampton, and Newcastle as being uneconomic production sites.

The constraints upon mineral input and other commodity availability at each commodity source are not expected to 'bite', i.e. there is assumed to be sufficient of a particular commodity at any node at which it is available, according to Table 5.13, to meet any level of demand for the commodity. As a result, Swindon and Carlisle may be eliminated, since Monmouth and Teesside respectively are more favourably placed with respect to demand.

Comparison of Monmouth and Bristol and Monmouth and Cardiff would indicate on first sight that Monmouth may be eliminated. But the existence of economies of scale complicates matters somewhat, since Monmouth may be the cheapest site from which to supply Bristol and Cardiff. No clear-cut decision can be made, and all three will be considered as potential production sites. The same approach applies to Cambridge, Peterborough, and Norwich.

Similar considerations would appear to apply to Preston, Manchester, and Liverpool, but in this case the direct link from Manchester to Liverpool allows us to eliminate Preston and Liverpool as being uneconomic.

Our estimates of production costs enable us to eliminate Leicester, Birmingham, and Sheffield. In the cases of Leicester and Birmingham, the reduction in unit costs of concentrating production at Coventry, which is itself a town, is sufficient to offset the transport costs incurred in moving cement rather than mineral input to Leicester and Birmingham. Sheffield can be eliminated on the same criterion.

This process leaves us with fifteen potential production sites – these are listed in Table 5.15. We have also completed the estimation of the parameters of the static model for the cement study.

6 SOLUTION OF THE STATIC CEMENT STUDY

6.1 INTRODUCTION

In this chapter we shall analyse the calculated optimum distribution for the cement industry obtained from solution of the static model as estimated in Chapter 5.

We consider first the solution of the original model and examine the ways in which transport costs and economies of scale interact in determining the calculated optimum distribution of the industry. Secondly, we perform a sensitivity analysis to identify the extent to which the calculated optimum changes with changes in various of the parameters estimated in Chapter 5. Finally, we compare the calculated optimum with the actual distribution of the industry. In doing so we examine the changes in the actual distribution of the industry over the period 1950–1974 and the factors important in explaining these changes. We then indicate the extent to which the actual distribution is moving towards the calculated optimum.

6.2 THE CALCULATED OPTIMUM FOR THE STATIC STUDY

We present first a partial analysis of the type of problem with which we are dealing. This analysis abstracts from the interactions and interdependencies that are an essential feature of the complete model, but it does highlight some general properties which we would expect to find in the calculated optimum.

Assume two towns A and B such that the demand at A equals demand at B and such that all inputs to production are available at both towns. Assume further that production costs are identical in the two towns and exhibit economies of scale throughout the feasible range of output. Assume that this range is greater than the combined demand at A and B.

Consider now the production decision: should all production be concentrated at A, with B supplied from A, or should A and B each supply its own demand? Figure 6.1 can be used to analyse this decision. Total demand is given by $O_A B$ or $O_B A$, where $O_A A (= BA)$ = demand at A, and $O_B B$ (= AB) = demand at B. Unit costs of production at A and B are given by AP_A and AP_B respectively, and unit costs of transport for production at A by $O_A AD$. We assume that all production at A up to $O_A A$ is supplied to A and incurs no transport costs.[1] Production in excess of $O_A A$ is supplied to B.

Unit costs of meeting demand at B by production at B are given by BB' and from production at A by BT. Clearly, production will be concentrated at A if $BB' > BT$ and disaggregated to A and B if $BB' < BT$.[2]

The first point that can be made is that for any production process, concentration is more likely the less elastic are production costs over the scale range $(O_A A, O_A B)$ and the lower are unit transport costs BD. Secondly, for any *given* production cost elasticity, concentration of production is more likely the greater is the ratio of production costs at output $O_A A$ to unit transport costs on some fixed length of haul.

The elasticity of production costs will be lower the greater is MES (as defined by Pratten, 1971) relative to demand at A and B. Unit transport costs over the same range are directly proportional to the cost of transporting unit amount from A to B. Unit transport costs BD will be lower, therefore, the lower the transport rate per mile or the nearer are A and B.

Now consider the situation when demand at A exceeds that at B: this is illustrated by the dotted lines in Figure 6.1. The axis $O_A C_A$ and unit production cost function AP_A move to the left, and unit transport costs fall to $O'_A AD'$. BT is reduced by both influences, and the greater is demand at A relative to demand at B, the more likely is it that B will be supplied from A.

This very simple analysis indicates that the relationship between production and transport costs is not of itself sufficient to determine whether production should be more or less concentrated. The absolute level of demand and its spatial distribution will also be important determinants of the distribution of production.

Obviously these results will be modified in a full model, e.g. since the sites close to the major concentrations of demand may be distant from the input

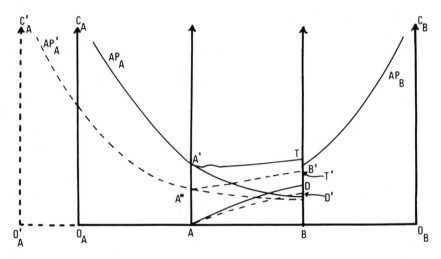

Figure 6.1.

sources. But in industries such as the cement industry, in which the major inputs are widely available, we should expect to find concentrations of production to emerge at or near towns that are major centres of demand and/or at locations that are central to a number of towns.

We examine the calculated optimum for the static model in the light of this analysis. This optimum is derived from a case study—denoted Case 0—defined by four sets of parameters estimated in Chapter 5:

I the graph G,
II the distribution of demand,
III transport costs,
IV production costs.

The main characteristics of the calculated optimum for the Case 0 study are summarised in Table 6.1 and illustrated in Figure 6.2.

We obtained as a by-product of the solution of the MIP the solution to the mathematical programme formed by treating all integer-constrained variables as continuous. When this is done each quasi production activity exhibits constant returns to scale. The resulting programming problem is, therefore, equivalent to a linear programme with the following objective function:

$$Z = v' \cdot x + t \cdot w \tag{6.2.1}$$
$$\text{where: } v'^i_{kv} = v^i_{kv} + m^i_{kv}/\hat{x}^i_{kv}$$

This may be simplified since:

Table 6.1. Calculated Optimum for Case 0

Node	Place Name	Predicted Capacity		Towns Supplied**	
		Case 0	LP	Case 0	LP
1	London	6.300	5.032	1,14	1
2	Shoreham	–	1.268		14
5	Cambridge	–	–		
6	Monmouth	–	–		
7	Nottingham	–	–		
8	High Peak	2.500	1.833	7,10,23,24,(20)	7,10,24
9	Hull	–	0.284		9
10	Leeds	–	–		
14	Southampton	–	–		
15	Plymouth	–	0.491		15
16	Bristol	1.293	0.802	15,16	16
17	Cardiff	0.898	0.898	17	17
18	Norwich	–	0.418		18
19	Peterborough	–	0.360		19
20	Leicester	–	–		
21	Coventry	2.537	1.916	18,19,21,22,(20)	20,21,22
22	Birmingham	–	–		
23	Stoke	–	0.510		23
24	Sheffield	–	–		
25	Manchester	2.138	2.138	25,26	25,26
26	Liverpool	–	–		
27	Teesside	1.334	1.050	9,27,28	27,28
28	Newcastle	–	–		
Tonne miles of cement transported (m.)		399.09	170.20		

**Figures in brackets indicate that the town is supplied from more than one production site.

(i) quasi production activity 4 is dominant in this new problem,
(ii) variable costs of operating quasi production activity 4 — excluding transport costs — are identical for all v.

Thus we have:

$$Z = v_k^4 \sum_v x_{kv}^4 + t \cdot w. \qquad (6.2.2)$$

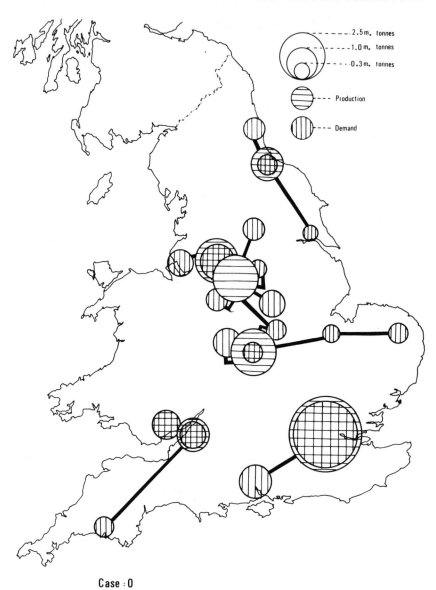

Case : 0

Figure 6.2.

At an optimum, since there is no joint production, we have:

$$Z^* = F \cdot v_k^4 + t \cdot w, \text{ where } F = \sum_v x_{kv}^4. \qquad (6.2.3)$$

It is clear that the optimum distribution for the LP formed by dropping the integer constraints in the MIP is that distribution of capacity for which transport costs are minimised. It is presented in Table 6.1 as a point of reference.

As can be seen from the calculated optimum for Case 0, economies of scale in cement production are sufficiently strong relative to transport costs to lead to a distribution of capacity somewhat more concentrated than that exhibited by the solution of the LP. In consequence, the calculated optimum for the Case 0 study is not that which minimises transport costs. Total market demand is met from only seven production sites as opposed to thirteen in the LP solution. Quasi activity 4 is used at two nodes, quasi activity 3 at two, and quasi activity 2 at three. It should be noted further that in one of the cases where quasi activity 3 is used, it is used to its maximum activity level.

Leicester (town 20) is the only town at which demand is supplied from more than one production site, demand being supplied from High Peak and Coventry. It is significant in this case that quasi activity 3 is used at one of the two production sites. Local demand conditions are such as to justify use of quasi activity 3 at High Peak, i.e. demand at Nottingham, Sheffield, and Leeds. Economies of scale are then sufficiently strong with respect to transport costs for this quasi activity to be used to its maximum activity level, additional output being supplied to Stoke and Leicester. But economies of scale are not sufficiently strong to justify use of the higher level quasi activity that would be necessary for High Peak to be the sole supplier for Leicester. In other words, while economies of scale in cement production encourage a highly concentrated pattern of production, transport costs and the distribution of demand are such as to impose effective constraints on the degree of concentration we find in the calculated optimum.

We can now recall the simple model analysed in the introduction to this section. Each of the production sites at which one of the two highest level quasi activities is used in the solution to Case 0 are sites at which the two central results of the simple analysis hold: they are nodes that are, or are close to, major concentrations of demand. Again, therefore, we see the importance of transport costs and the distribution of demand in determining the calculated optimum distribution of capacity.

6.3 SENSITIVITY ANALYSIS

We shall concentrate upon the sensitivity of the calculated optimum for Case 0 to parameters in the sets III and IV, but some mention will be made of the effects of changes in the parameters in the sets I and II.

Various measures of sensitivity of greater or lesser complexity could be used. We might consider, for example, the relationship between changes in each of the parameters in sets III and IV, and changes in the distribution of plant capacities, measured perhaps by changes in the capacity of the three largest plants as a percentage of total capacity. We feel, however, that the simplest measure of sensitivity with respect to a particular parameter is the change in tonne miles of cement transported.

If use is made of the LP solution associated with Case 0, tonne miles of cement transported has a more important advantage than that of simplicity. We have indicated that the LP distribution summarised in Table 6.1 is that for which total transport costs are minimised, given our estimates in Chapter 5 and our constraints on potential production sites as outlined in Table 5.15. More significantly for our purposes, however, it is that distribution of capacity for which the total of tonne miles of cement transported (referred to as tonne miles below) is minimised—again, of course, subject to the constraints mentioned above. In addition, this minimum measure of tonne miles is insensitive to uniform percentage changes in any of the parameters in sets III and IV, e.g. to a p% increase in transport costs or a q% reduction in labour costs. As a result, tonne miles for the LP can be used as a base against which we can compare tonne miles for the solutions to Case 0 and variants on Case 0. Expressing tonne miles for a particular variant of Case 0 as an index with tonne miles for the LP as base (=100) will indicate the extent to which, in that case, economies of scale in production are sufficient to offset diseconomies of transportation. Rather more important, however, is the property that the index of tonne miles for a particular case is directly related to the degree of spatial concentration exhibited by the calculated optimum for that case *over and above* that resulting from the concentration of demand.

Even with such a simple measure of sensitivity, care has to be exercised in its interpretation. Changes in the index of tonne miles for the solution to Case 0 will result from changes in the parameters in the sets III and IV. Clearly, variations in a particular parameter can also be expressed as an index, taking as base in this case the estimates in Chapter 5 (again = 100). If now the tonne miles index is plotted against the index of the parameter being varied, we shall obtain a sensitivity curve for that parameter. The first point to note is that this curve will be a step function. The indivisibilities in production costs and the discontinuities in the distribution of demand will give rise to a discontinuous reaction of the calculated optimum for Case 0, with a particular distribution of capacity being optimal for a range of values of the parameter.

Secondly, the form of the sensitivity curve has to be considered. Each of the parameters in the sets III and IV can be distinguished according to whether there are economies, diseconomies, or constant returns to that parameter from spatial concentration of production, e.g. there are diseconomies to transport costs from concentration: the greater the degree of concentration of production, the greater will be unit transport costs in meeting market demand. We can use this distinction to define three further sets of parameters from the parameter sets III and IV:

(i) the set E: parameters for which there are economies of concentration
(ii) the set D: parameters for which there are diseconomies of concentration
(iii) the set C: the remaining parameters.

As the cost index for a parameter in the set D (E) is increased from the base index, there will be a reduction (increase) in spatial concentration of production relative to the calculated optimum for Case 0; while as the index is reduced from the base, there will be an increase (reduction) in concentration. In addition, at high indices of parameters in D (E), we would expect to find convergence on the limiting case of complete disaggregation (aggregation) of production: the higher the cost index for a particular parameter, the more dominant will these costs become relative to other costs. The behavior of the sensitivity curve at very low indices is much less easy to judge, but in these inflationary times is also much less critical.

Ignoring the indivisibilities and discontinuities which characterise our model, we should therefore expect the sensitivity curve to be as in Figure 6.3(a) for parameters in the set D and 6.3(b) for those in the set E. The sensitivity curve for parameters in the set C is derived in paragraph 6.3.1.

The final point is that the more sensitive is the calculated optimum for Case 0 to changes in a particular parameter, the greater will be the arc elasticity of the sensitivity curve, at least for intermediate indices of the parameter. We have to use arc elasticity rather than point elasticity since, as has been indicated, the sensitivity curves will be step curves; the point elasticity of such a curve is zero everywhere but at a step, where it is infinite. This limitation also extends to arc elasticities unless one end of the arc is fixed. We therefore define the arc elasticity of the sensitivity curve for any of the parameters in the sets III and IV as:

$$\frac{TMCT - TMCT_{100}}{P - 100} \cdot \frac{P + 100}{TMCT + TMCT_{100}} \qquad (6.3.1)$$

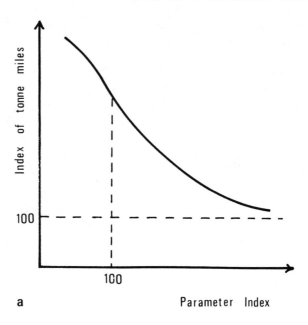

a

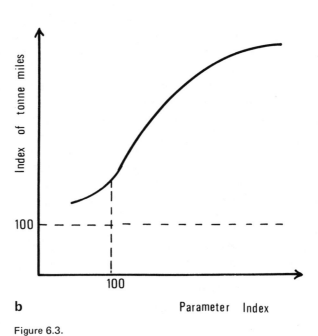

b

Figure 6.3.

where: P = parameter index

TMCT = index of tonne miles at parameter index P

$TMCT_{100}$ = index of tonne miles at parameter index 100.

This definition is such that the elasticity is measured with respect to the point on the sensitivity curve derived from the calculated optimum for Case 0. Thus an arc elasticity of e, say, would indicate that a change in the parameter index from 100 to $100 + p$ would lead to a change in the index of tonne miles from $TMCT_{100}$ to $TMCT_{100}(1 + e \cdot p/100)$. It is important to note, however, that we cannot use the definition of arc elasticity in (6.3.1) to estimate the elasticity of the sensitivity curve when the parameter index is changed from P to P' (P,P' $\neq$ 100).

The sensitivity of the calculated optimum to each of the parameters in the sets III and IV can now be compared by comparing either the positions of the various sensitivity curves or their arc elasticities.

6.3.1 Energy Costs in Production

In Chapter 5 we indicated that there were constant returns to energy costs. As a result an increase in energy costs would lead to a rotation of the spline, as in Figure 6.4. Unit variable costs for each segment of the spline would increase by the same amount, but there would be no change in the cost components m_{kv}^i or in the abscissas of the knots.

The same situation holds for any parameter in the set C, i.e. any parameter for which unit costs of meeting market demand are independent of the degree of concentration of production.

It is easy to show that the calculated optimum for Case 0 is insensitive to changes in cost indices for all parameters in the set C. As has been indicated, the effect of a change in the cost index for such a parameter is to increase the cost component v_{kv}^i for each quasi production activity by a constant amount. Thus the cost component v_{kv}^i for quasi activity $k^i v$ becomes $(v_{kv}^i + \bar{v})$.

The new objective function is:

$$Z' = \left(\sum_i \sum_v (v_{kv}^i + \bar{v}) x_{kv}^i \right) + t \cdot w + \gamma \cdot m$$

$$= v \cdot x + t \cdot w + \gamma \cdot m + \bar{v} \sum_i \sum_v x_{kv}^i.$$

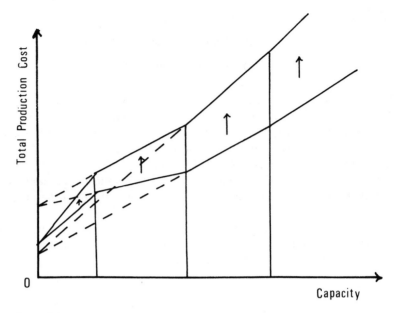

Figure 6.4.

But for the Case 0 study,

$$\sum_i \sum_v x^i_{kv} = \text{total final demand for cement} = \text{constant} = F.$$

Thus

$$Z' = Z + F \cdot \bar{v}, \text{ and}$$

$$\min_{x,w,\gamma} (Z') = \min_{x,w,\gamma} (Z) + F \cdot \bar{v},$$

i.e. those activity levels x^*, w^*, γ^* which minimise total cost Z in Case 0 also minimise Z'. Thus the solution for Case 0 is totally insensitive to changes in the cost index for any parameter in the set C and the senstivity curve for such a parameter is as in Figure 6.5.

Two points should be made about this result:

(i) It is independent of the contraints in Chapter 5 on potential production sites since it relies solely on the property that $\Sigma_i \Sigma_v x^i_{kv} = F$.

(ii) It is dependent upon the assumption that the demand for cement is perfectly price inelastic.

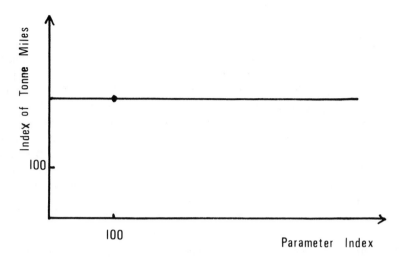

Figure 6.5.

We may generalise the result to other industrial situations provided certain conditions are satisifed. Consider a cost parameter P_i that enters into the production costs of production activities from which commodity nv is net output. Assume that P_i and nv are such that:

(i) P_i enters into *all* production activities from which commodity nv is net output,

(ii) there are constant returns to spatial concentration to the parameter P_i,

(iii) *either* commodity nv is a final product, the demand for which is perfectly price inelastic, *or* commodity nv is an inermediate product to which there are constant returns to scale in all production activities to which it is net input, and for which there are no substitutes in the industry being studied.

Then the calculated optimum will be independent of the cost index for parameter P_i.

6.3.2 Transport, Capital and Labour Costs

As the discussion in the introduction to this section indicates, we would expect the calculated optimum for Case 0 to exhibit some sensitivity to changes in transport, capital, and labour costs. Four sets of experiments were conducted in order to analyse the sensitivity of Case 0 to changes in

(i) transport costs,
(ii) mileage costs,

(iii) labour costs in production, and

(iv) capital costs in production.

We should perhaps elaborate briefly on (ii). We felt that, in the light of events over the period 1970–75, it would be worthwhile to try to identify the impact on Case 0 of changes in the fuel cost element of transport costs. A change in fuel costs will not have a symmetric effect on loading and mileage costs, but loading costs do contain a fuel element. In the absence of information to the contrary, therefore, we assume that a p% increase in mileage costs arising from some increase in fuel costs will give rise to $1/2$p% increase in loading costs. Whenever we refer below to the index of mileage costs, we assume that the loading cost index is such that if the mileage cost index is $100 + $ p, then the loading cost index is $100 + 1/2$p.

We report in detail on two of the experiments in the sets above, and will refer to the remainder in the light of discussion of the various sensitivity curves. The two experiments to be considered in detail are: firstly, that in which transport costs were increased by 100%—denoted Case 1—and, secondly, that in which capital costs were increased by 50%—denoted Case 2. Note that Case 1 (2) differs from Case 0 in one respect alone: transport (capital) costs have been increased by 100 (50) %.

The calculated optima for Cases 1 and 2 are summarised in Tables 6.2 and 6.3 and illustrated in Figures 6.6 and 6.7.

The 100% increase in transport costs (Case 1) has resulted in a general reduction in plant capacities. Eleven plants are operated in the calculated optimum for Case 1; one using quasi activity 4, three using quasi activity 3, four using quasi activity 2, and three using quasi activity 1.

The changes in the distribution of capacity are: firstly, a reduction in capacity at London, since the higher transport costs make it economic to operate a plant at Shoreham; and secondly, small scale plants operated at Hull, Plymouth, and Norwich, each of which supplies only local demand, with consequent reductions in capacity at Teesside, Bristol, and Coventry, respectively.

The 50% increase in capital costs (Case 2) has, on the other hand, resulted in a general increase in plant capacities. Such an increase in capital costs decreases the elasticity of total production costs with respect to scale sufficiently for it to be economic to supply total market demand from only five plants. Local demand supplied from Cardiff in the calculated optimum for Case 0 is supplied in that for Case 2 from Bristol, while demand supplied in Case 0 from High Peak is supplied in Case 2 from Coventry, Manchester, and Teesside. In this latter case, economies of scale are sufficiently strong to encourage concentration of production, but transport costs remain sufficiently important to ensure that production is expanded at potential production sites that also have at least some local demand.

Table 6.2. Calculated Optimum for Case 1

Node	Place Name	Predicted Capacity		Towns Supplied**	
		Case 1	Case 0	Case 1	Case 0
1	London	5.032	6.300	1	1,14
2	Shoreham	1.268	–	14	
5	Cambridge	–	–		
6	Monmouth	–	–		
7	Nottingham	–	–		
8	High Peak	2.343	2.500	7,10,23,24	7,10,23,24,(20)
9	Hull	0.284	–	9	
10	Leeds	–	–		
14	Southampton	–	–		
15	Plymouth	0.491	–	15	
16	Bristol	0.802	1.293	16	15,16
17	Cardiff	0.898	0.898	17	17
18	Norwich	0.418	–	18	
19	Peterborough	–	–		
20	Leicester	–	–		
21	Coventry	2.276	2.537	19,20,21,22	18,19,21,22,(20)
22	Birmingham	–	–		
23	Stoke	–	–		
24	Sheffield	–	–		
25	Manchester	2.138	2.138	25,26	25,26
26	Liverpool	–	–		
27	Teesside	1.050	1.334	27,28	9,27,28
28	Newcastle	–	–		
Tonne miles of cement transported (m.)		204.55	399.09		

**Figures in brackets indicate that the town is supplied from more than one production site.

The distribution of capacity in the calculated optimum for Case 2 is such that each plant supplies a spatially distinct sub-market. In addition, quasi activity 4 is used at all but two of the production sites. The constraints imposed in Chapter 5 on the activity level at which economies of scale are considered to run out are then such that we would expect to find no further concentration of production as the capital cost index is raised.

Given the results of the various sets of experiments and the changes in the distribution of capacity with which they are associated, we were able to identify the sensitivity curves for transport, mileage, labour, and capital costs. These

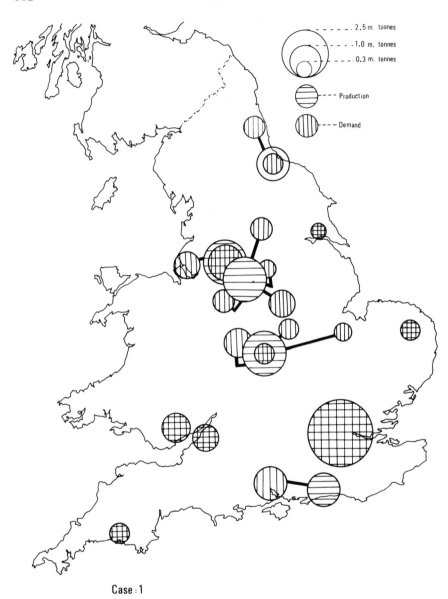

Case : 1

Figure 6.6.

Table 6.3. Calculated Optimum for Case 2

		Predicted Capacity		Towns Supplied**	
Node	Place Name	Case 2	Case 0	Case 2	Case 0
1	London	6.300	6.300	1,14	1,14
2	Shoreham	–	–		
5	Cambridge	–	–		
6	Monmouth	–	–		
7	Nottingham	–	–		
8	High Peak	–	2.500		7,10,23,24,(20)
9	Hull	–	–		
10	Leeds	–	–		
14	Southampton	–	–		
15	Plymouth	–	–		
16	Bristol	2.191	1.293	15,16,17	15,16
17	Cardiff	–	0.898		17
18	Norwich	–	–		
19	Peterborough	–	–		
20	Leicester	–	–		
21	Coventry	3.529	2.537	7,18,19,20 21,22	18,19,21,22,(20)
22	Birmingham	–	–		
23	Stoke	–	–		
24	Sheffield	–	–		
25	Manchester	3.048	2.138	23,24,25,26	25,26
26	Liverpool	–	–		
27	Teesside	1.932	1.334	9,10,27,28	9,27,28
28	Newcastle	–	–		
Tonne miles of cement transported (m.)		476.82	399.09		

**Figures in brackets indicate that the town is supplied from more than one production site.

sensitivity curves are illustrated in Figures 6.8 through 6.11 and the elasticities of the curves are illustrated in Figures 6.12 through 6.15. Point A on the various sensitivity curves refers to the calculated optimum for Case 0, and point B to the calculated optima for Cases 1 and 2 as appropriate.

Figure 6.8 indicates that the sensitivity curve for transport costs falls steeply as the index of transport costs is raised from 100 to 200.[3] At a transport cost index of 121, demand at Leicester is supplied totally from Coventry with a

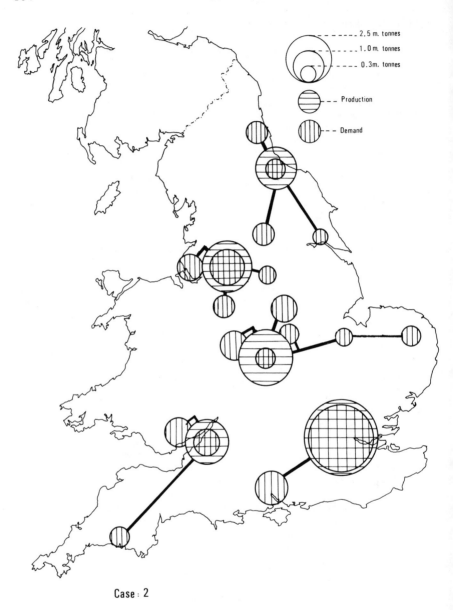

Case: 2

Figure 6.7.

reduction in capacity at High Peak. At an index of 128, local production is economic at Norwich with a reduction in capacity at Coventry; and, at an index of 154, production is economic at Plymouth with a consequent reduction in capacity at Bristol. Production is economic at Shoreham at an index of 158, and at Hull, Peterborough, and Stoke at indices of 196, 205, and 237, respectively.

The calculated optimum for transport cost indices in excess of 237 is identical with the calculated optimum for the LP. Transport costs are now sufficiently strong with respect to production costs as to completely dominate economies of scale to production.

It can also be seen that the sensitivity curve rises steeply as the index of transport costs is reduced from 100. At an index of 80, production is concentrated as in the calculated optimum for Case 2. Thus further reductions in transport costs will have no impact on production concentration. Production at High Peak is economic at an index of 82 and at Cardiff at an index of 96.

A similar sensitivity curve is obtained for mileage costs—see Figure 6.9—but it can be seen that the calculated optimum for Case 0 is less sensitive to changes

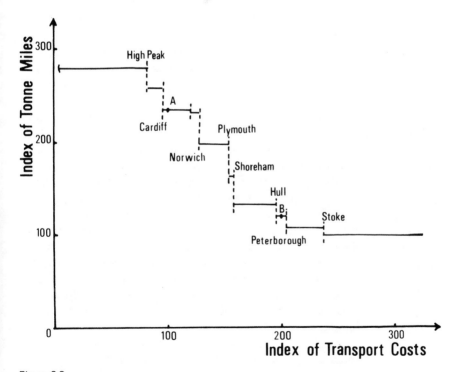

Figure 6.8.

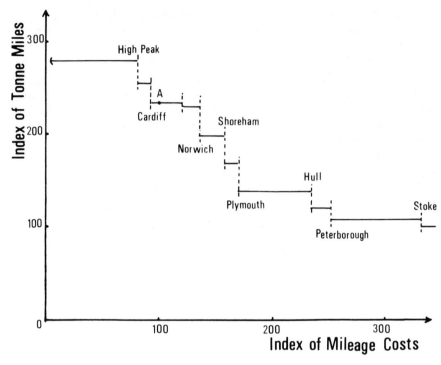

Figure 6.9.

in mileage costs than to changes in transport costs as a whole: complete disaggregation is not achieved until the mileage cost index is raised to 332.[4] One corollary of this is that if non-local haulage involves greater loading/unloading costs than local haulage (perhaps because commodities have to be more securely packed, require refrigeration, etc.), then greater disaggregation of production is to be expected.

Figure 6.10 indicates that the calculated optimum for Case 0 is not sensitive to changes in labour costs in production. This is to be expected from our estimates in Chapter 5. There are significant economies of scale to labour, but labour costs form a small proportion of total production costs. A reduction in labour costs does not alter the calculated optimum distribution for Case 0, while an increase in the labour cost index to 160 is required to produce any increase in production concentration.

A rather different picture emerges with respect to capital costs. Figure 6.11 confirms our impression that the calculated optimum for Case 0 would be sensitive to our estimates of capital costs. When the index is raised to 107, produc-

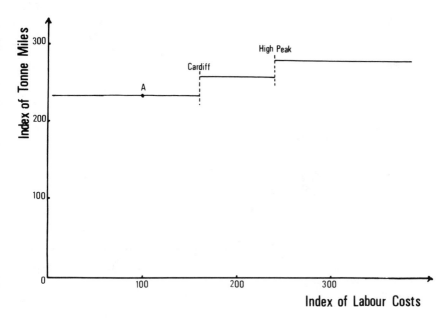

Figure 6.10.

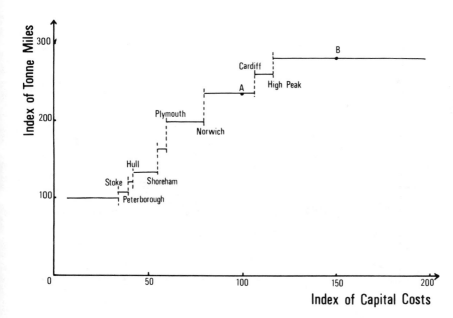

Figure 6.11.

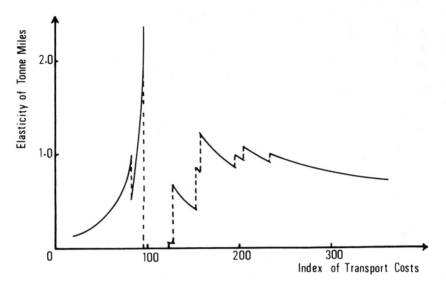

Figure 6.12.

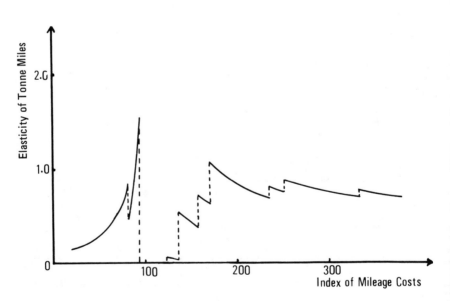

Figure 6.13.

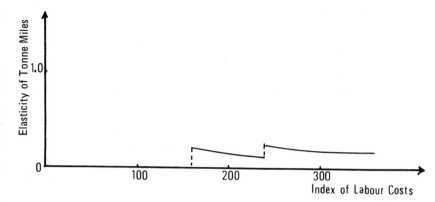

Figure 6.14.

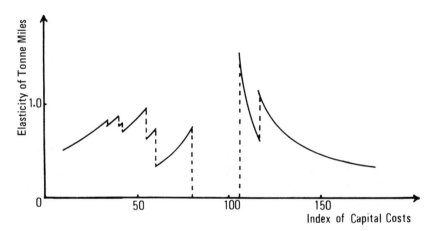

Figure 6.15.

tion is no longer economic at Cardiff, and at an index of 117, production is uneconomic at High Peak. As we have indicated, at this point the degree of spatial concentration is at the maximum attainable given the specification of the model.[5]

The calculated optimum for Case 0 is also sensitive to reduction in the capital cost index. Reduction in the index to 80 would result in production being economic at Norwich, entailing a reduction in capacity at Coventry. Production at Plymouth is economic at an index of 60, and at Shoreham at an index of 55. Production at Hull, Peterborough, and Stoke is economic at indices of 42, 40 and 34, respectively.

It should be noted that complete disaggregation of production is attained at capital cost indices below 34. There are still some economies of scale to production costs below this index, but these are not sufficient to offset to any extent the diseconomies of transport costs. This also implies that economies of scale to labour in production, assuming constant returns to all other production costs, would not be sufficient to encourage any degree of spatial concentration over and above that induced by the concentration of demand.

The arc elasticities in Figures 6.12 through 6.15 can also be used to assess the relative sensitivity of Case 0 to changes in the various cost parameters. The arc elasticity for transport costs is generally in excess of 0.7, while the elasticity for mileage and capital costs is generally in excess of 0.6. Elasticity with respect to labour costs, on the other hand, rarely exceeds 0.2.

6.3.3 Joint Sensitivity with respect to Transport and Capital Costs

The analysis in paragraph 6.3.2 indicates that the calculated optimum for Case 0 is sensitive to both capital and transport costs. It is difficult to say, however, whether the calculated optimum is more sensitive to one or the other, particularly since changes in these cost parameters affect the calculated optimum in opposite ways. We therefore conducted a further set of experiments in which capital and transport costs were varied simultaneously. The capital cost index was allowed to vary from 10 to 190 in steps of 20, i.e. capital costs were changed by p% for p = -90, -70, . . . +70, +90. For each capital cost index the MIP was solved with transport cost indices in the range 25 to 200 in steps of 25, i.e. for a p% increase in transport costs with p = -75, -50, . . . +75, +100.

These experiments identified eight points on the sensitivity curve for each capital cost index. Rather than attempt to identify the full sensitivity curve, however, Figure 6.16 presents the results of the analysis together with a subjective set of sensitivity curves; the number associated with each such sensitivity curve is the capital cost index for that curve.

This figure is sufficient for our purposes. It indicates that an increase of p% in both capital and transport costs will be roughly equal in its effect on the calculated optimum for Case 0 for p greater than -30%. In other words, the tendency to concentration of production caused by an increase in capital costs is almost exactly offset by the tendency to disaggregation of production coming from an equal increase in transport costs. As p falls below -30% however, some concentration of production does tend to emerge. At very low transport and capital cost levels, economies of scale to labour and capital are sufficient to offset the transport cost penalty of production concentration.

Our tentative conclusion, therefore, is that the calculated optimum for Case 0 is equally sensitive to changes in transport and capital costs.

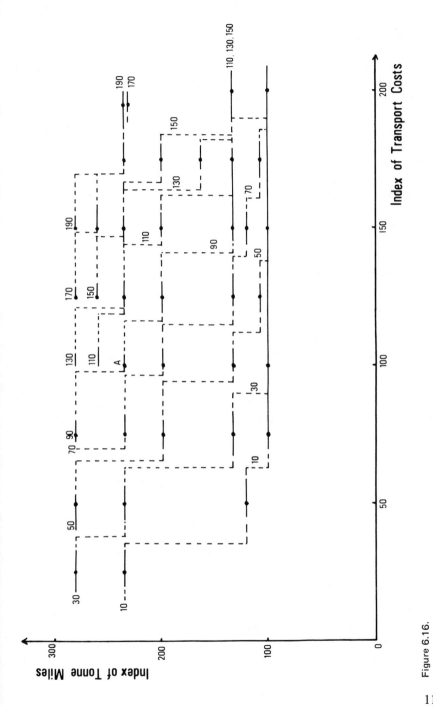

Figure 6.16.

111

6.3.4 Demand Distribution and Transport Network

We have already noted that the distribution of demand has a strong influence on the calculated optimum distribution of capacity. As a result, any sharp changes in demand distribution would give rise to similarly sharp changes in the predicted distribution of capacity.

This conclusion would be important if it could be shown that demand varied widely from town to town over a period of years. Data supplied by the Cement Makers Federation indicated, however, that while there have been some changes in demand distribution, these have been relatively small.

The absolute magnitude of total market demand will also have some influence. Since we have imposed an upper limit on the scale range over which economies of scale are available, the greater is total demand, the more plants there will be in the calculated optimum. It was for precisely this reason that we took 17 m. tonnes as our estimate of total demand – see Chapter 5.

Again we conclude that any reasonable variation in total demand would affect the fine detail of the calculated optimum distribution of capacity but would not give rise to any significant changes in this distribution.

The transport network was related to the network of major roads existing in England and Wales in 1966. Clearly there have been advances since then, both in the number of such roads and in their nature. The effect of such improvements has been, for example, to improve communications between London and the Midlands and South West, and between the Midlands and the North. There have also been some improvements in communication within the Midlands, e.g. movement between High Peak and Manchester is probably more direct than is implied by Figure 5.8.

But the calculated optimum for Case 0 and the results of the sensitivity analysis indicate that the total England and Wales market can be partitioned into a series of sub-markets which operate practically independently of each other. Thus we could define the following four sub-markets:

(i) London and the South East,
(ii) the South West and South Wales,
(iii) East Anglia, the Midlands, Manchester, and North Wales,
(iv) the North East.

They are illustrated in Figure 6.17.

Optimisation of the MIP for Case 0 could have been achieved by optimising the MIP's for each of these sub-markets.

Improvements in the transport network between the sub-markets would be equivalent to a decrease in transport costs between them. The results of our sensitivity analysis imply that, even with no improvement in communications

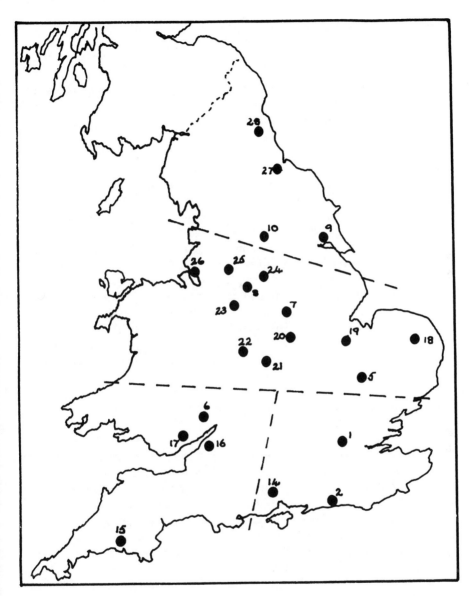

Figure 6.17.

within a sub-market, substantial changes in inter-market transport costs would be necessary to disturb the calculated optimum for Case 0.

This conclusion carries through to situations in which we consider the effects of introducing alternative modes of transport, e.g. rail or sea links. Empirical investigations have shown that rail and sea transport is economic with respect to road transport only over long hauls. As a result, the introduction of additional transport modes is equivalent to a reduction in inter-sub-market transport costs and so is subject to the same remarks.

Improvements in intra-sub-market communications would lead to some changes in the calculated optimum distribution for Case 0. In this case we can use the results of our sensitivity analysis directly, and note that if such improvements were equivalent to a 4 per cent reduction in transport costs, some change in the calculated optimum for Case 0 would result. (We would assume, of course, that the improvements also extended to the loading cost component of transport costs.) If, on the other hand, the only change in intra-sub-market communications is the construction of additional roads, e.g. between High Peak and Manchester, then there would be no significant changes in the calculated optimum distribution, although it might prove less sensitive to changes in transport costs.

We conclude, therefore, that although the assumptions made in Chapter 5 in defining the graph for the cement study do affect the fine detail of the calculated optimum distribution, there would have to be a sharp departure from these assumptions for there to be any significant change in the calculated optimum.

6.3.5 Solution of the Cement Study with Updated Cost Estimates

We indicated in Chapter 2 that sensitivity analysis is limited in that it is a comparative static device in which only one parameter can be varied at a time. In principle, of course, there is nothing to prevent us varying all the parameters simultaneously and analysing the results, but even with a small number of parameters the possible variations become very numerous and therefore unjustifiably expensive in computer time, as can be seen from paragraph 6.3.3.

We felt, however, that it would be useful to re-estimate the calculated optimum, taking account of the changes in the parameters in the sets III and IV over the period 1963-72, i.e. to present an updated calculated optimum based on 1972 costs. (We chose 1972 since this is the last year for which we could obtain reasonable estimates of labour costs in cement production.)

Indices of the various cost parameters are given in Table 6.4.

These indices were used to estimate the change in transport costs over the period 1963-72 on the following assumptions:

(i) the capital cost index applies to depreciation charges in transport,

Table 6.4.   Indices of Cost Parameters

Parameter	Cost Index (end of Year)		% change
	1963	1972	
Capital Costs	77.8	116.6	50
Labour Costs	100.0	173.9	74
Fuel Costs	100.0	199.5	100

Source: Capital costs, NIER 3/76; Fuel costs, Shell (U.K.) Ltd.; Labour costs, Census of Production 1963, 1972.

(ii) the labour cost index applies to labour costs in transport (we were not able to identify an index of labour costs specific to transport),

(iii) labour and transport costs have equal weights in the 1963 transport cost estimates.

Clearly these assumptions are not the only assumptions that could be made, but data limitations preclude a more sophisticated approach.

The average increase in labour and capital costs is then 62%. Using the estimate (footnote 4.) of the fuel element of transport costs, the mileage cost index for 1972 is estimated to be 180 and the loading cost index 170.

We re-estimated the linear spline, assuming a 74% increase in labour costs and a 50% increase in capital costs. Once more the abscissas of the knots were constrained to 0.5 and 1.6 m. tonnes with no significant changes in our estimates.[6]

Our estimates of the magnitude and distribution of demand were maintained; these had altered to some extent but only sufficiently to affect the detailed distribution of capacity in the calculated optimum.

The resulting model — denoted Case 3 — was solved to give the results in Table 6.5 and illustrated in Figure 6.18. Comparison with Figures 6.2 and 6.6 indicates that the calculated optimum for Case 3 is intermediate between those for Cases 0 and 1. The increase in transport costs relative to those elements of production costs that exhibit economies of scale is sufficient to produce some disaggregation of production relative to the Case 0 distribution. In particular, production is economic at Plymouth and Norwich entailing a reduction in capacity at Bristol and Coventry, and all demand at Leicester is supplied from Coventry, with a consequent reduction in capacity at High Peak.

The calculated optimum for Case 3 was found to be relatively sensitive to changes in transport costs. A further increase of 5% in transport costs (including loading costs) is sufficient to make production at Shoreham economic, with a reduction in the production concentration at London. Transport costs would

Table 6.5. Calculated Optimum for Case 3

Node	Place Name	Predicted Capacity		Towns Supplied**	
		Case 3	Case 0	Case 3	Case 0
1	London	6.300	6.300	1,14	1,14
2	Shoreham	–	–		
5	Cambridge	–	–		
6	Monmouth	–	–		
7	Nottingham	–	–		
8	High Peak	2.343	2.500	7,10,23,24	7,10,23,24,(20)
9	Hull	–	–		
10	Leeds	–	–		
14	Southampton	–	–		
15	Plymouth	0.491	–	15	
16	Bristol	0.802	1.293	16	15,16
17	Cardiff	0.898	0.898	17	17
18	Norwich	0.418	–	18	
19	Peterborough	–	–		
20	Leicester	–			
21	Coventry	2.276	2.537	19,20,21,22	18,19,21,22,(20)
22	Birmingham	–	–		
23	Stoke	–	–		
24	Sheffield	–	–		
25	Manchester	2.138	2.138	25,26	25,26
26	Liverpool	–	–		
27	Teesside	1.334	1.334	9,27,28	9,27,28
28	Newcastle	–	–		

**Figures in brackets indicate that the town is supplied from more than one production site.

then have to increase by something in excess of 30%, however, to secure any further changes in the distribution of production.

It should be noted that inflation in fuel costs has accelerated since 1972: taking 1972 as base, the fuel cost index in 1974 was 148.6, the capital cost index was 125.8, and the index of weekly wage rates in 'manufacturing and other' employment was 136.3. The relative increase in fuel costs is sufficient for us to expect that the calculated optimum based on 1974 costs would be somewhat more disaggregated than that for Case 3, but the additional disaggregation is not likely to be particularly great—it would probably involve local production at Shoreham. As a result we did not feel that additional computer tests were justified.

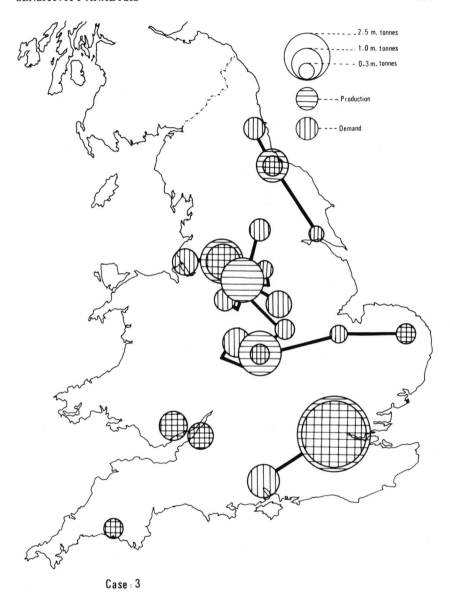

Case: 3

Figure 6.18.

6.4 COMPARISON OF ACTUAL AND CALCULATED DISTRIBUTIONS

6.4.1 The Actual Distribution of the Industry

A necessary preliminary to the comparison of actual and calculated location patterns in the cement industry is some consideration of the existing locational characteristics of the industry. The Cement Makers' Federal (CMF) kindly made available details of cement capacity by plant for the years 1956, 1960, and 1965, and by county for the years 1950 and 1974. Cement capacity by plant for 1970 was obtained from the *European Cement Association* (1972). Data giving cement deliveries by county for each of the indicated years were also supplied by the CMF. These data were used to derive cement capacities for each of the indicated years at each of the potential production sites derived in Chapter 5. The results are given in Table 6.6.

We can identify the changing spatial patterns of production over the period 1960–74 from the data summarised in Table 6.6, but can say nothing about the change in plant capacities. In order to analyse the latter factor we compared in-

Table 6.6.   Cement Capacity (m. tonnes) England and Wales

Nodes	1950	1956	1960	1965	1970	1974
London (1)	5.647	6.729	7.316	7.869	7.484	7.478
Shoreham (2)	0.238	0.680	0.698	0.735	0.460	0.532
Cambridge (5)	0.205	0.434	0.412	0.657	0.554	0.549
Monmouth (6)	—	—	—	—	—	—
High Peak (8)	0.383	0.615	0.620	0.652	1.216	1.554
Hull (9)	0.691	0.887	0.758	0.753	0.904	0.911
Plymouth (15)	—	—	0.070	0.216	0.536	0.535
Bristol (16)	—	—	—	0.641	0.613	0.623
Cardiff (17)	0.446	0.527	0.662	0.825	0.569	0.793
Norwich (18)	0.053	0.198	0.200	0.210	0.402	0.424
P'borough (19)	0.237	0.330	0.342	0.523	0.622	0.616
Coventry (21)	0.596	0.738	0.931	1.138	1.028	1.075
Stoke (23)	—	—	0.187	0.717	0.651	0.671
Manchester (25)	0.151	0.713	0.732	0.962	1.461	1.260
Teesside (27)	0.220	0.350	0.360	1.080**	0.670	0.761
Total	8.867	12.201	13.288	16.978	17.170	17.782

Source: see text.
**Includes ICI plant closed 1966 and APCM plant opened 1964.

dividual plant capacities for the years 1956 and 1970. Frequency distributions of these plants are given in Table 6.7. The data for 'all plants' indicate a general shift in the distribution towards plant capacities in excess of 350 th. tonnes p.a. Total capacity in England and Wales increased by 41% over the period 1956-70, while the number of plants in existence fell from 42 to 32; mean plant capacity increased by 85% and median capacity by 55%—see Table 6.8.

Table 6.7. Frequency Distribution of Plant Capacities

	All Plants		Surviving Plants	
Capacity Range (th. tonnes p.a.)	1956	1970	1956	1970
over 0 & under 50	—	} —	—	—
" 50 " 100	4		—	—
" 100 " 150	6	} 3	4	3
" 150 " 200	6		3	—
" 200 " 250	4	} 4	2	1
" 250 " 300	6		6	2
" 300 " 350	5	2	2	2
" 350 " 400	2	7	2	6
" 400 " 500	3	3	2	3
" 500 " 750	5	8	3	4
" 750 " 1000	1	2	1	2
" 1000 " 1500	—	2	—	2
" 1500 " 2000	—	—	—	—
over 2000	—	1	—	—
Number of Plants	42	32	25	25
Mean capacity	290.5	536.6	324.1	457.3
Median capacity	258.3	400.0	279.2	387.5

Source: CMF and European Cement Association (1972).

Table 6.8. Comparison of Plant Size Distributions

	Mean			Median		
	1956	1970	% change	1956	1970	% change
All plants	290.5	536.6	84.7	258.3	400.0	54.9
Surviving plants	324.1	457.3	41.1	279.2	387.5	38.8
New plants	—	987.1	—	—	640.0	—

Source: as for Table 6.7.

This change in the size distribution of plants was the result of several factors. Firstly, there was a general expansion in the capacities of surviving plants—those plants in operation in 1970 which were also in operation in 1956. Secondly, the plants closed over the period were predominantly small-scale plants—eleven of the seventeen plants closed had capacities in 1956 of less than 250 th. tonnes p.a. Thirdly, of the seven new plants opened in the period, five either had initial capacities in excess of 500 th. tonnes p.a. or had attained at least this capacity by 1970.

The different factors at work in changing the plant size distribution arose from differences in the behaviour of the individual firms in the industry. Of the seventeen plants closed, APCM (the market leader) owned thirteen, of which eleven were located in the London area. In addition, six of the seven new plants opened in the period were owned by APCM. Only one of these plants was located in London, but this plant—at Northfleet—had a 1970 capacity of nearly 4 m. tonnes p.a. Finally, twelve of the twenty-five surviving plants were owned by APCM. Of these twelve, only two increased in capacity over the period; the remainder had static or reduced capacities. The remaining thirteen surviving plants exhibited an average increase in capacity of 75%; the increase was relatively evenly spread over these plants.

These results indicate that the market leader reacted to the growth in demand and to the changing spatial distribution of demand in two ways. Firstly, in those regions outside the London area in which APCM was not represented, new medium-scale plants (with capacities in excess of 500 th. tonnes p.a.) were opened. Secondly, in the London area, old plant was closed down and capacity rationalised into a new large-scale plant. The remaining firms in the industry, on the other hand, continued to operate on their existing sites, increasing capacity either by adding new kilns or by replacing old kilns with new larger-capacity kilns.

The changes in the size distribution of cement plants is related to the change in the spatial distribution of these plants. In 1956 APCM had a virtual monopoly of cement making capacity in the South East, but was poorly represented elsewhere. By 1970, while retaining the dominant position in the South East, APCM had expanded into many of the major markets in other parts of the country.

Plymouth (15), Bristol (16), Stoke (23) and Manchester (25) are all nodes where capacity grew fastest over the period, and where new plants were opened and brought rapidly on-line. The plant at Norwich was small-scale (see Table 6.6) and the growth in capacity was achieved by adding further small-scale units. High Peak is the only node at which the growth of capacity resulted from the expansion of large-scale existing plant. It is significant in this case that the production site occupies a position convenient for many of the towns defined in Chapter 5, and that the plant involved is operated by APCM.

The adjustment of capacity at the remaining nodes was achieved in the majority of cases by adding additional units to existing plants.

Regressions were performed to identify those factors important in explaining the changing distribution of capacity over the period 1950-74. In this respect we noted in our analysis of the calculated optimum that the distribution of demand had a major influence on the locational pattern of production. To test for this factor, demand at each of the potential production sites listed in Table 6.6 was taken to be the sum of demands in those counties for which the particular node was the nearest potential supplier.

We assume that the reaction of capacity to changes in demand, etc., conditions is uniform across the various nodes. As a result, there are fourteen observations on capacity and demand for each of six periods. These observations were used to derive vectors C_t for capacity and D_t for demand, where:

$$C_t = (c_{11}, \ldots c_{16}, c_{21}, \ldots c_{26}, \ldots, c_{S1}, \ldots c_{S6})$$

$$D_t = (d_{11}, \ldots d_{16}, d_{21}, \ldots d_{26}, \ldots, d_{S1}, \ldots d_{S6})$$

(6.4.1)

where: c_{st} = capacity at node s in G at time t,

d_{st} = demand at node s in G at time t, (t=1 ... 6).

It should be noted that when lags are introduced to form the vectors C_{t-1}, C_{t+1}, etc., fourteen observations are lost for each period lagged (one for each of the fourteen nodes). Thus for regressions involving variables lagged to (t-1), t and (t+1), say, there will be fifty-six observations.

The observations for London indicated that London operated under a different regime from the remaining nodes and these observations were dropped. The preferred equation was then:

$$C_{t+1} - C_t = 0.073 + 0.025\ C_t + 0.205(D_t - C_t) \qquad (R^2 = 0.48; \quad (6.4.2)$$
$$\phantom{C_{t+1} - C_t = 0.073 + } (0.009) \quad (0.051) \qquad\qquad 65\ \text{d.f.})$$

where the vector $D_t - C_t$ is the vector of excess demands
at each node in each time period.

Figures in parentheses are the standard errors of the estimated coefficients. All coefficients are significant at the 1% level of significance.

The equation, therefore, supports the hypothesis that the distribution of demand is an important determinant of the distribution of capacity.

Further experiments were conducted using the change in excess demand (absolute and percentage), the growth in demand, and predicted excess demand.[7] In no case was there any significant improvement on (6.4.2), nor did any of the alternative parameters perform better than those in (6.4.2).

The estimated equation is a dynamic equation relating the response of capacity at each node to any excess or deficiency of capacity with respect to demand at that node. The 'half-life' of this response can be estimated by rewriting the equation as follows:

$$\Delta C_t + a_1 C_t = g_t \tag{6.4.3}$$

where: $a_1 = 0.205 - 0.025$

$$g_t = 0.073 + 0.205 D_t$$

The solution to (6.4.3) is, from Casson (1973) p. 340:

$$C_T = \sum_{t=0}^{T-1} \{(1-a_1)^t \cdot g(T-1-t)\} + (1-a_1)^T C_o. \tag{6.4.4}$$

The half-life of the response of capacity is then given by that value of T for which:

$$(1-a_1)^T = 0.50, \text{ i.e. } T = 3.5. \tag{6.4.5}$$

In other words, 50% of the adjustment of capacity to demand will take place in 3.5 periods, i.e. 17.5 years. If the term $0.025 C_t$ were dropped from equation (6.4.2), the half-life of response would shorten to 3.0 periods, i.e. 15 years. This implies that the existing distribution of capacity imposes a brake on changes in this distribution, but it can be seen that the braking process is not particularly strong.

If London operated under the same regime as the remaining nodes, then applying (6.4.2) to the observations for London would give rise to the time path illustrated in Figure 6.19. It can be seen that while actual capacity at London has been affected by the existence of excess capacity, the speed of response of capacity is much slower than that implied by (6.4.2).

6.4.2 Comparison of Predicted and Actual Distributions

In order to compare the actual and predicted optimal distributions of the UK cement industry, we expressed actual capacity at each node for the years 1950, 1965, and 1974, and calculated optimum capacity at each node for Cases 0 and 3 as a percentage of total capacity for the same year or case. The results are illustrated in Figure 6.20.

As might be expected, the actual distribution is, on the one hand, more disaggregated, and, on the other, shows a heavier concentration of capacity in the London area than the calculated optimum for Case 0.

With reference to the latter point, we have already noted that the dominance of the South East has been steadily eroded over the period 1950–74. We can claim, therefore, that the distribution of capacity is, in this respect, evolving towards our calculated optimum. In addition, those concentrations of produc-

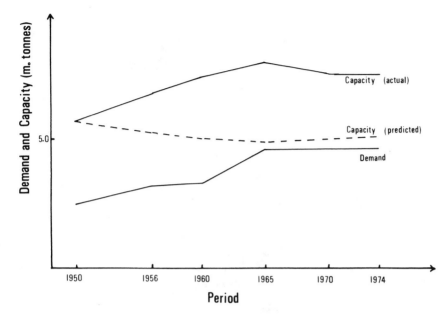

Figure 6.19.

tion which remain unchanged in the calculated optima for Cases 0 and 3 tend to occur at nodes in which the actual capacity has been expanding over the period 1950-74, e.g. Manchester and Teesside. (In Figure 6.20 the indicated capacity at Teesside includes the ICI plant closed in 1966.)

These comments are also consistent, however, with our feeling that the actual distribution of capacity is converging on a distribution more closely related to the calculated optimum for Case 3 than for Case 0. At two of the nodes where capacity in Case 3 is less than in Case 0 – Bristol and Coventry – the growth in actual capacity has also reversed, while our discussion of the Case 3 solution indicated that we might expect a further reduction in capacity at London with the emergence of production at Shoreham.

Convergence on the calculated optimum for Case 3 is to be expected when we consider, firstly, that the calculated optimum for Case 0 refers to a base date of 1963 while the actual distribution refers to the period 1950-74. We noted in paragraph 6.3.6 that cost conditions have changed significantly over this period, making the Case 3 solution the more relevant. Secondly, our findings with respect to the rate of adjustment would imply that plans are altered sufficiently quickly for us to expect adjustment to Case 3 rather than Case 0.

There remains a number of areas in which the actual distribution of capacity

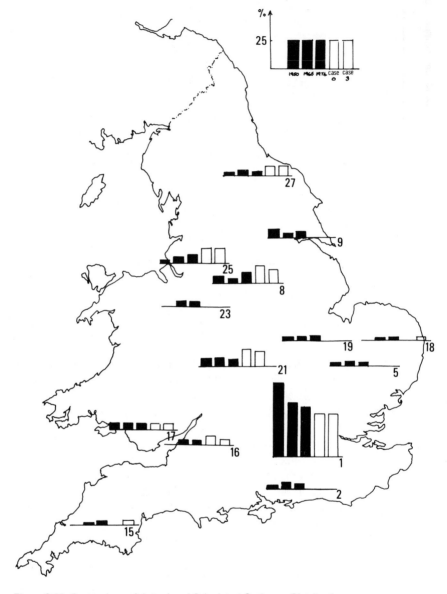

Figure 6.20. Comparison of Actual and Calculated Optimum Distribution.

deviates quite sharply from the calculated optimum for Case 3—Cambridge, Hull, Peterborough, Shoreham, Coventry, and Stoke. At three of these nodes, however—Cambridge, Peterborough, and Coventry—the plants are operated by firms other than APCM, on sites which they have occupied for some considerable time. In these cases competitive conditions in the industry would appear to operate to maintain a rather more spatially dispersed pattern of production than would otherwise be optimal.

In a fourth case, Shoreham, we noted in paragraph 6.3.6 that the further increase in transport costs in the period 1972–74 would result in local production being economic, with a consequent reduction in capacity at London. Actual capacity at both nodes is operated by APCM. Finally, in the case of Stoke, production was begun in the late 1950s when APCM opened a new plant. After an initial period of rapid growth—see Table 6.6—capacity declined, as the major growth in production was taken up at High Peak. This is in line with our expectations, given the calculated optima for Cases 0 and 3.

6.5 CONCLUSION

The discussion in 6.4.2 goes a long way towards reconciling the differences between the calculated optimum and actual distributions. Nevertheless, the adjustment of the industry to our calculated optimum is neither perfect nor uniform. We have already indicated the role of the competitive structure of the industry in slowing, or indeed preventing, the adjustment process. Two other factors should also be considered. Firstly, we have ignored the historical distribution of capacity in formulating the version of the model analysed in this chapter. But the regression results and the discussion of the changing frequency distribution of plants do indicate that the existing capacity and the growth of demand affect the process of spatial concentration. So long as raw materials are available, it may well be economic to keep old, small-scale plant in operation (i) since there have been no major technological innovations over the period 1930–74 and (ii) since the capital cost component of TPC for old plant will be rather less than that estimated in Chapter 5. Extension at existing sites and replacement of existing kilns may also incur lower capital costs than opening a new site; savings may be made on site clearance and erection costs and from the sale of old equipment as scrap.

Secondly, our simplifying assumptions, in particular the process of spatial aggregation involved in defining the market area, will influence the calculated optimum we obtain.

In Chapter 7 we present a multiperiod version of the model for one of the sub-regions defined above, and examine in more detail the effects of the time dimension on production allocation over space. As might be expected, we shall find that the calculated optima derived above are somewhat modified. Nevertheless, the variations between calculated and actual distributions cannot be completely explained by history and/or our simplifying assumptions. The discussion in paragraph 6.4.2 does indicate that we have obtained a calculated optimum which reflects the essential features of the UK cement industry. We can conclude therefore:

(i) that a further degree of spatial concentration is justified in certain areas, while some disaggregation is required – particularly from London,
(ii) that the results of the sensitivity analysis are indicative of the sensitivity of the optimal locational pattern to various of the cost parameters, and so give an indication of the extent to which this pattern will react to changes in the cost parameters,
(iii) that the regression analysis and the discussion in 6.4.2 can be used to indicate the time scale involved in securing any major reorganisation of the spatial and size distribution of the industry.

7 THE MULTIPERIOD VERSION OF THE MODEL

7.1 INTRODUCTION

One major limitation of the results in Chapter 6 is that they take no account of the history of the industry. A static model is presented in which capacity is to be allocated over a series of green-field sites.

The major reason for presenting the model in this way is that computer capacity constraints severely limit the size of problem that can be handled. In our discussion in paragraph 6.3.4, however, we noted that the cement study could have been solved by partitioning the market area into a number of sub-markets and solving the resulting mixed integer programme (MIP) for each sub-market.

Clearly, the MIP for a particular sub-market will be smaller than that for the whole graph. Advantage can be taken of the savings in computer capacity so achieved to define a multiperiod version of the cement study for each sub-market. Our comments on the limitations imposed by ignoring history can then be made more precise.

Extension of the model to a multiperiod form introduces a completely new class of decisions for the producer. He has to decide not only where and how, but also when capacity should be installed. Consider a very simple situation. De-

mand for final product at a town v is assumed to be expanding as in Figure
7.1(a), and v is assumed to be a potential production site at which average production costs are as in Figure 7.1(b). The planning curve in Figure 7.1(b) is the
traditional long-run average cost curve, and $SRAC_1$ is an associated short-run
average cost curve. For simplicity we ignore the effects of discounting costs to
period 0 and we assume that there is no inflation. We also assume that there is
no pre-existing capacity at v, and that capacity installed in period t is operational
in that period.

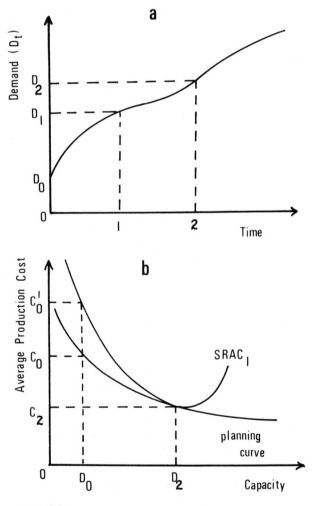

Figure 7.1.

A number of strategies are open to the producer. The simplest approach would be to expand capacity in each period by the increment in demand over the previous period. Thus D_0 units of capacity would be installed in period 0, $(D_1 - D_0)$ units in period 1 and $(D_2 - D_1)$ in period 2. Clearly, the slower is the growth of demand and/or the lower the elasticity of the total production cost function with respect to scale over the range $0 - D_2$, the higher will be the unit costs of production associated with this approach.

An alternative approach might be to instal OD_2 units of capacity in period 0. If this capacity is less than fully utilised in any period, average production costs will be given by $SRAC_1$, e.g. if only OD_0 units of capacity are utilised in period 0, unit production costs in that period will be OC_0'. On the other hand, the producer may fully utilise the capacity and either export the excess production to distant towns or store it at v against the short-fall in capacity which will arise after period 2.

Once the full set of interdependencies are recognised, the alternative strategies can become very complex. Simple or complex, however, the choice of strategy will obviously be dependent upon the relative importance of economies of scale, the rate of change of demand, transport costs, and storage costs.

7.2 RESTATEMENT OF THE OBJECTIVE

The objective assumed to face the industry is to find that use of existing capacity and pattern of installation of new capacity within the sub-market that will minimise the present cost at period 0 of satisfying price-inelastic demand at each town within the sub-market over the planning period $0 - T$, subject to constraints imposed by the availability of inputs to the production process.

In stating the objective in this fashion we drop the assumption of green-field sites which characterised the static version of the model. We shall examine the extent to which existing capacity remains in use, is extended, or is replaced by new capacity.

7.3 DECISION VARIABLES

Formally, the extension of the model to include the time dimension is straightforward. Commodities are now differentiated by type, location, and time, i.e. are subscripted

$$nvt \quad (t = 0 \ldots T; n = 1 \ldots N; v = 1 \ldots V). \qquad (7.3.1)$$

Activity vectors and activity levels are also differentiated by time, i.e. we define the activity vectors

$$\mathbf{a}_{kvt} = \begin{bmatrix} a_{0kvt} \\ \cdot \\ \cdot \\ \cdot \\ a_{Nkvt} \end{bmatrix} \qquad \text{(all } k,v,t) \qquad\qquad (7.3.2)$$

with associated activity levels

$$x_{kvt} \geq 0 \qquad \text{(all } k,v,t). \qquad\qquad (7.3.3)$$

The activity vectors and activity levels have exactly the same properties as the activity vectors and activity levels defined in Chapter 3.

For simplicity, we assume that $\mathbf{a}_{kvt}$ is invariant over the planning period, i.e.

$$\mathbf{a}_{kvt} = \mathbf{a}_{kv} \qquad \text{(all } k,v,t). \qquad\qquad (7.3.4)$$

The graph representation of the market area is formally the same (with the exception that in the case study we shall be concerned with allocation over a subset of the whole graph) but now contains a set of oriented branches

$$(v_t, v_{t+1}) \qquad \text{(all } v; t = 1 \ldots T\text{-}1). \qquad\qquad (7.3.5)$$

The implication of defining branches in this fashion is that transport over time (i.e. storage) is only available from one period to the next and, of course, it is not possible to move commodities from period t to period t–1. As a result, transport activities fulfil one of two roles. They either change the location of a good in a particular time period, in which case we define the activity levels

$$w_{nvut} \geq 0 \qquad \text{(all } n \neq 0; \text{ all } v,u,t), \qquad\qquad (7.3.6)$$

or they move a good at a particular location from one period to the next, in which case we define the activity levels

$$s_{nvt} \geq 0 \qquad \text{(all } n \neq 0; \text{ all } v,t \ (t \neq T)) \qquad\qquad (7.3.7)$$

indicating the amount of good n stored at node v in time t. Obviously, appropriate combination of the activity levels (7.3.7) will allow transfer of a good from any period to any future period up to T.

Note that we do not define activity levels (7.3.7) for labour. We assume that the labour services available in any period appear as a flow (with the exception of certain fixed labour services discussed more fully in paragraph 7.4.3). Any labour services made available in period t but not employed in production in t cannot then be stored for use in t+1.

The activity levels (7.3.6) incur transport costs as defined in Chapter 3. For the activity levels (7.3.7), however, the costs incurred are more properly storage costs.

Appropriate respecification of the cost, availability, requirement, and other parameters defined in Chapter 3 follow in a straightforward fashion, and the resulting linear programme is changed very little from that presented in Chapter 3. Of more interest is a multiperiod specification of the MIP in Chapter 4, i.e. of the model assuming economies of scale in production.

In a single period model or a model in which market conditions are assumed to remain constant indefinitely, all capacity will be installed at the beginning of the history of the economy and will be fully utilised throughout its life. Given the existence of economies of scale, however, and a situation in which final demand is changing over time, it may well be economic to instal capacity in period t, say, which will not be fully utilised until period $t + \tau$. Thus we have to distinguish between the capacity installed in any period and the extent to which it is used in that period and subsequent periods.

We define the addition to capacity of activity kv in period t to be

$$y_{kvt} \geq 0 \quad \text{(all k,v,t)}. \tag{7.3.8}$$

There is a number of assumptions implicit in this definition:

(i) We can define activity levels (7.3.3) such that

$$0 \leq x_{kvt} \leq \sum_{\tau=0}^{t} y_{kv\tau} \quad \text{(all k,v,t)} \tag{7.3.9}$$

i.e. the maximum activity level of activity kv in time t is the sum of installed capacity up to time t.

(ii) Following from (7.3.9) there is the assumption that capacity installed in time t is operational in time t. Clearly this is not crucial to the model, but it does have the merit of simplicity.

(iii) The variable costs incurred in operating activity kv are independent of the vintage of the equipment involved in the activity – this will be considered further in section 7.4.

(iv) If y_{kvt} units of capacity are installed in time t, this capacity is fully available up to time T. There is nothing in principle to prevent us varying the attainable capacity of particular items of equipment with the life of that equipment – this would merely involve changing the coefficients on the $y_{kv\tau}$ in the summation (7.3.9). Similarly, if the expected life of plant is r periods, where $r < T$, we could rewrite (7.3.9) as

$$0 \leq x_{kvt} \leq \sum_{\tau=\max(0,t-r)}^{t} y_{kv\tau} \tag{7.3.9'}$$

But while the principle is straightforward, the data requirements are not. We therefore maintain the assumptions (i) and (iv).

The final set of decision variables which will be defined in this section are those relating to the utilisation of existing capacity. We define the available capacity in period 0 and all subsequent periods of a pre-existing activity $k^e v$ to be

$$y^e_{kv} \geq 0 \quad \text{(all k,v).} \tag{7.3.10}$$

The activity vectors associated with these activities are assumed to be

$$a^e_{kv}. \tag{7.3.11}$$

These activity vectors have the same properties as those defined in (7.3.2). In particular, we can define production activity levels on this capacity

$$x^e_{kvt} \geq 0 \quad \text{(all k,v,t).} \tag{7.3.12}$$

Existing capacity is treated in this way since we shall wish to distinguish between the activity vectors, activity levels, and costs involved in operating new and existing capacity.

Installing new capacity will involve some capital expenditure which might be expected to exhibit economies of scale. A further set of decision variables has to be defined—as in Chapter 4—to take this into account. They will be integer-constrained and are best considered in conjunction with our discussion of the cost parameters in the multiperiod model.

7.4 COST PARAMETERS

Unless otherwise stated, all costs referred to below will be assumed to have been discounted to present values at $t = 0$.

7.4.1 Capital Costs

We assume that the capital cost incurred in installing new capacity in activity kv at time t will be as in the smooth curve in Figure 7.2. We then adopt the same trick as in Chapter 4 and approximate this curve by a linear spline. The unit capital cost of installing y_{kvt} units of capacity will vary with the segment of the spline in which y_{kvt} lies. Thus if y_{kvt} is in the interval $[\hat{y}^{i-1}_{kvt}, \hat{y}^i_{kvt})$ (i = 1 ... I), capital costs involved in installing y_{kvt} units of capacity are

$$
\begin{aligned}
C(y_{kvt}) &= m^i_{kvt} + b^i_{kvt} y_{kvt} & \text{if } y^{i-1}_{kvt} \in [\hat{y}^i_{kvt}, \hat{y}_{kvt}) \text{ (all i)} \\
&= 0 & \text{if } y_{kvt} = 0.
\end{aligned} \tag{7.4.1}
$$

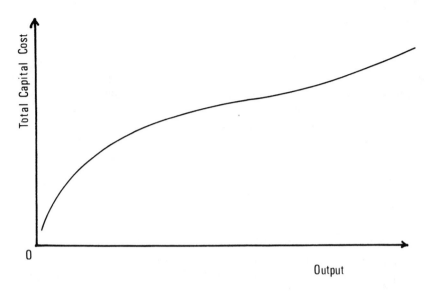

Figure 7.2.

Equation (7.4.1) indicates that the cost parameters that are operative in the objective function will vary with the interval in which y_{kvt} lies. Thus if we introduce decision variables γ^i_{kvt} analogous to the γ_{kv} defined in Chapter 4 we would have

$$C(y_{kvt}) = \sum_i (m^i_{kvt}\gamma^i_{kvt} + b^i_{kvt}y_{kvt}) \qquad (7.4.2)$$

$$\text{where: } \gamma^i_{kvt} = 1 \text{ if } y_{kvt} \geq \hat{y}^{i-1}_{kvt} \text{ and } y_{kvt} < \hat{y}^i_{kvt}$$

$$= 0 \text{ otherwise.}$$

The conditions on γ^i_{kvt} are rather awkward to handle. We feel that the simplest approach is to define a further set of decision variables y^i_{kvt} and rewrite (7.4.2) as

$$C(y_{kvt}) = \sum_i (m^i_{kvt}\gamma^i_{kvt} + b^i_{kvt}y^i_{kvt}) \qquad (7.4.3)$$

subject to the constraints

(i)
$$y_{kvt} = \sum_i y^i_{kvt}$$

(ii) $$y^i_{kvt} \geq \gamma^i_{kvt} \hat{y}^{i-1}_{kvt}$$ (7.4.4)

(iii) $$y^i_{kvt} < \gamma^i_{kvt} \hat{y}^i_{kvt}$$

(iv) $$\gamma^i_{kvt} = 0 \text{ or } 1.$$

Treating capital costs in this way makes the decision variables y_{kvt} redundant. The y^i_{kvt} have exactly the same interpretation as the y_{kvt} but are differentiated according to the range of capacities to which they apply. The constraints (7.3.9) can therefore be rewritten

$$0 \leq x_{kvt} \leq \sum_i \sum_{\tau=0}^{t} y^i_{kv\tau} \quad \text{(all k,v,t)}$$ (7.4.5)

We have presented equations (7.4.1) and (7.4.3) without any consideration of the assumptions and complications involved in defining 'capital cost' in a multi-period model. The first point that should be noted is that our treatment of capital costs is such that installing y^i_{kvt} units of capacity in activity kv is independent of whether capacity in the same activity has been installed in previous periods. Thus we assume that adding 100 th. tonnes p.a. capacity in period 3 to an activity kv installed in period 0, say, will incur the same site clearance, machinery erection, and other costs as installing 100 th. tonnes p.a. capacity in activity kv in period 3 on a green-field site.

Secondly, a multiperiod model introduces an extra dimension of scale to the production unit – the total output of the unit over the planning period. We must then allow for distorting edge effects in our treatment of capital costs. Consider, for example, the choice between installing z units of capacity in activity kv in period t or t+1. Capital costs are respectively $C(z_{kvt})$ and $C(z_{kv(t+1)})$. If no allowance is made for the edge effect of stopping the economy at the finite time T, there will be a bias against the decision to instal capacity in time t+1, since total output from the capacity will be greater the earlier it is installed. Two different methods for removing this bias are presented and discussed in section 7.5. In the meantime, we shall assume that the cost parameters m^i_{kvt} and b^i_{kvt} take account of these.

Thirdly, we should consider the treatment of maintenance costs. At least part of such costs for a particular activity will be related to the installed capacity of that activity and so can be discounted to present values at $t = 0$ and added to our estimates of capital costs. Other elements of maintenance costs might be expected to vary with the utilisation of installed capacity, however, and give rise to more awkward problems. If these elements of maintenance costs vary with the vintage of plant, then our equation (7.4.5) no longer holds since it relies on the assumption that variable costs are independent of vintage. We would have to define activity levels

$$x_{kvt}^{\tau} \geq 0 \quad (\tau = 0 \ldots T, \tau \leq t; \text{all } k,v,t), \qquad (7.4.6)$$

i.e. we would have to specify separately the activity level in period t of capacity in activity kv installed in period τ ($\tau = 0 \ldots$ t). Clearly, this would involve a sharp increase in the number of decision variables. We make the heroic asssumption, therefore, that maintenance costs that are related to the activity level of a production activity are linearly proportional to the activity level and independent of the vintage of the capital equipment to which they refer. As a result this element of maintenance costs can be incorporated in the variable costs of operating activity kv.

7.4.2 Labour Costs

Labour costs per period in activity kv are assumed to consist of a fixed cost independent of the installed capacity of the activity or of its activity level, plus an amount linear in the activity level. Thus we assume that once activity kv is opened—at time t, say—subsequent additions to the capacity of this activity will not incur additional fixed labour charges. This assumption implies that the labour commodity involved in production on new capacity is of two types. There is a fixed element—perhaps of management, scientific, and clerical staff— independent of the scale of operation, and a variable element related linearly to the activity level. This variable element may, of course, include some technical and other services. There is the further implication that the element of labour services that is independent of scale constitutes a stock—once it is employed it is contracted and is therefore available in each period. But it also constitutes a charge in each period whether or not the activity is operated. Finally, we assume that economies of scale to labour arise solely from spreading the fixed labour charge over an increased output.

Thus labour costs at time t are

$$L(x_{kvt}) = g_{kvt} + d_{kvt}x_{kvt} \qquad \text{if } \sum_{i} \sum_{\tau=0}^{t} y_{kv\tau}^{i} > 0$$

$$\qquad (7.4.7)$$

$$= 0 \qquad \text{if } \sum_{i} \sum_{\tau=0}^{t} y_{kv\tau}^{i} = 0$$

which can be rewritten as

$$L(x_{kvt}) = g_{kvt}\rho_{kvt} + d_{kvt}x_{kvt} \qquad (7.4.8)$$

subject to the constraints

(i) $$0 \leq x_{kvt} \leq \sum_{i} \sum_{\tau=0}^{t} y_{kv\tau}^{i} \qquad \text{(all k,v,t)}$$

(7.4.9)

(ii) $$x_{kvt} \leq \rho_{kvt} L \qquad\qquad \text{where L is 'very large'} \\ \text{(all k,v,t)}$$

(iii) $$\rho_{kvt} = 0 \text{ or } 1 \qquad\qquad \text{(all k,v,t).}$$

Constraints (i) are those we have already met. The constraints (ii) and (iii) are such that (a) if $\Sigma_i \Sigma_{\tau=0}^{t} y_{kv\tau}^{i} > 0$: Capacity can only be operated by choosing $\rho_{kvt} = 1$, i.e. by incurring the fixed labour charge g_{kvt} since setting $\rho_{kvt} = 0$ would impose the constraint $x_{kvt} \leq 0$. Note that since L is 'very large', setting $\rho_{kvt} = 1$ imposes no constraints upon the choice of x_{kvt} additional to those imposed by constraints (i). (b) if $\Sigma_i \Sigma_{\tau=0}^{t} y_{kv\tau}^{i} = 0$: Cost minimisation will force $\rho_{kvt} = 0$, i.e. no labour charges will be incurred if no capacity has been installed.

7.4.3 Variable Costs

Materials, energy, and other variable costs are assumed linear in the activity levels and independent of the vintage of the capital equipment — see equation (7.3.9). However, variable labour costs refer only to the variable labour input and do not include any element of fixed labour costs. The variable cost of operating activity kv in period t at unit activity level is then

$$v_{kvt} = d_{kvt} - \sum_{n=1}^{N} a_{nkv} c_{nvt} + e_{kvt} = d_{kvt} + u_{kvt} + e_{kvt} \qquad (7.4.10)$$

where: d_{kvt} is as in (7.4.8),

c_{nvt} has the same properties as c_n in Chapter 3, i.e. c_{nvt} is the unit cost of commodity nvt to the producer. The negative sign of this component arises since $a_{nkv} < 0$ if n is an input to the production activity,

e_{kvt} is the maintenance cost component related to output,

$$u_{kvt} = - \sum_{n} a_{nkv} c_{nvt}.$$

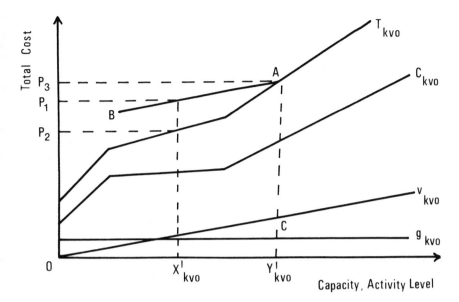

Figure 7.3.

Our treatment of production costs associated with capacity installed in the planning period is such that we draw a distinction between the cost of installing an activity and the cost of operating that activity. Thus we assume that a fixed cost is incurred at the installation stage — made up of capital costs, some element of maintenance costs, and, in certain circumstances outlined above, fixed labour charges. If we ignore the fixed labour costs, costs are only incurred subsequent to installation if the capacity is operated. Further, these latter costs are linear in the activity level and are independent of the vintage of the capital equipment.

To see what this implies, consider the situation in which y'_{kv0} units of capacity in activity kv are installed in period 0, but in which the activity level in period 0, x'_{kv0}, is less than y'_{kv0}. Figure 7.3 illustrates this situation. $T_{kv0} = C_{kv0} + v_{kv0} + g_{kv0}$; BA is parallel to OC.

Total production costs in period 0 are OP_1 whereas

(i) if installed capacity were fully utilised total production costs in period 0 would be OP_3 and

(ii) if x'_{kv0} units of capacity had been installed total production costs would have been OP_2.

If no further additions to capacity are made in period 1, production costs in period 1 would be

$$g_{kv1} + v_{kv1}x_{kv1} \quad \text{where } 0 \leq x_{kv1} \leq y'_{kv0}. \tag{7.4.11}$$

Alteratively, if further capacity of y''_{kv1} is installed in period 1, production costs incurred in period 1 would be

$$C(y''_{kv1}) + g_{kv1} + v_{kv1}x_{kv1} \tag{7.4.12}$$

$$\text{where now: } x_{kv1} \leq y'_{kv0} + y''_{kv1}.$$

In terms of traditional analysis, AB is the short run total cost curve associated with a plant of capacity y'_{kv0} and T_{kv0} is the long run total cost curve. Note that we do not allow operation at activity levels in excess of installed capacity, even in the short run.

7.4.4 Transport and Storage Costs

Transport costs associated with the activity levels w_{nvut} are assumed to be as defined in Chapter 3, i.e. to consist of loading and mileage charges, both linear in the quantity transported. Storage costs r_{nvt} associated with the activity levels s_{nvt} are assumed to be linear in the amount stored. Thus we assume that the storage activity does not involve any fixed costs associated with the provision of storage space. Total costs of storage and transport are then

$$\sum_n \sum_v \sum_u \sum_t t_{nvut}w_{nvut} + \sum_n \sum_v \sum_t r_{nvt}s_{nvt}. \tag{7.4.13}$$

7.4.5 Costs of Operating Pre-Existing Capacity

We assume that the only costs incurred in operating pre-existing capacity are variable costs, but that these might involve elements of depreciation and maintenance charges. The variable cost of operating activity $k^e v$ at activity level x^e_{kvt} is then

$$v^e_{kvt}x^e_{kvt} \quad \text{(all k,v,t).} \tag{7.4.14}$$

7.4.6 Disposal Costs

Disposal activities and costs can be handled exactly as in Chapters 3 and 4. In the empirical testing of the model, however, our estimates of capital costs include an element relating to control of dust emission in cement production. As a result, we shall present the model without explicit consideration of disposal costs or activities.

7.5 EDGE EFFECTS ASSOCIATED WITH CAPITAL COSTS

We indicated in paragraph 7.4.1 that our choice of a finite time horizon T will give rise to distorting edge effects with respect to investment decisions within the planning period. Two methods will be suggested in this section for dealing with these distortions. No choice will be made between them, however, since it will be interesting to compare their implications for the calculated optimum in our case study.

The first method is that suggested by Kendrick (1967). Capital costs are

'converted to the equivalent uniform payments series, and the payments . . . cut off at the end of the period covered by the model.' (Kendrick 1967, p. 84)

We assume that the capacity installed in time t is also operational in time t. It seems reasonable, therefore, to require that the first of the uniform payments be paid in time t. As a result, our equation for the adjusted capital costs is slightly different from that suggested by Kendrick. Specifically, the uniform payments series for capacity installed in activity kv in time t is

$$P(y_{kvt}) = \frac{C'(y_{kvt}) \cdot R \cdot (1+R)^{r-1}}{((1+R)^r - 1)} \tag{7.5.1}$$

where: $C'(y_{kvt})$ = undiscounted cost of installing y_{kvt} units of capacity in activity kv at time t,

R = discount rate,

r = expected life of equipment.

The discounted capital cost of installing y_{kvt} units of capacity in activity kv at time t adjusted for edge effects by the Kendrick method is then

$$C(y_{kvt}) = P(y_{kvt}) \left[\frac{1}{(1+R)^t} + \frac{1}{(1+R)^{t+1}} + \frac{1}{(1+R)^{t+2}} + \cdots \frac{1}{(1+R)^T} \right]. \tag{7.5.2}$$

The Kendrick method might be considered to be myopic since it is concerned solely with optimality within the planning period. This leads us to an alternative method which might be put as follows. We assume that market conditions—in particular the magnitude and distribution of demand for final products, and the cost parameters—will remain constant at the values they attain in time T for all periods subsequent to T. In addition, we assume that no changes can be made to the distribution of capacity, the activity levels on this capacity, and the transport activity levels, all evaluated at time T, in any period subsequent to T. Note that this second assumption requires that:

(i) any primary factor availability constraints that do not bite before T do not bite thereafter, and

(ii) any pre-existing capacity being operated at time T at activity levels x_{kvt}^e will continue to be available and operated at the same activity levels after T.

As a result, we can associate with an investment decision in time t not only the capital costs $C'(y_{kvt})$—see equation (7.5.1)—but also the stream of replacement costs to which this investment decision gives rise. Assuming as before an expected life of new capacity of r years, the discounted capital cost of installing y_{kvt} units of capacity in activity kv at time t adjusted for edge effects by this approach is

$$C(y_{kvt}) = \frac{C'(y_{kvt})}{(1+R)^t} + \frac{1}{(1+R)^t}\left[\frac{C'(y_{kvT})}{(1+R)^r} + \frac{C'(y_{kvT})}{(1+R)^{2r}} + \ldots\right]. \qquad (7.5.3)$$

Hence:

$$C(y_{kvt}) = \frac{1}{(1+R)^t}\left[C'(y_{kvt}) + \frac{C'(y_{kvT})}{(1+R)^r-1}\right]. \qquad (7.5.4)$$

The difference in the time stream of replacement costs incurred by installing capacity in time t rather than t+1 is then

$$\Delta C(y_{kvt}) = \frac{1}{(1+R)^t}\left[C'(y_{kvt}) - \frac{C'(y_{kv(t+1)})}{(1+R)}\right] +$$
$$\frac{R}{(1+R)^{t+1}} \cdot \frac{C'(y_{kvT})}{(1+R)^r-1}. \qquad (7.5.5)$$

The second term in (7.5.5) is positive, while the first term will be positive if the rate of inflation of capital costs from t to t+1 is less than the discount rate. A positive difference $\Delta C(y_{kvt})$ implies that earlier installation of capital equipment will give rise to a higher future time stream of replacement costs.

If we adopt this infinite horizon method for countering the biasing edge effects, we must take account of the fact that *all* costs at time T other than capital costs represent infinite future cost streams. Thus, for example, the variable cost of operating activity kv at unit activity level in time T in the Kendrick approach will be v_{kvT} as defined in equation (7.4.10). With the infinite horizon approach, however, operating activity kv at unit activity level in time T will commit the producer to that level of operation thereafter, and so will incur the infinite cost stream given by

$$v_{kvT} + \frac{v_{kvT}}{(1+R)} + \ldots = v_{kvT} + \frac{v_{kvT}}{R}. \tag{7.5.6}$$

It should be recalled that v_{kvT} is a cost discounted to $t = 0$.

The fixed labour charge g_{kvT} is a flow per period and so is treated in the same way as v_{kvT}. The adjustment (7.5.6) is therefore applied to the cost parameters v_{kvT}, v_{kvT}^{e}, g_{kvT} and t_{nvuT}.

As things stand there is nothing in the infinite horizon method to prevent demand in period T being produced and moved to the appropriate town in period T–1 and stored there until T, thereby avoiding the artifically increased variable costs of production and transport in period T. Adjusting the cost parameters $r_{nv(T-1)}$, as in (7.5.6), would not overcome this limitation since storage will generally incur lower costs than production and transportation. But it seems reasonable to require that capacity in period T and the activity levels on that capacity in T be sufficient to meet demand for final products in T, and so in all subsequent periods, without the need for storage.[1] Thus, with the infinite horizon method, we associate infinite costs with the storage activities $s_{nv(T-1)}$ to ensure that at an optimum

$$s_{nv(T-1)}^{*} = 0 \quad \text{(all n,v)}. \tag{7.5.7}$$

We should also consider a further limitation of the infinite horizon method that is not so easily removed. Our definition of capital costs with this method is such that the producer is committed forever to every investment decision he makes in the planning period. Thus, if capacity is installed in period 1, say, we assume that it will be replaced in period 1+r, 1+2r, etc. This assumption will not be too restrictive if there are no sharp changes in the distribution of demand in the planning period and/or if the planning period is short relative to the expected life of plant. If these conditions do not hold, however, then we would prefer a formulation which allows for equipment to be taken out of service. In these circumstances we would have to differentiate capacity in each period by its vintage – see equation (7.4.6) – and require that the infinite time stream of replacement costs be incurred only on that capacity for which $x_{kvT}^{\tau} > 0$, i.e. that capacity of vintage τ still in service in period T. As we indicated in paragraph 7.4.1, defining the activity levels x_{kvt}^{τ} is very expensive in computer capacity. In addition, we shall find in our case study that the conditions mentioned above are satisfied. We note this limitation, therefore, but shall not respecify the model to take account of it.

The Kendrick method removes the biasing edge effects by reducing the capital costs of installing new capacity the later that capacity is installed. As indicated, therefore, it is myopic in that it is concerned solely with optimality in the planning period. The infinite horizon method, on the other hand, works by introducing a counter bias. Investment decisions made in periods closer to T than 0 will presumably be better adjusted to market conditions in T and so to the market conditions assumed to hold after T. Since we assume that the pattern of production and distribution attained in T will be unchanged after T, the better adjusted the industry is to market conditions in T, the lower will be the cost penalty incurred. Nevertheless, the additional dimension of scale introduced in the multiperiod model may encourage installation of capacity early rather than late. Equation (7.5.5) then indicates that this will generally involve a higher time stream of replacement costs.[2]

7.6 THE MULTIPERIOD PROGRAMMING MODEL

To economise on notation we shall refer to the cost parameters v_{kvT}, t_{nvuT}, etc., and shall rely on the context to indicate whether we are referring to these cost parameters as defined for the Kendrick method or for the infinite horizon method.

7.6.1 The Objective Function

The objective function can be stated very simply. We wish to find the nonnegative activity levels x_{kvt}, x_{kvt}^e, w_{nvut} and s_{nvt}, the nonnegative additions to capacity y_{kvt}^i, and the integer constrained variables γ_{kvt}^i, ρ_{kvt} to minimise total cost given by

$$Z = \sum_i \sum_k \sum_v \sum_t (m_{kvt}^i \gamma_{kvt}^i + b_{kvt}^i y_{kvt}^i) + \sum_k \sum_v \sum_t g_{kvt} \rho_{kvt}$$

$$+ \sum_k \sum_v \sum_t (v_{kvt} x_{kvt} + v_{kvt}^e x_{kvt}^e) + \sum_n \sum_v \sum_u \sum_t t_{nvut} w_{nvut}$$

$$+ \sum_n \sum_v \sum_t r_{nvt} s_{nvt}. \tag{7.6.1}$$

The first term in Z is the sum of capital costs associated with new capacity installed in the planning period, while the second term gives the fixed labour costs associated with this capacity. The third term is the sum of variable production costs on new and pre-existing capacity, and the final two terms give the costs of transport and storage respectively.

7.6.2 Supply and Demand Constraints

7.6.2.1 The Labour Constraints. We maintain the assumptions in Chapter 3 and add the assumption that labour cannot be stored.

Labour availability ℓ_{vt} at node v in period t is defined net of the fixed labour input. It should be clear, however, that if $\ell_{vt} = 0$, then $x^*_{kvt} = 0$ (all k). We then require that the amount of labour involved in production at node v in time t should not exceed the labour available at v in t:

$$\sum_k (a_{0kvt} x_{kvt} + a^e_{0kvt} x^e_{kvt}) \geq \ell_{vt} \qquad \text{(all v,t)} \qquad (7.6.2)$$

the sign of the inequality arising since labour is net input to production.

7.6.2.2 Primary Factors of Production. No primary factor can be net output from any production activity. In addition, the initial endowment $p_{nv} \leq 0$ of primary factor n at node v constitutes a stock which cannot be replenished. Thus we require that the input of primary factor nv plus net exports of n from v plus net storage of n at v in all periods up to and including t (t = 0 ... T) should not exceed the endowment of primary factor nv:

$$\sum_{\tau=0}^{t} \left[\sum_k (a_{nkv\tau} x_{kv\tau} + a^e_{nkv\tau} x^e_{kv\tau}) + \sum_u (w_{nuv\tau} - w_{nvu\tau}) \right]$$

$$+ \sum_{\tau=0}^{t-1} s_{nv\tau} - s_{nvt} \geq p_{nv} \qquad \text{(nv a primary factor; all v,t)} \qquad (7.6.3)$$

where we define $\displaystyle\sum_{\tau=0}^{t-1} s_{nv\tau} = 0$ when t = 0 all n,v.

7.6.2.3 Intermediate Commodities. No more of an intermediate commodity can be input to production at, exported from, or put into storage at any node v in period t than is produced at, moved to, or available in storage at that node in that period:

$$\sum_{\tau=0}^{t} \left[\sum_{k} (a_{nkv\tau}x_{kv\tau} + a_{nkv\tau}^{e}x_{kv\tau}^{e}) + \sum_{u} (w_{nuv\tau} - w_{nvu\tau}) \right]$$

$$+ \sum_{\tau=0}^{t-1} s_{nv\tau} - s_{nvt} \geq 0 \qquad \begin{array}{l}\text{(nv an intermediate commodity;} \\ \text{all t,v)}\end{array} \tag{7.6.4}$$

7.6.2.4 Final Products. The producer is constrained to meet a price-inelastic demand $f_{nvt} \geq 0$ for final product nv in each period t. Thus in each period the net output of final product nv plus net imports of n to v less the availability of n in storage at v must be sufficient to meet demand for final product n at v plus the amount of nv put into storage at time t:

$$\sum_{\tau=0}^{t} \left[\sum_{k} (a_{nkv\tau}x_{kv\tau} + a_{nkv\tau}^{e}x_{kv\tau}^{e}) + \sum_{u} (w_{nuv\tau} - w_{nvu\tau}) \right]$$

$$+ \sum_{\tau=0}^{t-1} s_{nv\tau} - s_{nvt} \geq f_{nvt} \qquad \text{(nv a final product; all v,t)} \tag{7.6.5}$$

7.6.3 Other Constraints

The remaining constraints are those presented in equations (7.4.4) and (7.4.9) plus nonnegativity constraints on all of the decision variables. Thus we wish to find nonnegative x_{kvt}^{*}, x_{kvt}^{e*}, w_{nvut}^{*}, s_{nvt}^{*}, y_{kvt}^{i*}, γ_{kvt}^{i*} and ρ_{kvt}^{*} (all n,k,v,t) to minimise (7.6.1) subject to the constraints (7.6.2) through (7.6.5), (7.4.4) and (7.4.9).

7.7 CASE STUDY: INTRODUCTION

We apply the theoretical model developed above to the UK cement industry, assuming a planning horizon of four periods – 1960, 1965, 1970, and 1975. Each of these periods is assumed to be the mid-point of a five-year interval, and for each interval we assume that:

(i) demand is constant within the interval, changing solely at the end of each interval,
(ii) undiscounted cost conditions at 1960, 1965, etc., represent mean undiscounted cost conditions over the appropriate interval.

We further assume that the discount rate does not change over time. The discount factor to be applied to all noncapital costs is then:

$$D_t = \frac{1}{(1+R)^{5(t-1)}} + \frac{1}{(1+R)^{5(t-1)+1}} + \cdots \frac{1}{(1+R)^{5(t-1)+4}} \qquad (7.7.1)$$

$$\text{where: } D_t = \text{discount factor}$$
$$R \ = \text{discount rate} \qquad (t = 1 \ldots 4).$$
$$t \ = \text{time period}$$

It should be noted that equation (7.7.1) takes account of the fact that demand estimates and noncapital cost estimates presented below are expressed initially as flows per annum, while the interval between the periods is five years. Application of the discount factor D_t converts all such costs to discounted costs per five-year period.

The choice of interval is forced on us by data limitations, while the length of the planning period is a compromise between computer constraints and the desire to choose a horizon long enough to require some adjustment to changing market conditions. One drawback of defining a five-year interval, however, is that it becomes somewhat unrealistic to consider storage of commodities between periods. As a result, we shall not define the variables s_{nvt} in our case study.

7.8 MARKET AREA

We shall concentrate upon the allocation of production in the sub-markets (i) and (ii) defined in Chapter 6, i.e. the sub-markets consisting of London, South Wales, and Southern England—see Figure 6.17.

We assume that throughout the planning period these sub-markets are closed with respect to the other sub-markets defined in Chapter 6, and with respect to markets external to England and Wales.

The distribution of primary commodities and the transport network are assumed invariant over the planning period and to be as estimated in Chapter 5. Pre-existing capacity is taken to be that capacity existing in 1960—see Table 6.6, Chapter 6. Primary commodities and labour when available at a node v in the sub-market in 1960 are assumed to be available in sufficient quantity to allow production at any activity level at node v throughout the planning period. We then apply the suboptimising techniques of Chapter 5 to eliminate nodes 3,4,13, and 14 as potential production sites.

Demand is assumed price inelastic and is estimated as in Chapter 5. Table 7.1 gives the demand estimates for each of the time periods.[3]

Table 7.1.   Demand Estimates (m. tonnes p.a.)

Node	1960	1965	1970	1975
1 London	3.376	4.660	4.674	4.742
14 Southampton	.734	1.174	1.132	1.225
15 Plymouth	.346	.455	.564	.622
16 Bristol	.570	.743	.943	.993
17 Cardiff	.781	.831	.881	1.000

7.9 COST ESTIMATES

7.9.1 Capital Costs

Table 5.7 gives engineering estimates of the relationship between plant capacity and capital cost for the West German industry. To obtain estimates in 1963 prices for the UK industry, an adjustment factor of 0.133 was applied to the West German estimates. We take these adjusted estimates as our starting point and fit a linear spline to them as described in Chapter 5. The adjusted capital costs are given in Table 7.2 and the linear spline in Table 7.3.

Estimates of capital costs in each period are based on this spline. The spline

Table 7.2.   Capital Cost Estimates UK Industry 1963 (£m.)

Capacity (m. tonnes)	Capital Cost (£m)	Capacity (m. tonnes)	Capital Cost (£m)
0.0825	2.633	0.9075	16.531
0.099	3.098	0.990	17.250
0.132	4.003	1.155	18.886
0.166	4.868	1.320	20.538
0.2475	6.929	1.485	22.317
0.330	8.738	1.650	24.366
0.4125	10.321	1.980	28.329
0.495	11.784	2.310	32.266
0.5775	12.981	2.640	36.176
0.660	14.045	2.970	40.299
0.7425	14.909	3.300	43.890
0.825	15.800		

Table 7.3.   Linear Spline for Capital Costs

i	m^i_{kvt}	b^i_{kvt}	$\hat{y}^{i-1}_{kvt}$	$\hat{y}^i_{kvt}$
1	0.58	22.15	0.00	0.55
2	7.13	10.14	0.55	1.50
3	4.26	12.06	1.50	—

Table 7.4.   Minimum Efficient Scale

Year	MES (m. tonnes p.a.)
1960	1.0
1965	2.0
1970	3.0
1975	3.0

has been derived, however, on the assumption that economies of scale are available to capital costs for plant capacities up to 3.3 m. tonnes p.a. We discussed in Chapter 5 the implications of this assumption and noted that the minimum efficient scale (MES) in cement production exhibited a rapid increase over the period 1950–71. Two approaches are then open to us for those periods in which MES is less than 3 m. tonnes p.a. We might assume that any plant constructed with annual capacity in excess of MES will exhibit diseconomies of scale to capital, i.e. replication will lead to an increase in unit capital costs. Alternatively, we might assume that replication will not involve a capital cost penalty, i.e. that there are constant returns to capital costs for plant capacities in excess of MES.

The latter approach is the one we shall adopt. It is computationally simpler and does not appear too unreasonable. Estimates of capital costs in each period unadjusted for edge effects and undiscounted, i.e. estimates of $C'(y_{kvt})$, are then derived as follows:

(i) We assume that MES in each period is as in Table 7.4.
(ii) 1963 capital costs are adjusted to costs in time t by applying the index of capital costs of 'plant, vehicles, etc.' obtained from the NIER. The indices are given in Table 7.5, column (1). These adjusted costs are then discounted and further adjusted for edge effects assuming, as in Chapter 5, a discount rate of 10% and an expected life of plant of forty years. The composite index to be applied to the capital cost estimates is given in Table 7.5, columns (3) and (5); the resulting estimates are given in Table 7.6.

Table 7.5.   Index of Capital Costs (1963=100)

			Kendrick			Infinite Horizon	
Year	τ	Index of $C'(y_{kv\tau})$ (1)	Edge Effect Adjustment* (2)	Index of $C(y_{kv\tau})$ (3)	Edge Effect Adjustment** (4)	Index of $C(y_{kv\tau})$ (5)
1960	2	74.1	0.693	51.4	0.886	65.7
1965	7	106.2	0.373	39.6	0.539	57.2
1970	12	128.5	0.174	22.4	0.332	42.7
1975	17	236.8	0.050	11.8	0.202	47.8

Notes: *: Adjustment = $(1+R)^{r-T-1} \{(1+R)^{T-\tau+1}-1\}/\{(1+R)^r-1\}$
  **: Adjustment = $(1 + I_\tau/\{(1+R)^r-1\})/(1+R)$
  where: $r = 40$, $T = 19$, $R = 0.10$, $I_\tau = C'(y_{kvT})/C'(y_{kv\tau})$.

Table 7.6.   Adjusted Linear Splines for Capital Costs

				Kendrick				Infinite Horizon	
Year	i	m^i_{kvt}	b^i_{kvt}	$\hat{y}^{i-1}_{kvt}$	$\hat{y}^i_{kvt}$	m^i_{kvt}	b^i_{kvt}	$\hat{y}^{i-1}_{kvt}$	$\hat{y}^i_{kvt}$
	1	0.27	11.39	0.00	0.55	0.35	14.55	0.00	0.55
1960	2	3.66	5.21	0.55	1.00	4.68	6.66	0.55	1.00
	3	0.00	8.87	1.00	—	0.00	11.34	1.00	—
	1	0.21	8.77	0.00	0.55	0.30	12.67	0.00	0.55
1965	2	2.82	4.02	0.55	1.50	4.08	5.80	0.55	1.50
	3	1.69	4.78	1.50	2.00	2.44	6.90	1.50	2.00
	4	0.00	5.62	2.00	—	0.00	8.12	2.00	—
	1	0.12	4.96	0.00	0.55	0.23	9.46	0.00	0.55
1970	2	1.60	2.27	0.55	1.50	3.04	4.33	0.55	1.50
	3	0.95	2.70	1.50	3.00	1.82	5.15	1.50	3.00
	4	0.00	3.02	3.00	—	0.00	5.76	3.00	—
	1	0.06	2.61	0.00	0.55	0.25	10.59	0.00	0.55
1975	2	0.84	1.20	0.55	1.50	3.41	4.85	0.55	1.50
	3	0.50	1.42	1.50	3.00	2.04	5.76	1.50	3.00
	4	0.00	1.59	3.00	—	0.00	6.44	3.00	—

7.9.2 Labour Costs

We assume that labour costs consist of a fixed charge plus an amount linear in the output of the plant,[4] and that the estimated relationship reported in Chapter 5 holds throughout the planning period.[5]

Thus labour input in each period is given by:

$$E_{kvt} = 92.51 + 0.4318\, X_{kvt} \qquad (7.9.1)$$

where: E_{kvt} = employment (number) in activity kv at t

X_{kvt} = output (th.t.p.a.) of activity kv at t.

We estimate labour costs by applying to (7.9.1) the discounted average wage for the particular period. Let this wage be $W_t' D_t$ ($t = 1 \ldots 4$). Then discounted labour costs are given by

$$L_{kvt} = W_t' D_t (92.51 + 0.4318\, X_{kvt}) \qquad (7.9.2)$$

where D_t is as in equation (7.7.1).

Relating this to (7.4.8) we assume therefore that

(i) $$g_{kvt} = 92.51\, W_t' D_t \qquad (7.9.3)$$

(ii) $$d_{kvt} = 0.4318\, W_t' D_t.$$

To estimate W_t', we first estimated an index of average wage rates in UK cement production, using data on employment and total wage bill from the *Census of Production*. Secondly, we calculated an index of 'hourly earnings in manufacturing' from data published in NIER. Wage indices for 1960, 1965, and 1970 were interpolated from the *Census of Production* series using the NIER series as base, e.g. the index for 1960 is (from Table 7.7): $74.1 + (87.0 - 77.7)$ $\cdot (100 - 74.1)/(100 - 77.7) = 84.9$. The index for 1975 was estimated assuming that the rate of growth of wages and salaries in cement production from 1972–1975 was as for 'hourly earnings in manufacturing'. The various estimates are given in Table 7.7.

Table 7.7.   Index of Labour Costs in UK Cement Production (1963=100)

Year	Index of Ave. Wage Rates	Index of Hourly Earnings in Manufacturing	Index of Wage Rates in Cement Production (W_t')
1958	74.1	77.7	–
1960	–	87.0	84.9
1963	100.0	100.0	100.0
1965	–	115.8	110.4
1968	126.3	139.8	–
1970	135.6	171.5	135.6
1972	173.9	220.1	–
1975	–	372.8	294.5

Source: col. (1) Census of Production; col. (2) NIER

Table 7.8. Labour Costs UK Cement Production

Year	t	W'_t (£th.)	D_t	g_{kvt} (£m)	d_{kvt} (£m)
1960	1	0.843	4.170	0.325	1.518
1965	2	1.096	2.589	0.262	1.226
1970	3	1.347	1.608	0.200	0.935
1975	4	2.924	0.907* 2.633**	0.245* 0.712**	1.145* 3.325**

Notes: *Kendrick; **Infinite Horizon.

Our estimates of W'_t are, then, the wage indices multiplied by the average wage rate in 1963, i.e. £993 (see Chapter 5). The discount factors D_t were calculated from equations (7.5.6) and (7.7.1), assuming a discount rate of 10%. Equations (7.9.3) were then used to estimate g_{kvt} and d_{kvt}. The results are given in Table 7.8.

7.9.3 Transport Costs

We repeat the procedure in Chapter 6 to estimate transport costs. The indices of the various cost parameters are given in Table 7.9, and the resulting mileage and loading cost indices in Table 7.10. The indices in Table 7.10 are then applied to the transport costs estimated in Chapter 5.

7.9.4 Variable Production Costs

Variable production costs as estimated in Chapter 5 consist of fuel, energy, raw material, and packaging costs. We assume that the physical inputs of each of these goods per unit of cement output is invariant with scale and time and would

Table 7.9. Indices of Input Costs to Transport (1963=100)

Year	Capital Cost Index	Labour Cost Index	Fuel Cost Index
1960	74.1	84.9	97.0
1965	106.2	110.4	110.0
1970	128.5	135.6	180.0
1975	236.8	294.5	310.0

Source: text and Shell (UK).

Table 7.10. Indices of Transport Costs (1963=100)

Year	Undiscounted Index		Discounted Index	
	Mileage	Loading	Mileage	Loading
1960	88	84	367	350
1965	109	109	282	282
1970	155	144	249	232
1975	287	276	260* 756**	250* 727**

Notes: *Kendrick; ** Infinite Horizon.

then have preferred to estimate a separate cost index for each good. This did not prove possible, however. As a result, we use as indices the indices of 'materials' and 'fuel' purchased by manufacturing activities as published in the *Annual Abstract of Statistics*. The indices are given in Table 7.11, columns (1) and (3).[6] Variable cost at 1963 was estimated in Chapter 5 as £1.89, of which £0.74 were 'materials' and £1.15 'fuel' costs. Estimates of discounted variable costs u_{kvt} are, then, as in Table 7.11, column (5).

7.9.5 Costs of Operating Pre-existing Capacity

Data reported in the *Census of Production* 1963 indicate that unit materials, labour, and fuel costs in cement production were £3.20 per tonne in 1963. To

Table 7.11. Variable Costs (u_{kvt}) in Cement Production

Year	Materials Index[a] Undisc'd (1)	Discounted[c] (2)	Fuel Index[b] Undisc'd (3)	Discounted[c] (4)	Discounted Unit Variable Costs (£) (5)
1960	100	417.0	92.6	386.1	7.53
1965	100	258.9	108.6	281.2	5.15
1970	128.3	206.3	128.1	206.0	3.90
1975	312.5	283.4* 822.8**	201.9	183.1* 531.6**	4.20* 12.20**

Notes: *Kendrick; **Infinite Horizon; (a) Includes fuel oil; (b) Coal, gas and electricity; (c) Discount factors from Table 7.8.

Table 7.12. Operating Costs on Pre-Existing Capacity

Year	Discounted Cost Index (1963 = 100)	Unit Production Costs on Pre-existing Capacity (v^e_{kvt}) (£)
1960	377.1	13.31
1965	275.6	9.73
1970	210.0	7.41
1975	256.4* 744.3**	9.05* 26.27**

Notes: *Kendrick; ** Infinite Horizon.

this we add a depreciation allowance of £0.33 per tonne (see *NBPI Report No. 38, 1967*) to give a 1963 estimate for unit production costs on pre-existing capacity of £3.53 per tonne, the costs being in the ratio 58:32:10, materials and fuel:labour:depreciation. These ratios were used to derive the composite (discounted) indices of costs given in Table 7.12, from which were then estimated the operating costs also reported in Table 7.12.

7.9.6 Maintenance Costs

We were unable to obtain direct estimates of maintenance costs, but presumably labour costs will include some element of maintenance, and our estimates of capital costs include an allowance for 'spares', etc. We assume, therefore, that $e_{kvt} = 0$ (all k,v,t).

7.10 SOLUTION OF THE MULTIPERIOD MODEL

The predicted optima for the Kendrick and Infinite Horizon versions of the model are detailed in Table 7.13.

In both versions the distribution of new capacity—capacity installed within the planning horizon—is almost identical by period 4 with the distribution of demand in period 4, a picture which is much more disaggregated than that presented by the calculated optimum for Case 0 in Chapter 6.

The inflation of transport costs relative to capital and other costs over the planning horizon explains part of this outcome, but the introduction of the time dimension is equally important in explaining the relative lack of production concentration.

Table 7.13. Calculated Optima for the Multi Period Model

Node and Period v	t	Demand	Existing Capacity	Kendrick Version						Infinite Horizon Version					
				Activity Level x^g_{kvt}	Capacity Installed in t y_{kvt}	Total New Capacity Σy_{kvt}	Activity Level x_{kvt}	Imports**	Exports	Activity Level x^g_{kvt}	Capacity Installed in t y_{kvt}	Total New Capacity Σy_{kvt}	Activity Level x_{kvt}	Imports**	Exports
London (1)	1	3.376	7.316	0.042	3.334	3.334	3.334	–	–	–	3.376	3.376	3.376	–	–
	2	4.660		–	1.500	4.834	4.834		0.174	–	1.591	4.967	4.834		0.174
	3	4.674		–	–	4.834	4.806		0.132	–	–	4.967	4.806		0.132
	4	4.742		–	–	4.834	4.834		0.092	–	–	4.967	4.967		0.225
Shoreham (2)	1	0.734*	0.698	–	1.000	1.000	0.734	–		–	1.000	1.000	0.734	–	
	2	0.174*		–	–	1.000	1.000	0.174(1)		–	–	1.000	1.000	0.174(1)	
	3	1.132*		–	0.133	1.133	1.000	0.132(1)		–	–	1.000	1.000	0.132(1)	
	4	1.225*		–	–	1.133	1.133	0.092(1)		–	–	1.000	1.000	0.225(1)	
Plymouth (15)	1	0.346	–	–	0.374	0.374	0.346	–		–	0.346	0.346	0.346	–	
	2	0.455		–	–	0.374	0.374	0.081(16)		–	–	0.346	0.346	0.109(16)	
	3	0.564		–	0.190	0.564	0.564	–		–	0.276	0.622	0.564	–	
	4	0.622		–	0.058	0.622	0.622	–		–	–	0.622	0.622	–	
Bristol (16)	1	0.570	–	–	0.993	0.993	0.993	–	0.423	–	0.993	0.993	0.993	–	0.423
	2	0.743		–	–	0.993	0.993	–	0.250	–	–	0.993	0.852	–	0.109
	3	0.943		–	–	0.993	0.943	–	–	–	–	0.993	0.943	–	–
	4	0.993		–	–	0.993	0.993	–	–	–	–	0.993	0.993	–	–
Cardiff (17)	1	0.781		0.358	–	–	–	0.423(16)		0.358	–	–	–	0.423(16)	
	2	0.831	0.662	0.662	–	–	–	0.169(16)		–	1.000	1.000	0.831	–	
	3	0.881		–	1.000	1.000	0.881	–		–	–	1.000	0.881	–	
	4	1.000		–	–	1.000	1.000	–		–	–	1.000	1.000	–	

*Demand is demand at Southampton: imports are imports to Southampton:

** Figures in brackets indicate the exporting node.

153

Obviously, a more concentrated pattern of production in period 4 is equivalent to having some proportion of capacity spatially distinct from the markets it serves in this period. If full advantage is to be taken in period 4 of economies of scale to production, this capacity should contain a high proportion of large-scale units (relative to MES). Given the pattern of growth of demand for cement, however, such a configuration of capacity could be achieved only at the expense, in earlier periods, of either

(i) low rates of capacity utilisation, or
(ii) relatively high expenditures on transport costs.

To see why this is so, consider a production concentration at some node v, and denote the set of towns supplied from v in period 4 by V_4. Situation (i) arises if the large-scale units of capacity installed at node v in anticipation of the growth in demand at towns in V_4 are used in periods prior to period 4 to supply solely the towns in V_4. Attempts to achieve higher rates of capacity utilisation in these periods will introduce situation (ii), since in these circumstances excess capacity will have to be used to supply towns outside V_4.

It is a simple matter to envisage cases in which it would be optimal to adopt either of these approaches. For example, if economies of scale are 'important' and transport costs are low relative to production costs, the cost penalty incurred in using excess capacity to supply distant towns may well be less than the cost advantage of large-scale production. Alternatively, if demand growth were either much more rapid or much slower than that exhibited by the cement industry, then the cost penalty (i) would be much less severe.

If, on the other hand, capacity in a more concentrated configuration is made up of relatively small-scale units, high rates of capacity utilisation will certainly be achieved. However, additional transport costs (with respect to the calculated optima for the Kendrick and Infinite Horizon versions) will be incurred with no offsetting advantages from economies of scale.

Thus while the cement industry is characterised by economies of scale, these are not sufficiently strong to justify the low rates of capacity utilisation or high expenditures on transport costs which would be associated with the early lives of large-scale plants in a concentrated pattern of production. Transport costs are then sufficiently great to ensure that small-scale plants are located near to the markets they serve.

This is not to say, however, that economies of scale in cement production are completely dominated by transport costs and the effects of history. The near identity of the distribution of capacity and demand in period 4 is not repeated in earlier periods to anything like the same extent, implying that economies of scale will lead to some concentration of production. There is some tendency in these earlier periods for the growth in capacity at particular nodes to anticipate the growth in demand at the same or nearby nodes. Excess capacity is then used to supply more distant nodes, either until local demand grows sufficiently to exhaust local capacity or until demand at the distant nodes grows sufficiently to justify local production at those nodes. For example, sufficient capacity is installed at Bristol in period 1 to meet demand at Bristol in each period up to period 4. Excess capacity is used to supply part of demand at Cardiff and Plymouth until the growth in demand at these latter nodes justifies local production.

We can take this discussion further by comparing the calculated optima for the Kendrick and Infinite Horizon versions of the model. As has been indicated, the overall distributions achieved by period 4 are practically identical. But the ways in which these distributions are reached are somewhat different in the two versions of the model.

Table 7.13 indicates that the production units in operation in period 4 in the Kendrick version are generally of lower capacity than those operated in the Infinite Horizon version. This is associated with a greater use of pre-existing capacity in the Kendrick solution[7] and with a tendency for new capacity to be installed earlier and less fully utilised in its early life in the Infinite Horizon solution.

These differences between the two solutions arise from the differing cost structures associated with the two versions of the model. In the Kendrick version, capital costs are smaller with respect to other costs than in the Infinite Horizon version, particularly in later periods. As a result, in the Kendrick version of the model economies of scale are less important relative to the diseconomies of transportation and of anticipating demand growth, and the capital cost penalty of installing new capacity is relatively low in later periods. We would, therefore, expect the exhibited pattern for the Kendrick solution: distribution of production relatively well adjusted to the distribution of demand in early periods by use of pre-existing capacity, and in later periods by installing small scale units of new capacity.

One final point is worth noting. We found in Chapter 6 that even with a concentrated pattern of production, the calculated optimum would contain a number of production units with capacities considerably below MES as conventionally defined. This finding is reinforced by the solution of the multiperiod model. In both Kendrick and Infinite Horizon calculated optima, the units of capacity installed in each period are almost without exception considerably smaller than estimated MES for that period. The influence of transport costs and of time—past, present and future—are together sufficient to make the choice of small-scale units of capacity a perfectly efficient choice.

This has the corollary that the actual locational pattern of the industry may well be more efficient than was implied by Chapter 6 and by other writings.

As we have indicated, the influence of 'time' is to introduce a further diseconomy to production concentration. If this is not offset by, for example, very rapid (or very slow) demand growth, then an industry in making locational decisions may well be forced to sacrifice economies of scale which are apparently available if attention is confined to estimates of minimum efficient scale and the shape of the planning curve.

8 A COMPETITIVE MODEL ASSUMING FREE ENTRY

8.1 INTRODUCTION

The model used to generate the results in Chapters 6 and 7 is Weberian in origin and implicitly assumes that the industry being studied is operating within a monopolistic market structure. Competition between plants in the industry, either for particular production locations or particular customers, is resolved on the basis of what is best for the industry as a whole, rather than for the individual plant. Indeed, given that there are economies of scale to production, we would expect in general that optimality with respect to each particular plant would not be consistent with optimality for the industry. The monopolistic market structure also leads to calculated optimal distributions of production that take full advantage of the available economies of scale in production (taking account, of course, of the impact of transport and other costs).

As we indicated in the conclusions to Chapter 6, therefore, the exclusion of competitive elements from the model may, in part, explain why our calculated optima exhibit greater concentration of production than the actual distribution of the industry. In order to test this, we felt that it would be useful and informative to present a 'competitive' model and apply it to the UK cement industry.

Our discussion in Chapter 1 of the work of both Lösch and Hotelling noted that the development of *operational* competitive models is fraught with difficulties. Firstly, there are the purely technical problems involved in developing models that lend themselves to solution, whether by analytic or computational methods, and yet capture the major elements in which we are interested: the interplay between economies of scale, transport costs, distribution of demand, etc. Secondly, a competitive model is only as good as the behavioural rules attributed to the competitors. But the more complex these rules the more severe will be the analytic and computational problems to be overcome.

The model presented below is based on fairly simple behavioural rules, but it has the advantage of being amenable to computer solution.[1] More complex models have been developed, e.g. by Rothschild (*op. cit.*), but they have not been applied to market areas as complex as that developed for the cement study.

8.2 THE MODEL

The model presented below relies heavily on the work of Gee (1976). It is intended to analyse the pattern of entry of competitive firms to a bounded, two-dimensional, market area. Computational constraints are such that the market area is defined as a set of points on a lattice. Each such point is a potential production site, and consumers are evenly distributed over the points in a known, and fixed, way. All consumers are assumed to be identical and (in the initial version of the model) to consume one unit of a single, homogeneous product in each 'period'.[2,3]

The costs of production at each point i are given by:

$$C_i(Q) = F + v_i \cdot Q \tag{8.2.1}$$

where: F = fixed production costs,

v_i = variable costs of production at point i,

Q = output.

As can be seen, we have found it necessary to considerably simplify the production cost function: in terms of the model developed in Chapter 4, only one quasi production activity is defined. Variable costs of production are assumed to include transport costs incurred in obtaining the inputs to production, i.e. we assume a heterogeneous resource base, but also assume that each input is in perfectly elastic supply at all of its sources.

Transport costs of delivery of the final product to consumers are assumed linear in distance and weight,[4] i.e. transport costs involved in moving Q units of output from point i to point j are:

$$T_{ij}(Q) = t \cdot d_{ij} \cdot Q \qquad\qquad (8.2.2)$$

where: d_{ij} = distance from point i to point j, given
by the standard Euclidean metric,

t = transport cost per unit of weight, per
unit distance.

Firms are assumed to compete in terms of the price they charge at any point in the market area. The pricing policy adopted by each firm can be described as follows:

Assume for simplicity that the market is linear[5] and that it contains two firms, A and B, located at O_A and O_B respectively in Figure 8.1. Variable costs of production at O_A and O_B are given by v_A and v_B respectively, and of production and transportation by $v_A A'$ and $v_B B'$.

The price charged by firm A to any consumer is the variable cost of production and transportation from firm B. For example, the price charged by A to consumers located at T is $O_A P$, while the variable costs of supplying them from A are $O_A V$. Hence, ignoring fixed costs of production, firm A will profit from sales to all consumers on $O_A D^*$ but lose on any sales to consumers on $O_B D^*$. Firm A will therefore supply all consumers on $O_A D^*$ and firm B all consumers on $O_B D^*$.

The market area is regarded initially as a series of green-field sites, and firms are assumed to enter sequentially, each sequence being taken as 'one period'. Since demand is assumed price inelastic, the location of the first firm is indeterminate, and must be set as a parameter.[6] We assume that each firm (after the first) is a profit maximiser, and that location decisions, once made, cannot be

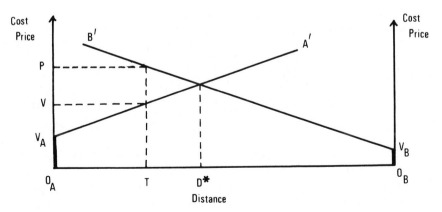

Figure 8.1.

revised and do not take account of the actions of future potential entrants to the market. The second firm will, therefore, enter at that location at which it will make the maximum profit, given that the location of firm 1 is fixed. Similarly, a third firm will enter at that location which maximises its profit, given that the locations of firms 1 and 2 are fixed, and so on.

As more firms enter the market, the profits made by some existing firms will be reduced—more constraints are imposed on the maximum price certain firms will be able to charge. If then the profit of any firm falls below a set minimum profit constraint, this firm will be removed from the market. Similarly, if there are no points of entry that satisfy the minimum profit constraint, no further firms will enter the market.

We define market stability to be a situation in which no existing firm wishes to leave the market, and no potential entrant wishes to enter the market. It should be noted that this definition of stability is consistent with the existence of some supernormal profits: profits in excess of the minimum profit constraint.[7]

8.3 APPLICATION TO THE CEMENT STUDY

8.3.1 The Market Area

We imposed a regular grid on the market area defined in Chapter 5 to generate the set of consumption locations illustrated in Figure 8.2; demand at each such location was taken from Table 5.12. To maintain comparability with the results in Chapter 6, we limited the set of feasible production sites to those given in Table 5.15; these are also illustrated in Figure 8.2.

8.3.2 Operating Costs and Profit Constraint

Production costs excluding input transport costs were estimated from Table 5.9 using ordinary least squares. The estimated function was:

$$C(Q) = 0.5309 + 0.003498 Q \quad (R^2 = 0.99; 21 \text{ d.f.}) \quad (8.3.1)$$

where: Q is measured in th. tonnes.

Transport costs were taken from Deakin and Seward (op. cit.) Table 2.10. They are summarised in Table 8.1.

Finally, we must specify the minimum profit constraint. The estimates in Table 5.9 already include an allowance for profit, since capital costs have been expressed as an annual charge assuming a return to capital of 10%. We felt, there-

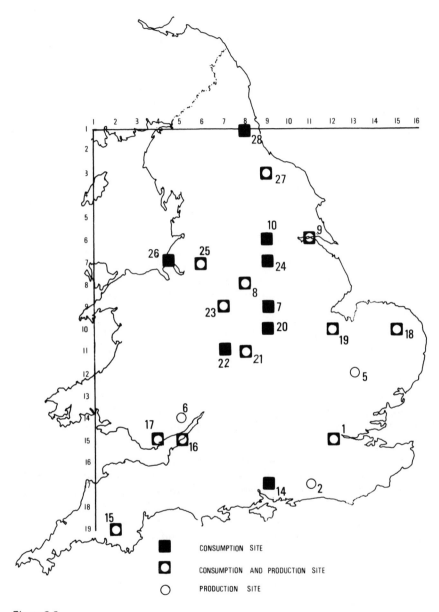

Figure 8.2.

Table 8.1.   Transport Costs 1966

Commodity	Transport Cost (pence per ton-mile)
Cement	4.23
Crude Minerals	4.92
Coal and Coke	5.63

Source: see text.

fore, that the minimum profit constraint should be taken to be the fixed cost element in equation (8.3.1).

8.4 SOLUTION OF THE MODEL

The solution to the model specified in section 8.3 is summarised in Table 8.2 and illustrated in Figure 8.3. A total of nine firms have entered the market, and no firm has been forced to exit. Comparison with the calculated optimum for Case 0 indicates, as we expected, that production is rather more dispersed in the competitive model. Plants have entered at Shoreham, Plymouth, and Peterborough that were not economic in the calculated optimum for Case 0 in the monopolistic model.

There are two exceptions to this process of production dispersion. Firstly, demand at Bristol is supplied from Cardiff, and secondly, there is a greater production concentration at High Peak. Both are in part the result, however, of the discontinuous nature of the lattice and the lack of constraints on the transport system. For example, High Peak is 'nearer' to Hull and Leeds than is Teesside in the competitive model, but not in the monopolistic model.

There is some possibility that the production distribution presented in Table 8.2 is sensitive to our choice of location for the first plant. If a plant were placed at Bristol, for example, would it survive or would it be forced out of the market by competitive entrants? In order to test this aspect of the model, we ran four cases assuming the pre-existence of two plants as follows:

Case 1: plants at London and Bristol,
Case 2: plants at London and Norwich,
Case 3: plants at London and Hull,
Case 4: plants at London and Stoke.

Only in Cases 1 and 2 did the second plant survive. Consumers supplied from a plant at Cardiff in the original run are supplied from Bristol in the solution

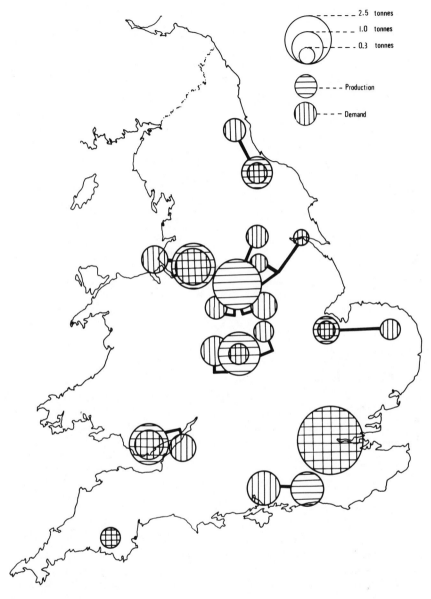

Figure 8.3.

Table 8.2. Solution to the Competitive Model

Node	Place Name	Predicted Capacity		Towns Supplied	
		Competitive Model	Case 0	Competitive Model	Case 0
1	London	5.032	6.300	1	1,14
2	Shoreham	1.268	–	14	
5	Cambridge	–	–		
6	Monmouth	–	–		
8	High Peak	2.627	2.500	7,9,10,23,24	7,10,23,24,(20)
9	Hull	–	–		
15	Plymouth	0.491	–	15	
16	Bristol	–	1.293		15,16
17	Cardiff	1.700	0.898	16,17	17
18	Norwich	–	–		
19	Peterborough	0.778	–	18,19	
21	Coventry	1.916	2.537	20,21,22	18,19,21,22,(20)
23	Stoke	–	–		
25	Manchester	2.138	2.138	25,26	25,26
27	Teesside	1.050	1.334	27,28	9,27,28

for Case 1, while consumers supplied from Peterborough are supplied in Case 2 from Norwich. In both Cases 3 and 4, the second plant is rapidly driven out of the market and the market stabilises on the distribution summarised in Table 8.2. There is, therefore, sensitivity to initial conditions in the model, but the distribution of production generated by the original version of the model (Table 8.2) can be taken as a reasonable approximation to the competitive distribution.

8.5 THE MODEL ASSUMING ELASTIC DEMAND

Throughout our analysis in this and previous chapters, we have assumed demand to be price inelastic. Such an assumption was necessary for the programming model developed in Chapters 3 and 4: any other assumption would have involved the use of some variant of quadratic programming.[8] We can, however, relax this assumption with respect to the competitive model by appealing to the considerable literature now available on spatial pricing policies.

The analysis of spatial pricing policies goes back at least to the work of Hoover (1937) and Singer (1938). Their work was subsequently developed by, for

example, Greenhut and Greenhut (1977) to identify the basic equation charac-
terising optimal spatial pricing policy for a profit maximiser:

$$p(r) \left[1 - \frac{1}{e(r)} \right] = t \cdot r + v \qquad (8.5.1)$$

where: $p(r)$ = delivered price at distance r from the producer,

$e(r)$ = elasticity of demand at price $p(r)$,

t = unit transport cost per unit distance,

v = marginal production cost.

If we assume that the demand curve is linear, i.e.

$$q = a - b \cdot p \quad (a, b > 0), \qquad (8.5.2)$$

then (8.5.1) gives:

$$p(r) = \tfrac{1}{2} \cdot a/b + \tfrac{1}{2}(t \cdot r + v). \qquad (8.5.3)$$

The profit maximiser serving consumers with identical, linear demand curves
should absorb one half of transport costs to his consumers.

In addition, Norman (1977 b) has shown that, given constant marginal costs
of production, the optimal spatial pricing policy (8.5.1) and (8.5.3) is independent of both the distribution of consumers and the size of the market area
served by the producer. As a result, there are no technical constraints involved in
introducing the linear demand schedule (8.5.2) to the model outlined in section
8.2: we need only replace the pricing policy illustrated in Figure 8.1 by the pricing policy (8.5.3)[9] and make the appropriate adjustments to the profit calculation procedures.

There remains the operational problem of choosing appropriate values for a
and b in (8.5.2) when we apply the model to the cement industry. We were
unable to obtain any estimates of the demand curve for cement, and therefore
assumed two demand curves as follows:

Demand Curve 1: $q = 4.0 - \tfrac{2}{3} p$

Demand Curve 2: $q = 2.5 - \tfrac{1}{3} p$

$(8.5.4)$

These are illustrated in Figure 8.4.

The only rationale behind these demand curves is that each consumer purchases
one unit of cement at a price of £4.50 — the approximate average price of cement
in the United Kingdom in 1963. It should be noted that demand curve 2 is more
elastic than demand curve 1 at every price.

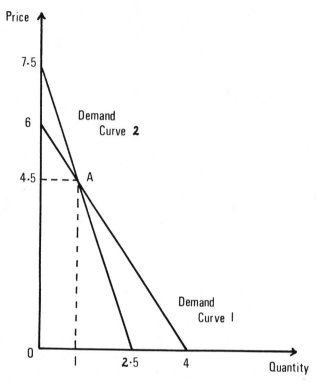

Figure 8.4.

8.6 SOLUTION ASSUMING ELASTIC DEMAND

Table 8.3 and Figures 8.5 and 8.6 summarise the solutions for the two demand curves. As can be seen, more firms can enter the market if it is characterised by demand curve 2 rather than by demand curve 1. In other words, the more elastic demand curve supports a less disaggregated pattern of production in our competitive model.

It should be noted, however, that an increase in elasticity of demand[10] will not invariably lead to a decrease in the number of firms that can enter the market. The limiting case of perfect elasticity at a price of £4.50 will allow plants to enter and survive at all feasible production sites. This case is, in fact, indeterminate, but it should be clear that if demand is very elastic firms may well be able to enter and satisfy the minimum profit constraint at locations such as, for example, Norwich. The minimum price that would be charged at Norwich is approximately £4.15 (from (8.5.3) and production cost conditions), which gives

Table 8.3. Solution of the Model with Elastic Demand

Node	Place Name	Demand Curve 1				Demand Curve 2			
		Supplier Location	Price (£)	Quantity Demanded*	Capacity of Firm*	Supplier Location	Price (£)	Quantity Demanded*	Capacity of Firm*
1	London	London	4.84	3.906	4.405	London	5.59	3.211	3.211
2	Shoreham								0.643
5	Cambridge								—
6	Monmouth								—
7	Nottingham	High Peak	5.00	0.561		High Peak	5.74	0.489	
8	High Peak				1.636				1.175
9	Hull	High Peak	5.37	0.119		High Peak	6.12	0.130	—
10	Leeds	High Peak	5.13	0.345		High Peak	5.88	0.322	—
14	Southampton	London	5.46	0.456		Shoreham	5.98	0.643	—
15	Plymouth	Cardiff	5.55	0.146		Plymouth	5.67	0.299	0.299
16	Bristol	Bristol	4.77	0.658	0.658	Bristol	5.52	0.530	0.530
17	Cardiff	Cardiff	4.78	0.732	0.878	Cardiff	5.53	0.590	0.590
18	Norwich	London	5.85	0.043		P'borough	6.09	0.196	—
19	Peterborough	Coventry	5.46	0.129		P'borough	5.57	0.231	0.427
20	Leicester	Coventry	5.00	0.304		Coventry	5.74	0.265	—
21	Coventry	Coventry	4.75	0.377	1.539	Coventry	5.50	0.301	1.184
22	Birmingham	Coventry	4.92	0.729		Coventry	5.67	0.618	—
23	Stoke	High Peak	5.00	0.342		Stoke	5.56	0.330	0.330
24	Sheffield	High Peak	5.00	0.269		High Peak	5.74	0.234	—
25	Manchester	M'chester	4.76	1.150	1.594	M'chester	5.51	0.922	1.330
26	Liverpool	M'chester	5.11	0.444		M'chester	5.86	0.408	—
27	Teesside	Teesside	4.81	0.370	0.678	Teesside	5.57	0.302	0.601
28	Newcastle	Teesside	5.21	0.308		Teesside	5.96	0.299	—

Notes: *Million tonnes per annum. Demand is unit demand multiplied by number of consumers.

167

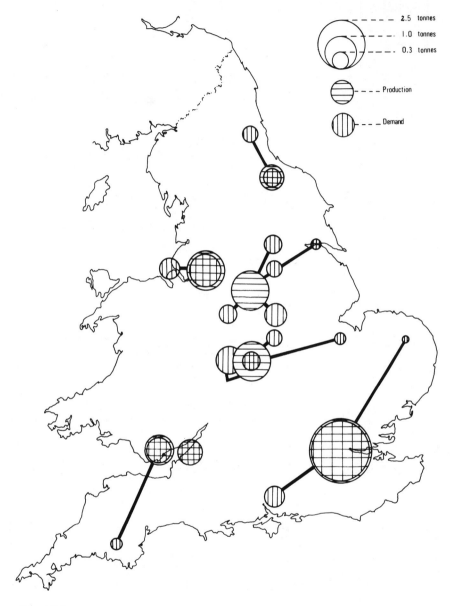

Figure 8.5.

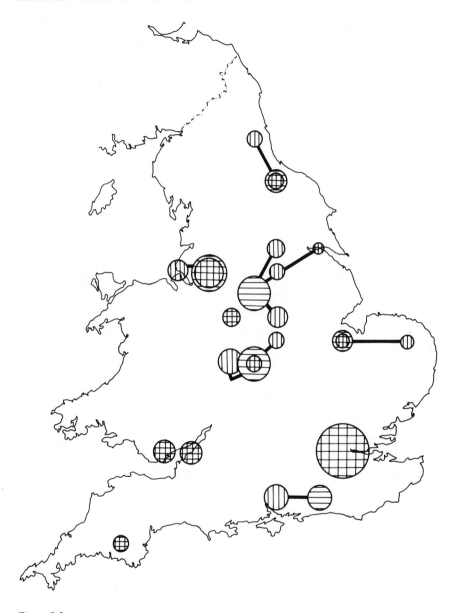

Figure 8.6.

a profit over variable costs of approximately £0.35. Therefore, if demand is such that each consumer demands 3.7 units at a price of £4.15, the minimum profit constraint will be satisfied.

To summarise, given the assumption that all consumers have identical linear demand curves as in Figure 8.4, then the more elastic the demand curve is, up to some limit, the fewer the number of firms that will be able to enter the market. Beyond that limit, however, an increase in elasticity of demand will increase the number of firms able to enter the market.

8.7 CONCLUSIONS

Direct comparison with the results in Chapter 6 is possible only for the model presented in sections 8.2 through 8.4. We then note that, although the production cost function (8.3.1) exhibits generally stronger economies of scale than that used in Chapter 6, more firms are supported in the market in our competitive model. In other words, part of the divergence between our calculated optima in Chapter 6 and the actual distribution of the cement industry can be explained by the competitive elements in the industry.

No direct comparison can be made for the model incorporating a linear demand curve. We noted, however, that the more inelastic is demand, the greater the number of firms that will enter the market in this version of the competitive model. The majority of cement consumers consume cement as an intermediate product, and we noted in Chapter 5 that cement is not an important input for these consumers. There is some reason to expect, therefore, that demand for cement will be price inelastic. This would lend further support to the hypothesis that competitive elements in the industry will support a somewhat more dispersed spatial allocation of production than that predicted in Chapter 6.

9 CONCLUSIONS

9.1 INTRODUCTION

The presence of nonconvexities does severe damage to conventional economic theories of the firm and of the individual. The essential contribution of location theory, however, is in a world in which there are nonconvexities. We have already indicated that if resources are uniformly distributed, and if the usual convexity assumptions are made, then all economic activity would be distributed evenly; there would be no concentration of production. Thus the statement which is usually made, that the standard results carry over to a world in which there is spatial choice, is too weak and fails to capture the essence of location theory.

Having said this, it should not be thought that the introduction of the spatial dimension will resolve the problems which nonconvexity introduces. We saw in Chapter 6, in the analysis of a very simple case, that there is no reason to believe production units will be operated in convex regions of their total cost curves (where total cost now includes transport costs). The introduction of the spatial dimension is interesting and fruitful when (perhaps, only when) there are nonconvexities, but it should not be thought that 'space' is a panacea whereby equilibrium theory can be rescued from the attacks of Lord Kaldor.

171

9.2 PROGRAMMING MODELS AND PLANNING

Since the model developed in the previous chapters is a programming model, it might be felt to have planning implications, and while we indicated in Chapter 2 that our model was not intended to have such implications, we should perhaps indicate some of the applications of programming to planning.

Discussions of decentralised planning procedures have a long history, but application of mathematical programming techniques to national planning had to await the development of large, fast, computer facilities. Examples can be found in Kornai (1967) for Hungary, and Ellman (1971, 1973) for the U.S.S.R. Such applications rely heavily on the principle that a planned economy can be characterised by a linear (or convex) programming problem, and therefore can be decentralised using shadow prices. If all agents maximise their individual objective functions according to these shadow prices, an efficient allocation of resources will be generated for the economy.

This is all very well providing everything is nicely convex, and in particular that production possibility sets are convex. But if production is characterised by economies of scale—as we would expect in many cases given the work, for example, of Pratten (1971)—the price-guided planning procedure based on a programming model begins to break down. As Kornai states:

'(the) class of programming problems where the objective function is . . . a concave function to be minimised or a convex function to be maximised . . . can *not* be solved by . . . the simplex method'. (Kornai 1967, p. 94)

This point is reinforced in subsequent work by Heal and others. Heal (1969), for example, develops a *quantity*-guided planning procedure, and Heal (1971), a price-guided system supplemented by command planning. The conclusion drawn from the latter work is that:

'the social optimum located by the planning process . . . cannot be supported by prices in the normal way, (but) there is a . . . structure of incentives that . . . make a departure from the social optimum against the interest of all agents taken together.' (Heal 1971, p. 291–292)

Calsamiglia (1977) takes this further by showing that, even in a very simple economy, it is not possible to design a decentralised resource allocation mechanism which yields optimal solutions in economies with increasing returns. As he indicates, his work does indeed 'bring into full daylight the extent to which increasing returns do make trouble.' (Calsamiglia 1977, p. 265)

Where do these considerations leave us? We can develop theoretical models in which the production process is characterised by economies of scale. Since such models do not satisfy the convexity assumptions, we can make very few theoretical statements about the ways in which an optimal distribution might be characterised. In addition, the conditions under which convexity would be restored by the influence of space would appear to be a matter for empirical investigation rather than theoretical generalisation.

The study presented in the chapters above is one step in this direction. Clearly, the results that are derived and the conclusions that are drawn are peculiar to the particular case study. But the industry we have analysed does exhibit many characteristics which allow of generalisation to other industrial situations.

9.3 NATURE OF ECONOMIES OF SCALE

Since our study is concerned almost exclusively with the role of transport costs and economies of scale in the industrial location decision, a major requirement was that estimates be made of the shape of total production costs for the cement industry. We found that the industry was indeed characterised by economies of scale, but noted that:

(i) the cost elasticity of scale with respect to each input and with respect to all inputs together is by no means independent of scale, and
(ii) marginal production costs increase beyond some plant scale, while remaining below average production costs, i.e. cost elasticity of scale increases with scale above some plant scale, while remaining less than unity.

These findings are in direct conflict with cost structures that assume either constant cost elasticity of scale or concave production costs. But it should be noted that the topology of cement production satisfies many of the classical properties which form the basis of such cost structures. As a result, we might expect our findings to generalise to other industrial situations.

In other words, fitting an equation of the form $C = aX^n$ to observations A, B and C in Figure 9.1 would give a very misleading impression of the underlying cost:scale relationship, at least for plant capacities in excess of X_2. We must accept, of course, that the paucity of data on the relationship between production costs and plant scales in most industries necessitates the introduction of simplifying assumptions. Indeed, our estimates in Chapter 5 are based on many such assumptions! But we should be aware of the dangers involved in both interpolation and extrapolation on the basis of an assumed constant cost elasticity of scale or concave total production cost function.

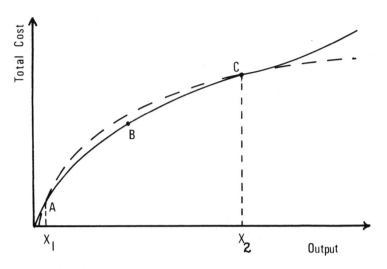

Figure 9.1.

9.4 LOCATIONAL INFLUENCE: STATIC MODEL

The analysis of the very simple model in the introduction to Chapter 6 indicated that we might expect the distribution of demand, the absolute levels of transport and production costs, and the elasticity of these costs with respect to scale and industrial concentration to be major determinants of locational choice.

The results of the case study supported these expectations. In the static model, the sensitivity analysis indicated the important and opposing roles played by transport costs and capital costs in determining the optimal distribution of production. We found that economies of scale to labour costs were of minor importance as a force leading to the concentration of production, but we also noted that labour costs form a small proportion of total production costs in cement production.

Clearly, these conclusions are specific to the cement industry, and are not easily generalised. However, we can conclude, firstly, that industrial location, in whatever industry is being studied, will be more sensitive to a particular cost parameter

(i) the stronger are economies or diseconomies of scale to that parameter, and
(ii) the more important is that parameter relative to other costs which are non-linearly related to scale.

Secondly, the more linear are the production cost relationships (excluding transport costs), the less sensitive will locational choice be to either production or transport costs.

We also found that the distribution of demand was an important determinant of location. Even within the concentrated patterns of production exhibited by the calculated optima in Chapter 6, demand distribution clearly determined the major features of production concentration. The importance of this influence was supported by our econometric investigation of the changes exhibited by the actual distribution of the industry over the period 1950–74.

Again, of course, these findings are industry-specific. The interregional resource base of the cement industry is relatively homogeneous, and, therefore, demand distribution might be expected to play an important role. For industries in which differences in the resource base are significant, however, and for which input transport costs are high, very different locational patterns might be expected to emerge.

A case in point is the Fletton brick industry. Fletton bricks are produced from a special clay known as 'Oxford clay' which is found in a 'thick stratum . . . in the areas round Peterborough, Bedford and Bletchley'. (NBPI, *Report No. 47,* 1967)

This of itself is not sufficient to explain the concentration of Fletton brick production in the Peterborough and other areas, of course. Weber (1929), for example, analyses the different locational patterns which will emerge in an area characterised by a highly concentrated resource base. Other inputs to Fletton brick production are relatively ubiquitous, however, while the weight loss in production and relative transport costs of inputs and outputs are likely to be biased, if anything, in favour of the concentrated input source. As a result, we find the exhibited, strongly localised, pattern of production dominated by one aspect of the resource base.

We should be careful, therefore, not to overemphasise the importance of the distribution of demand (or differences in the resource base) in determining the optimal locational structure of an industry. What we can state is that the distribution of demand will be a more important determinant of the distribution of production:

(i) the more widely available are inputs to the production process or the less dominant is any single input which is strongly localised,
(ii) the lower are transport costs on input commodities relative to production costs and output transport costs, and
(iii) the less evenly distributed is demand.

9.5 LOCATIONAL INFLUENCES: THE MULTIPERIOD MODEL

Most of the factors discussed in section 9.4 carry over to the multiperiod model. In addition, however, the introduction of time to locational decision-making introduces a further diseconomy to industrial concentration. Except in special circumstances, e.g. zero or very rapid (relative to MES) demand growth, large scale production in a multiperiod situation either entails the existence of idle capacity for part of the planning period, or incurs additional transport costs.

In our case study we noted that these diseconomies were sufficiently strong to encourage a highly disaggregated spatial pattern dominated by the distribution and growth of demand. Again, of course, this outcome is industry-specific. It is the result of the interplay between

(i) the pattern of growth of demand from an initial distribution,
(ii) the degree of economies of scale available to the production unit, and
(iii) the structure of transport costs.

Other industries will exhibit different resolutions to this interplay, but it should be recognised that 'time' is an important dimension of the locational decision, no matter what industry is being studied.

This has particular implications for the notion of minimum efficient scale (MES). In the calculated optima for both the single and multiperiod models, we found that a choice of plant size significantly less than MES could be a perfectly efficient choice. As a result, the notion of MES must be treated with some caution. In particular, its use in industrial economic analysis must be modified by a consideration of the distribution and pattern of growth of demand and of the configuration of production and transport costs.

9.6 THE COMPETITIVE MODEL

The multiperiod version of the model was presented, among other reasons, since we were concerned that the calculated optima presented in Chapter 6 ignored the influence of time, and so generated rather more production concentration than would, in fact, be optimal.

Similarly, the competitive model was introduced to examine the extent to which competition in the industry would generate spatial dispersion of production. The behavioural rules underlying the competitive model are relatively simple, but we feel that the results obtained are valuable. These results indicate that, even in the presence of a production function exhibiting quite strong economies of scale, a number of small-scale firms can enter the market and make the necessary minimum profit to allow long-run survival.

The results of the model were not tested for their sensitivity to changes in transport costs or capital costs. It should be clear, however, that the higher are transport costs (or the lower are capital costs), the greater the number of firms that would be able to enter the market.

We also noted that the price elasticity of demand for the final product influences the degree of production concentration generated by the competitive model. For any industry there would appear to be a definable point at which a decrease in overall elasticity of demand will lead to an increase in the number of firms which the market will support. Again we note, therefore, that the concept of minimum efficient scale may have to be modified, in this case by considering the nature of competition in an industry and the elasticity of demand for the final products of that industry.

9.7 THE IMPORTANCE OF TRANSPORT COSTS

The emphasis we have placed on transport costs as a determinant of industrial location is in direct conflict with the claim which is often made that transport costs are unimportant. This claim is based either on interview evidence from behavioural studies, or on the finding that transport costs actually incurred constitute a very small proportion of total production costs.

We have paid no attention to behavioural studies in this thesis, and do not feel that it is appropriate to introduce them in a discussion of our conclusions. We shall concentrate, therefore, on the second line of attack on the importance of transport costs.

With respect to certain industries the statement is probably acceptable, but to justify it on the basis of incurred transport costs is to confuse ex post and ex ante. If transport costs over some fixed length of haul are low relative to production costs, then the statement is trivially true and we might expect, other things being equal, to find a concentrated pattern of production with transport costs having little effect on plant size and location decisions. Alternatively, if transport costs are high relative to production costs (where transport costs are again measured over some fixed length of haul), we would expect plant size and location decisions to be such as to minimise transport costs while still obtaining some advantage from the available economies of scale. As a result, ex post analysis will indicate once more that transport costs are low relative to production costs, i.e. 'unimportant', when, in fact, the opposite is the case.[1]

We would, therefore, conclude that the relative importance of transport costs as a determinant of industrial location is industry-specific and is best judged either from regression studies of the type conducted by Scherer (1975) or by case study of the type presented in this monograph.

APPENDIX A

The additional notation for Chapter 3 is as follows:

$$\left.\begin{array}{ll} \mathbf{z}^v = (z_{0v}, \ldots, z_{Nv}) & (v = 1 \ldots V) \\ \mathbf{z} = (\mathbf{z}^1, \ldots, \mathbf{z}^V) \end{array}\right\} \quad (z = \lambda, y, c)$$

$$\mathbf{x}^v = (x_{1v}, \ldots, x_{K'_v}) \quad (v = 1 \ldots V)$$

$$\mathbf{x} = (\mathbf{x}^1, \ldots, \mathbf{x}^V)$$

$$\mathbf{w}_{vu} = (w_{0vu}, \ldots, w_{Nvu}) \quad (v,u = 1 \ldots V; w_{vv} = 0 \text{ all } v)$$

$$\mathbf{w} = (\mathbf{w}_{11}, \mathbf{w}_{12}, \ldots, \mathbf{w}_{1V}, \mathbf{w}_{21}, \ldots, \mathbf{w}_{2V}, \ldots, \mathbf{w}_{V1}, \ldots \mathbf{w}_{VV})$$

$$\mathbf{t}_{vu} = (t_{0vu}, \ldots, t_{Nvu})$$

$$\mathbf{t} = (t_{11}, t_{12}, \ldots, t_{1V}, t_{21}, \ldots, t_{2V}, \ldots, t_{V1}, \ldots, t_{VV})$$

$$\mathbf{d}^v = (d_{v1}, \ldots d_{vV}) \quad (v = 1 \ldots V; d_{vv} = 0 \text{ all } v)$$

$$\mathbf{d} = (\mathbf{d}^1, \ldots, \mathbf{d}^V)$$

$$T = \begin{bmatrix} T^1 0 \ldots \ldots 0 \\ 0\ T^2 \ldots \ldots 0 \\ \cdot \quad \cdot \\ \cdot \quad \cdot \\ 0 \qquad\quad T^V \end{bmatrix}$$

$W = \| e_{ij} \|$ where i denotes the ith. element of λ and j the jth. element of **w**. If i corresponds to commodity nv and j to element w_{nts} then:

(i) $e_{ij} = 1$ for all $(\vec{t,s})$ in G^B such that $s = v$,
(ii) $e_{ij} = -1$ for all $(\vec{t,s})$ in G^B such that $t = v$,
(iii) $e_{ij} = 0$ otherwise.

$$D = \begin{bmatrix} 1 \ldots 1\ 0 \ldots 0 & 0 \\ 0 \ldots 0\ 1 \ldots 1\ 0 & 0 \\ \cdot & \cdot \\ \cdot & \cdot \\ 0 & 1 \ldots 1 \end{bmatrix}$$

where the vth. row of D has (N+1) (V–1) zeros, then (N + 1) unities, and the remainder of the coefficients zero.

APPENDIX B
Summary of United Nations (1963) Study Data

Table B.1. Capacity, Capital Costs, Labour Requirements

Capacity (th. tons p.a.)	Capital Costs ($'000)	Labour Requirements	
		Direct (no.)	Indirect (no.)
100	6,500	75	"
120	7,000	75	12
200	10,800	96	"
210	11,250	95	17
260	13,200	105	19
340	16,000	130	21
400	18,000	128	"
430	19,000	145	21
500	21,500	150	"
510	21,000	150	21
1000	30,000	150	21

Table B.2. Physical Inputs per ton of Cement related to Capacity

Capacity (th. tons p.a.)	120	210	260	340	430	510	1,000
Limestone (tons)	1.6	1.6	1.6	1.6	1.6	1.6	1.6
Clay (tons)	0.3	0.3	0.3	0.3	0.3	0.3	0.3
Power (Kwh.)	115	115	115	115	115	115	115
Fuel (million BTU)	5.85	5.85	5.85	5.85	5.85	5.85	5.85
Gypsum (%kgs. of weight)	40	40	40	40	40	40	40

Source: United Nations (1963).

APPENDIX C
General Data for the U.K.
and U.S. Cement Industries

1. All data quoted below refer to 1963. The sources used were the Census of Production 1963 for the U.K. and the Census of Manufactures 1963 for the U.S.

2. The size distribution of the two industries by employment is summarised in Table C.1.

The definition of Net Output in the UK is 'the value added to materials by the process of production. (It) constitutes the fund from which (various) charges have to be met (including) depreciation. Net Output has been obtained by deducting from the gross output the cost of purchases adjusted for stock changes, payments for work given out to other firms, and payment to other organisations for transport.' (*Census of Production,* UK, 1963) Value added is obtained 'by subtracting the total cost of materials (including supplies, fuel, electricity, cost of resales, and miscellaneous receipts) from the value of shipments, and adjusting the resulting amount by the net change in finished products and work-in-progress inventories between the beginning and end of each year . . . it does not exclude . . . purchased services nor depreciation charges.' (*Census of Manufactures,* US, 1963) Thus the two measures can be taken to be roughly comparable. A selection of these data is graphed at Figures C.1 and C.2.

3. Comparison of the two series will be affected by the relatively high number of small establishments in the UK industry—small being defined as employ-

Table C.1. Size Distribution by Employment

			(a) UK Cement Manufacture			
Ave. No. Empl'd in Size Group	*Est's (no.)*	*Net[a] Output (£m.)*	*Total Empl't (th.)*	*Ave. Empl't (no.)*	*Net Output p. Est't (£'000)*	*Net Output p. Head (£'00)*
1- 5	3					
6- 10	4	0.5	0.1	10.7	35.7	33.4
11- 24	7					
25- 49	5	0.3	0.2	40.0	60.0	15.0
50- 99	8	2.0	0.6	75.0	250.0	33.4
100-199	13	5.3	1.9	146.0	415.0	28.4
200-299	11	9.3	2.8	254.5	854.4	33.6
300-399	7	6.8	2.4	343.0	985.7	28.8
400+	10	16.3	6.2	620.0	1,640.0	26.5
	68	40.4	14.2	—	—	—

		(b) US Cement Manufacture				
		b			b	b
1- 4	5					
5- 9	2	2116	0.05	5.6	235.1	42.0
10- 19	2					
20- 49	7	7123	0.3	36.9	1,017.7	27.6
50- 99	23	50116	1.9	81.5	2,180.0	26.8
100-249	112	436658	18.9	169.0	3,900.0	23.0
250-499	31	209738	9.9	321.0	6,770.0	21.1
500-999	6	79930	3.8	639.0	13,321.7	20.9
1000+	—	—	—	—	—	—
	188	785,681	34.9	—	—	—

Notes: [a]Value Added in US; [b]$'000.

ing less than 25 persons. A more useful analysis can be conducted if we confine our attention to those establishments with employment 25+ in the UK and 20+ in the US. We then obtain the data in Table C.2.

4. In using these data to estimate λ two points should be noted. Firstly, the *Census of Production* and *Census of Manufactures* data relate to *output* and employment in 1963, while the estimated equation (5.3.2) relates *capacity* and employment in 1970. We are, therefore, forced to the assumption that the relationship between capacity and output given by (5.3.3) holds for both countries

Table C.2. Comparison of Establishments: excluding small establishments

	UK	US	UK as % of US
Total employment	14200	34800	—
Total output (th. tons)*	13088	55700**	—
No. of establishments	54	179	—
Output per establishment (tons)	242	311	77.8
Output per operative (tons)	921	1600	57.6
Operatives per establishment	263	194	135.6

Source: see text.
*Portland Cement only
**99.6% of total output of cements

and for both years, i.e. for the US and UK in 1970 and 1963. The relationship between output and employment for the US is then:

$$E = 59.76 + 0.2790 \ X. \qquad (C.1)$$

Secondly, we do not use the data in Table C.1 to estimate the employment: output relationship directly because these data exhibit the type of bias discussed by Johnston (1963). Examination of the final column of Table C.1 would imply that there are diseconomies of scale to labour in both countries!

The approach we have adopted relies on the heavily concentrated nature of the UK and US industries by employment size of establishment. The modal ranges are the 100-299 range for the UK and 100-249 range for the US. There are some slight differences in the two distributions as indicated by the cumulative frequency curves plotted in Figure C.1; the UK having a slightly greater proportion of small and large establishments than the US. We cannot estimate the extent to which the effect of small establishments on output per establishment is offset by the effect of large establishments, and in the absence of better information we assume that the effect is symmetrical.

If we take $X_{US} = 311$ th. tons p.a. (278 th. tonnes p.a.) and $X_{UK} = 242$ th. tons p.a. (216 th. tonnes p.a.), equations (C.1) and (5.3.4) then imply estimates of operatives per establishment of

$$\hat{E}_{US} = 137; \hat{E}_{UK} = \lambda \cdot 120. \qquad (C.2)$$

We now assume that the ratio of estimated (1970) employment per establishment to actual (1963) employment per establishment is the same in the two countries, i.e.

$$\hat{E}_{US}/194 = \hat{E}_{UK}/263. \qquad (C.3)$$

Thus

$$\lambda = (263 \times 137)/(194 \times 120) = 1.548. \qquad\qquad (C.4)$$

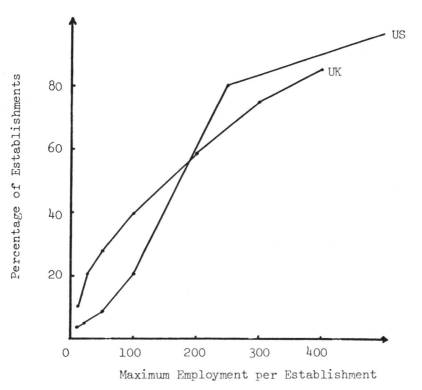

Figure C.1.

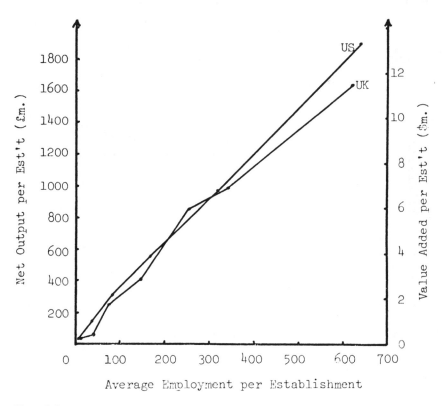

Figure C.2.

APPENDIX D
Regional and County Analysis of Cement Deliveries (1965)

Region	County	County Deliveries (%)	Regional Deliveries (%)
NORTHERN	Cumberland	0.58	6.18
	Durham	2.81	
	Northumberland	1.43	
	Westmorland	0.19	
	North Riding	1.17	
EAST & WEST RIDING			6.74
NORTH MIDLANDS	Derbyshire	2.72	9.61
	Leicestershire & Rutland	2.21	
	Lincolnshire	1.60	
	Northamptonshire	0.89	
	Nottinghamshire	2.19	
EASTERN	Bedfordshire	1.22	11.78
	Cambridgeshire	0.10	

(continued)

Region	County	County Deliveries (%)	Regional Deliveries (%)
EASTERN (cont.)	Essex	4.24	
	Hertfordshire	2.53	
	Huntingdonshire	0.31	
	Norfolk	1.29	
	Suffolk	1.17	
GREATER LONDON			11.63
SOUTHERN	Berkshire	1.79	8.99
	Buckinghamshire	1.51	
	Dorset	0.95	
	Hampshire	3.76	
	Oxfordshire	0.97	
SOUTH WESTERN	Cornwall & Devon	2.89	7.61
	Gloucestershire	2.56	
	Somerset	1.21	
	Wiltshire	0.95	
WALES	North Wales	1.51	6.44
	South Wales	4.93	
MIDLANDS	Herefordshire	0.34	11.51
	Shropshire	0.98	
	Staffordshire	4.82	
	Warwickshire	4.41	
	Worcestershire	0.95	
NORTH WESTERN	Cheshire	2.29	11.07
	Lancashire	8.78	
SOUTH EASTERN	Kent	3.95	8.44
	Surrey	1.75	
	Sussex	2.74	

Source: Cement Makers' Federation.

APPENDIX E
Estimated Road Distances

Branch (u,v)	Distance (Miles)	Branch (u,v)	Distance (Miles)
(1,3)	20	(9,10)	50
(1,4)	80	(9,27)	75
(1,5)	50	(10,24)	30
(1,13)	60	(10,27)	60
(1,14)	70	(11,25)	25
(1,15)	220	(11,26)	30
(1,21)	90	(12,25)	120
(2,3)	35	(12,28)	55
(2,14)	30	(14,15)	150
(3,14)	55	(15,16)	125
(4,16)	30	(16,22)	80
(5,18)	60	(18,19)	75
(5,19)	35	(19,20)	35
(6,16)	20	(20,21)	25
(6,17)	25	(21,22)	15
(7,8)	30	(22,23)	40
(7,20)	25	(23,25)	35
(7,24)	40	(24,25)	35
(8,23)	25	(25,26)	30
(8,24)	20	(27,28)	35

BIBLIOGRAPHY

Agin, N.R. 1966. 'Optimum Seeking with Branch and Bound'. *Management Science* 13: 176–85.

Alonso, W. 1964. 'Location Theory'. In *Regional Development and Planning: a Reader,* eds. Friedmann, J., and Alonso, W. Cambridge, Mass.: Massachusetts Institute of Technology Press.

Balinski, M.L. 1970. 'Integer programming, methods, uses, computation'. In *Proceedings of the Princeton Symposium on Mathematical Programming,* ed. Kuhn, H.W. Princeton, N.J.: Princeton University Press.

Beale, E.M.L., and Small, R.E. 1965. 'Mixed Integer Programming by a Branch and Bound Technique'. In *Proceedings of the IFIP Congress,* pp. 517–49.

Beckenstein, A.R. 1975. 'Scale Economies in the Multi Plant Firm: theory and empirical evidence'. *Bell Journal of Economics* 6: 644–60.

Berry, B.J.L., and Garrison, W.L. 1958. 'The functional bases of the central place hierarchy'. *Economic Geography* 34: 145–54.

Bollobas, B., and Stern, N. 1972. 'The Optimal Structure of Market Areas'. *Journal of Economic Theory* 4: 174–79.

Bos, H.C. 1965. 'Spatial Dispersal of Economic Activity'. Rotterdam: Rotterdam University Press.

Buckley, P.J., and Casson, M.C. 1976. *The Future of the Multinational Enterprise.* London: Macmillan Press.

Calsamiglia, X. 1977. 'Decentralized Resource Allocation and Increasing Returns'. *Journal of Economic Theory* 14: 263–83.

Casson, M.C. 1973. *Introduction to Mathematical Economics,* London: Nelson.

Cement and Concrete Association. 1951. *Cement in the Making.* London: Cement and Concrete Association.

Chamberlin, E. 1933. *The Theory of Monopolistic Competition.* Cambridge, Mass.: Harvard University Press.

Chisholm, M., and O'Sullivan, P. 1973. *Freight Flows and Spatial Aspects of the British Economy.* Cambridge: Cambridge University Press.

Christaller, W. 1966. *Central Places in Southern Germany,* trans. by Baskin, C.W., from *Die zentralen Orte in Suddeutschland.* 1933. Englewood Cliffs, N.J.: Prentice-Hall.

Cockerill, A. 1971. 'Economies of Scale in the Brewing Industry'. Unpublished dissertation for the degree of M. Phil., Leeds University.

Cockerill, A. 1974. *The Steel Industry: International Comparisons of Structure and Performance.* Cambridge: Cambridge University Press.

Cook, P. Lesley. 1958. *The Effects of Mergers.* London: Allen and Unwin.

Dantzig, G.B. 1963. *Linear Programming and Extensions.* Princeton, N.J.: Princeton University Press.

Dasgupta, P.S., and Heal, G.M. Forthcoming. *On the Optimal Depletion of Exhaustible Resources.*

Deakin, B.M., and Seward, T. 1969. *Productivity in Transport: a Study of Employment, Capital, Output, Productivity and Technical Change.* Cambridge: Cambridge University Press.

Deaton, A. 1974. 'NLFIML: Non-Linear, Full Information, Maximum Likelihood'. Unpublished study paper. Cambridge University.

Diwan, R.K. 1966. 'Alternative Specifications of Economies of Scale'. *Economica (New Series)* 33: 442–53.

Dorfman, R., Samuelson, P.A., and Solow, R.M. 1958. *Linear Programming and Economic Analysis.* New York: McGraw-Hill.

Dunford, M. 1969. 'Interregional Freight Flows: an application of linear programming'. Unpublished dissertation for B. Sc. degree, Department of Geography, University of Bristol.

Eaton, B.C., and Lipsey, R.G. 1975. 'The Principle of Minimum Differentiation Reconsidered: some new developments in the theory of spatial competition'. *Review of Economic Studies* 42: 27–50.

Eaton, B.C., and Lipsey, R.G. 1978. 'Freedom of Entry and Existence of Pure Profit'. *The Economic Journal* 88: 455–69.

Ellman, M. 1971. *Soviet Planning Today.* Occasional paper No. 25. Department of Applied Economics. Cambridge: University of Cambridge.

Ellman, M. 1973. *Planning Problems in the U.S.S.R.* Monographs, vol. 24. Department of Applied Economics. Cambridge: University of Cambridge.

Elshafei, A.N. 1965. 'An Approach to Locational Analysis'. *Operational Research Quarterly* 26: 167–81.

European Cement Association. 1972. *World Cement Directory*. Paris: Cembureau.

Farrell, M.J. 1957. 'The Measurement of Productive Efficiency'. *Journal of the Royal Statistical Society, Series (A)* 120: 253–81.

Farrell, M.J., and Fieldhouse, M. 1962. 'Estimating Efficient Production Functions under Increasing Returns to Scale'. *Journal of the Royal Statistical Society, Series (A)* 125: 252–67.

Gass, S.I. 1964. *Linear Programming: Methods and Applications*. 2nd. ed. New York: McGraw-Hill.

Gee, J.M.A. 1976. 'A Model of Location and Industrial Efficiency with Free Entry'. *Quarterly Journal of Economics* XC: 557–74.

Getis, A. 1963. 'The determination of the location of retail activities with the use of a map transformation'. *Economic Geography* 39: 14–22.

Gomory, R.E., and Baumol, W.J. 1960. 'Integer Programming and Pricing'. *Econometrica* 28: 521–50.

Greenhut, M.L. 1956. *Plant Location in Theory and Practice: the economics of space*. Chapel Hill: University of North Carolina Press.

Greenhut, M.L. 1963. *Microeconomics and the Space Economy*. Chicago: University of Chicago Press.

Greenhut, J., and Greenhut, M.L. 1977. 'Nonlinearity of Delivered Price Schedules and Predatory Pricing'. *Econometrica* 45: 1871–75.

Griliches, Z., and Ringstad, V. 1971. *Economies of Scale and the Form of the Production Function*. Amsterdam: North-Holland.

Guigou, J.-L. 1971. 'On French Location Models for Production Units'. *Regional and Urban Economics, operational methods*. Vol. 1: 107–38.

Hadley, G. 1962. *Linear Programming*. Reading, Mass.: Addison-Wesley Publishing Co.

Hadley, G. 1964. *Nonlinear and Dynamic Programming*. Reading, Mass.: Addison-Wesley Publishing Co.

Haldi, J., and Witcomb, D. 1967. 'Economies of Scale in Industrial Plants'. *Journal of Political Economy* 75: 373–85.

Heal, G.M. 1969. 'Planning without Prices'. *Review of Economic Studies* 36: 347–62.

Heal, G.M. 1971. 'Planning, Prices and Increasing Returns'. *Review of Economic Studies* 38: 281–94.

Heal, G.M. 1973. *Theory of Economic Planning*. Amsterdam: North-Holland.

Hoover, E.M. 1937. *Location Theory and the Shoe and Leather Industries*. Cambridge, Mass.: Harvard University Press.

Hoover, E.M. 1937. 'Spatial Price Discrimination'. *Review of Economic Studies* 4: 182–91.

Hoover, E.M. 1948. *The Location of Economic Activity*. New York: McGraw-Hill.

Hotelling, H. 1929. 'Stability in Competition'. *Economic Journal* 39: 41–57.

Intriligator, M.D. 1971. *Mathematical Optimisation and Economic Theory*. Englewood Cliffs, N.J.: Prentice-Hall.

Isard, W. 1956. *Location and Space Economy*. Cambridge, Mass.: Massachusetts Institute of Technology Press.

Isard, W. 1960. *Methods of Regional Analysis*. Cambridge, Mass.: Massachusetts Institute of Technology Press.

Johnston, J. 1960. *Statistical Cost Analysis*. New York: McGraw-Hill.

Koopmans, T.C., ed. 1951. *Activity Analysis of Production and Allocation*. Cowles Commission Monograph, no. 13. New York: Wiley & Sons.

Koopmans, T.C., and Beckmann, M. 1957. 'Assignment Problems and the Location of Economic Activities'. *Econometrica* 25: 53–76.

Kornai, J. 1967. *Mathematical Planning of Structural Decisions*. Amsterdam: North-Holland.

Kuhn, H.W., and Tucker, A.W. 1951. 'Nonlinear Programming'. In *Proceedings of the Second Berkeley Symposium on Mathematical Statistics and Probability*, ed. Neyman, J. Berkeley, Calif.: University of California Press.

Land, A.H., and Doig, A.G. 1960. 'An Automatic Method of Solving Discrete Programming Problems'. *Econometrica* 28: 497–520.

Land, A.H., and Powell, S. 1973. *Fortran Codes for Mathematical Programming, Linear, Quadratic, and Discrete*. London: Wiley.

Lea, A.C. 1973. 'Location-allocation systems; an annotated bibliography'. Discussion Paper No. 13. Department of Geography, University of Toronto.

Lösch, A. 1938. 'The Nature of Economic Regions'. *Southern Economic Journal* 5: 71–78.

Lösch, A. 1954. *The Economics of Location*, trans. by Woglom, W.H., from *Die räumliche Ordnung der Wirtschaft*. 1940. New Haven: Yale University Press.

Manne, A.S. 1967. *Investments for Capacity Expansion: Size, Location, and Time-Phasing*. London: George Allen and Unwin.

National Board for Prices and Incomes. 1967. *Portland Cement Prices*. Report No. 38, cmnd. 3381, H.M.S.O.

National Board for Prices and Incomes. 1967. *Prices of Fletton and Non-Fletton Bricks*. Report No. 47, cmnd. 3480, H.M.S.O.

National Institute Economic Review, 1974, 1976. National Institute of Economic and Social Research, London.

Nijkamp, P. 1977. *Theory and Application of Environmental Economics*. Amsterdam: North-Holland.

Norman, G. 1977(a). 'Pricing System, Distribution of Demand and Location'. *Regional Studies* 11: 183–89.

Norman, G. 1977(b). 'Spatial Price Discrimination and Plant Location'. *Discussion Papers in Economics, Series A, No. 96*. University of Reading.

Organisation for Economic Cooperation and Development 1972. *Manual of Industrial Project Analysis in Developing Countries*. Vol. 1, rev. ed. Paris: OECD Development Centre.

Paelinck, J.H., and Nijkamp, P. 1976. *Operational Theory and Method in Regional Economics*. Saxon House/Lexington, Westmead, Farnborough, Hants, England.

Parr, J.B. 1973. 'Structure and Size in the Urban System of Lösch'. *Economic Geography* 49: 185–212.

Pratten, C.F. 1971. *Economies of Scale in Manufacturing Industry.* Cambridge: Cambridge University Press.

Pratten, C.F., and Dean, R.M. 1965. (In collaboration with Silberston, A.) *The Economies of Large-Scale Production in British Industry: an Introductory Study.* Cambridge: Cambridge University Press.

Review of Economic Studies. 1974. *Symposium on the Economies of Exhaustible Resources.* Special supplement.

Robinson, E.A.G. 1931. *The Structure of Competitive Industry.* Cambridge Economic Handbooks. Cambridge: Cambridge University Press.

Rothschild, R. 1976. 'A Note on the Effect of Sequential Entry on Choice of Location'. *Journal of Industrial Economics* 24: 313–20.

Scherer, F.M., et al. 1975. *The Economics of Multi-Plant Operation: an International Comparisons Study.* Cambridge, Mass.: Harvard University Press.

Silberston, A. 1972. 'Economies of Scale in Theory and Practice'. *Economic Journal* 82(supplement): 369–91.

Singer, H.W. 1937. 'A Note on Spatial Price Discrimination'. *Review of Economic Studies* 5: 75–77.

Smithies, A.F. 1941. 'Optimum Location in Spatial Competition'. *Journal of Political Economy* 49: 423–39.

Soland, R.M. 1974. 'Optimal Facility Location with Concave Costs'. *Operations Research* 23: 373–82.

Starrett, D.A. 1974. 'Principles of Optimal Location in a Large Homogeneous Area'. *Journal of Economic Theory* 9: 418–48.

United Nations. 1963. *Studies in the Economics of Industry, 1.* New York: United Nations.

Vietorisz, T., and Manne, A.S. 1963. 'Chemical Processes, Plant Location and Economies of Scale'. In *Studies in Process Analysis,* eds. Manne, A.S., and Markowitz, H. New York: Wiley.

Walters, A.A. 1963. 'Production and Cost Functions: an econometric survey'. *Econometrics* 31: 1–66.

Weber, A. 1929. *Alfred Weber's Theory of Location of Industries,* trans. by Friedrich, C.J., from *Über den Standort der Industrien. 1909.* Chicago: University of Chicago Press.

White, C.H. 1970. 'Production Allocation with Set-up Penalties and Concave Material Costs'. *Operations Research* 18: 958–72.

NOTES

CHAPTER 1. INTRODUCTION

1. A significant exception, of course, is the work on monopolistic competition developed by Chamberlin (1933).

2. The distinction between 'interregional' and 'intraregional' is somewhat arbitrary, however, since Weber did not provide a coherent definition of what constituted a 'region'.

3. It is perhaps convenient to think of demand as being price-inelastic.

4. In constructing his materials index, Weber concentrates on the case in which transport costs are independent of the commodity transported, being determined by weight and distance alone. The formulation here modifies the analysis to allow for different transport rates for different commodities. Weber also thought that he could introduce transport costs varying with distance, but Isard (1956) for example, has shown that there is a logical flaw in Weber's analysis in this respect.

5. Obviously this imples that labour is ubiquitous but immobile, and is a departure from assumption (ii) — that the price of a factor is independent of location.

6. Note that these factors do not change the transportation relationships. Thus, for example, there will be no change in the relative weights of localised inputs and output as a result of agglomeration.

7. This is not the only case in which agglomeration will reduce production costs. If, for example, the critical isodapane for P_1^* did not intersect those for P_2^* and P_3^*, agglomeration would reduce costs:

'if the ratio of economies to deviation costs for *other* parts of the agglomeration is so favourable that a balance on the side of economy still remains for the agglomerated industry as a whole'. (Weber, p. 137)

8. See, for example, Vietorisz and Manne (1963).

9. These assumptions indicate the intellectual debt of Lösch to Chamberlin.

10. The 'distance' between P and F is expressed in cost terms. Division by the appropriate transport cost will convert this to miles.

11. For an analysis of the 'types' of industrial activities located at each central place see Parr (1973).

12. We shall however, maintain the assumption of linearity with weight transported.

CHAPTER 2. OBJECTIVES OF THE STUDY

1. An excellent discussion of these factors can be found in Heal 1973, Chapters 1, 3, and 10. The following paragraphs summarise some of the points made by Heal.

CHAPTER 3. STATIC MODEL ASSUMING CONSTANT RETURNS TO SCALE

1. We shall use the terminology of graph theory but none of the mathematical properties. For a brief discussion of the theory of graphs, see Hadley (1962) Chapter 10. A more extensive treatment of the role of graph theory in location analysis can be found in Guigou (1971).

2. We do not need to define location other than at nodes in G since transport is assumed to be timeless.

3. Negative rather than positive from our conventions outlined below regarding the signs of the components of the activity vectors.

4. Note that a net input has a negative sign in a production activity.

5. The quantity k now runs from 1 to K' with activities $(K+1)v \ldots K'v$ being disposal activities.

6. Koopmans (1951) applies disposal activities to waste products and to surpluses from joint production. In general, it would appear sensible to ignore this latter aspect of disposal since the surpluses are not a 'social evil'.

7. This approach avoids many of the problems associated with waste disposal. An extensive discussion of these problems can be found in Nijkamp (1977).

8. While disposal may be considered costless in this sense, costs will have been incurred in transporting a commodity, some of which will end up as waste. This cost will be made up of direct cost of transport and indirect (opportunity) cost of taking up limited transport capacity which could have been used to transport a nonwaste commodity.

9. For additional notation see Appendix A.

10. This formulation of the quantity demanded follows from the assumption of a perfectly price-inelastic demand.

11. This formulation assumes that the flow on (v,u) does not interfere with the flow on (u,v).

12. In adopting this approach, particularly for primary factors, we abstract from the

difficult question of exhaustible resources. Deposits of raw materials are finite and not replaceable and the 'true' cost to the economy of depleting these deposits need not be reflected in the selling price. Estimating such 'true' costs lies outside the scope of this study. The problems involved in doing so are discussed in P.S. Dasgupta and G.M. Heal: 'On the Optimal Depletion of Exhaustible Resources' (forthcoming), and in a special issue of the *Review of Economic Studies* (1975).

13. No distinction is made between row and column vectors. The context will indicate which type is being used.

14. The basic references are Dorfman, Samuelson and Solow (1958), Dantzig (1963), Hadley (1962), and Gass (1964).

CHAPTER 4. THE STATIC MODEL WITH INCREASING RETURNS

1. If assumptions 2 through 4 and the sufficient condition for assumption 1 are satisfied, 'output' and 'scale' are synonymous.

2. It should be noted that for those scale ranges for which elasticities I and II are less than unity, the appropriate envelope average cost curve will be downward sloping.

3. The theoretical and empirical literature on this subject is vast. Undoubtedly, however, one of the most important studies is Robinson (1931). Of the more recent work on economies of scale exhibited by production functions, Walters (1963) and Diwan (1966) are interesting examples of particular sectors, while Griliches and Ringstad (1971) provides a wider coverage. Economies of scale exhibited by cost functions were analysed by Haldi and Witcomb (1967). The most important recent work in this field however has been produced by Cockerill (1971, 1974), Pratten and Dean (1965) and Pratten (1971).

4. We assume that (i) commodity prices and labour costs are independent of location (see Chapter 3), (ii) TPC excludes all elements of transport costs, and (iii) capital costs are independent of location. As a result $T_k(\ )$ is independent of location.

5. We assume that the labour availability constraints are expressed net of fixed labour inputs.

6. In the interests of simplicity we shall drop the subscripts kv in this section and the bulk of section 4.4.

7. Calculations have been simplified (i) by ignoring the effect of truncation to the left at x=0 (which will be negligible in most cases) and (ii) by assuming no limit on the above capacity operation of plant. This assumption understates $V_2(x,Z)$ in the subsequent analysis.

8. Algorithms do exist which can be applied if T(x) is strictly concave – see Scherer (1975) – but we allow (T(x) to be of general form.

9. Note that in the same way that T(x) is independent of location, so the parameters of TT(x) will generally be independent of location.

10. Since they exclude capital and fixed labour costs.

11. Mixed integer programmes have been specified by other researchers in 'applied' location studies. These programmes tend to assume, however, that the cost function consists of either

(i) a fixed cost plus an element linear in output – see, for example, Bos (1965), Vietorisz and Manne (1963) – or
(ii) a number of segments forming a concave total cost function – see, for example, Elshafei (1975).

The advantage of the MIP specified in this study is that it can handle cost functions of general form.

12. We shall consider below what we mean by 'capacity' in such cases.

13. These problems are also discussed in Paelinck and Nijkamp (1976), especially sections 5.8 and 5.19. The method Paelinck and Nijkamp suggest for solving their model when it is specified to include economies of scale has the same underlying philosophy as the method we shall use to solve the MIP.

CHAPTER 5. CASE STUDY — THE CEMENT INDUSTRY

1. See Chapter 3, footnote 12.

2. The claim is occasionally made that UK manufacturers in general do not take as full advantage of available economies of scale as do manufacturers in the United States.

This claim has two conflicting interpretations. The first is that establishments in any particular UK industry operate at generally lower scales than establishments in the same industry in the US, as a result, perhaps, of different market size or costs of serving a given market area. But this interpretation is consistent with the elasticity of output with respect to labour input being the same in the two countries.

The alternative interpretation is that the elasticity of output with respect to labour input is greater in the US than in the UK. In other words, the degree of economies of scale to labour available to US manufacture is greater than that available to UK manufacture *at every scale.*

There is no viable method for testing the two interpretations on the basis of the data at Appendix C. One implication derivable from the latter, however, would be that output per establishment in the US would diverge *at an increasing rate* from that in the UK as employment per establishment increases. This is not confirmed by the data graphed in Appendix C, Figure C.2, which would appear to indicate that the two measures are in constant proportion as employment expands.

This test is not conclusive, of course. It is still possible that a divergence exists between the two countries, since labour in the US and UK will differ in such factors as trade union organisation, etc. These differences may well put UK manufacturers at a disadvantage relative to the US in their ability to reduce labour input per unit of output as scale expands. As it is impossible to estimate their extent, we assume that employment elasticity of scale is the same in the two countries.

3. Comparison of the United States capital cost data at Appendix B with the West German data in Table 5.7 would indicate on first sight that the elasticity of capital costs with respect to scale was lower in the US (in the period 1956–60) than in West Germany (in 1970) for plant capacities in the range 0.1 - 1.0 m. tonnes p.a. The following table indicates the relative elasticities.

One possible explanation of the apparent difference is that the data in Appendix B exhibit a consistent bias in capital costs. These data are taken from Appendix I of the United Nations report and represent a sample of seven observations from a total of eighteen. The study team report in the main text that on the basis of all eighteen observations the elasticity of capital costs over the range 0.1 - 1.0 m. tonnes p.a. was 0.77. Applying the ratio 0.77/0.69 to the estimated elasticities in col. (1) above gives the results in col. (3) which are much more in line with the West German estimates.

Capacity			Elasticity of Capital Costs*		
United States		West Germany			
m. tons p.a.	m. tonnes p.a.	m. tonnes p.a.	US (1)	WG (2)	US** (3)
0.120	0.107	0.099	0.76	0.84	0.85
0.510	0.455	0.4125	0.53 0.69	0.60 0.77	0.59
1.000	0.893	0.9074			

*Estimated from a relationship $Y = aX^n$ where n = elasticity of Y with respect to X.
**See text above.

4. It is informative to compare the estimate of μ with the DM/£ exchange rate. Over the period 1960–65, this rate averaged £0.089 per DM. Converting the German estimates to £ by applying the exchange rate would therefore lead to a substantial underestimate of UK capital costs.

5. These estimates are based on comments in the *NBPI Report no. 38 (op. cit.)*. The NBPI reported that in evidence to a 1961 Restrictive Practices Court it was indicated that cement producers 'had been content to accept a rate of return of under 10 per cent from capital . . . invested in new works.' The NBPI's recommendation was in fact based upon a return of 10%. Further, they reported that 'kilns tend to have a long life of up to 40 years or more'.

6. Note that we have assumed that the production unit is the cement plant. In addition we assume that restrictions on dust emission, etc., are reflected in the capital cost estimates. As a result, the subscript k is such that k = 1.

7. Transport costs for chalk, clay, gypsum, limestone, and shale are assumed to be those estimated for 'crude minerals'.

8. This is the graph G': see Chapter 3.

9. As we expected (Chapter 3), the capacity constraints upon the transport network had to be dropped from the analysis.

10. Clearly, projected demand should be used rather than demand at 1963. In addition, cement deliveries, i.e. demand, exhibited little variation around 17.0 m. tonnes p.a. over the period we have taken.

CHAPTER 6. SOLUTION OF THE STATIC CEMENT STUDY

1. The unit transport cost function has the form $t_{AB}x/(A+x)$ where: t_{AB} = cost of transporting one unit of output from A to B, x = amount transported from A to B, A = demand at A.

2. In the interests of simplicity we have ignored the possibility of an intermediate position involving production at A and B in conjunction with some demand at B being supplied from A. The first order condition for a minimum cost allocation of production is that:

$$t_{AB} + MC(x_A) = MC(x_B) \tag{1}$$

where $MC(x_A)$ = marginal production cost at A at output x_A

$MC(x_B)$ = marginal production cost at B at output x_B.

We assume that x_A is greater than demand at A and x_B is less than demand at B. If we further assume that MC is monotonic decreasing then (1) is a maximum and the intermediate position would not occur.

If, on the other hand, we have a TPC function such as that derived for the cement industry, MC is increasing for capacities in excess of some capacity C'. Thus if demand at A and B are such that x_A and x_B in (1) are both greater than C', (1) is necessary and sufficient for a minimum cost allocation, i.e. the intermediate position should be chosen.

Finally, if $x_A > C'$ and $x_B < C'$ then (1) may be a maximum or minimum. These considerations do not change our conclusions fundamentally, however; firstly since x_A and x_B are strongly influenced by demand at A and B respectively, and secondly since $x_A > C'$ implies that the majority of scale economies to production at A have been exhausted.

3. It should be noted that in this and subsequent sensitivity curves each measure of tonne miles is associated with a unique distribution of capacity.

4. Estimates based upon a National Economic Development Office (NEDO) analysis of energy costs indicate that a 100% increase in fuel costs would lead to a 48% increase in transport costs.

5. This is partly a result of our assumption of constant returns to scale for plant capacities in excess of 2.5 m. tonnes p.a.

6. We did not re-estimate materials and energy costs in view of our findings in para. 6.3.1.

7. Predicted excess demand was estimated by applying to $\mathbf{D}_t$ the growth rate of demand from (t–1) to t, giving the vector $\mathbf{D}_{t+1}^*$, and forming the vector $\mathbf{D}_{t+1}^* - \mathbf{C}_t$.

CHAPTER 7. THE MULTI-PERIOD VERSION OF THE MODEL

1. Since we are considering an infinite time horizon, dropping this requirement would mean that an infinite amount would have to be put into storage in period T.

2. It should be noted that capital costs in the Infinite Horizon version always exceed those in the Kendrick version.

3. Demand estimates for 1975 are assumed to be as for 1974.

4. We realise that this conflicts with the hypothesis in Chapter 5 of a fixed relationship between output and capacity. Maintaining the approach in Chapter 5 is straightforward: we add to b_{kvt}^i the estimated variable labour cost and maintain our assumptions regarding d_{kvt}. In the multiperiod version, however, we feel that it is more reasonable to relate labour input to output rather than capacity.

5. The relationship we use is that estimated in Appendix C, equation (C.1), adjusted by our estimate of $\lambda = 1.548$.

6. The indices for 1975 were estimated assuming that materials and fuel prices increased in the same proportion as 'materials used in manufacture' (N.I.E.S.R.) over the period 1974–75.

7. Note that in both versions pre-existing capacity is used solely to 'top up' new capacity.

CHAPTER 8. A COMPETITIVE MODEL
ASSUMING FREE ENTRY

1. I am grateful to Linda Roberts for developing the computer programme used in this chapter.

2. Demand is therefore assumed to be price inelastic. This assumption is relaxed in section 8.5.

3. The meaning of a 'period' will be made clear below.

4. It was not possible to incorporate loading and unloading costs, or to impose constraints on the transport network.

5. This is solely for expository purposes.

6. We assume that the first firm is located at London in most of our applications of the model to the cement study.

7. It is interesting to note that Eaton and Lipsey (1978) find that pure profit may well persist in a spatial model with free entry.

8. Norman (1977 a) examines some of the implications for location decisions consequent upon the introduction of a linear demand schedule, but does so in a highly simplified model.

9. This is only possible if we assume that the profit maximiser also adopts a profit maximising policy with respect to his pricing system. Other pricing systems are possible, e.g. uniform pricing or mill pricing, but Norman (1977 b) indicates that the optimal uniform or mill price is *not* independent of market size or consumer distribution.

10. Throughout this discussion we confine our attention to demand curves which are such that one unit is demanded at a price of £4.50, i.e. which pass through the point A in Figure 8.3.

CHAPTER 9. CONCLUSIONS

1. This type of consideration underlies the Scherer (1975) work which indicates that transport cost on some fixed length of haul is a significant determinant of plant size decisions in twelve industries.

INDEX

Activity analysis, 14, 19
  disposal activities, 30, 31 ff
  production activities, 29, 30, 54 ff
  transport activities, 29, 30
Activity level, 30, 130, 131
Activity vector, 30, 54 ff, 129
Agglomeration,
  economies of, 5 ff, 14
  forces of, 2 ff, 11
Agin, N. R., 59
Alonso, W., 3, 6

Balinski, M. L., 59
Baumol, W. J., 53
Beale, E. M. L., 59
Beckenstein, A. R., 6
Beckmann, M., 39
Behavioural rules, 158
Berry, B. J. L., 10
Bollobas, B., 7
Bos, H. C., 197 n

Branch and bound, 59 ff
Brick industry, 175
Buckley, P. J., 6

Calsamiglia, X., 172
Casson, M. C., 6, 122
Cement industry, 14, 60 ff, 182 ff
  actual distribution, 118 ff
  economies of scale, 46
  exports, 62
  imports, 62
  mineral consumption, 65
  optimal distribution, 90, 100, 152, 162
  plant capacities, 119 ff
  production unit, 45
  technology, 61, 74
Cement study
  calculated optimum, 91 ff
  comparison with actual, 118 ff
Chamberlin, E., 195 n
Chisholm, M., 18

202

Christaller, W., 9
Commodity, 29, 129
   final products, 29, 33, 144
   intermediate, 29, 33, 143
   primary factors, 29, 33, 143
   waste products, 29, 31
Competitive model, 158, 162, 176
Concentration *see also* spatial concentra-
     tion
   index, 62
   production, 93, 154ff, 166, 170, 171,
     176
Constant returns to scale, 95, 110
   model, 26ff
   production unit, 50
   sensitivity curve, 98
Convexity, 11, 56, 171
Cook, P. L., 61
Cost function, 46ff, 128, 158, 170
Costs
   capital, 19, 69ff, 99ff, 132, 146
   commodity, 35
   disposal, 31ff, 138, 196n
   fuel, 100
   labour, 67ff, 99, 135ff, 149ff
   loading/unloading, 28, 100
   maintenance, 134
   mileage, 100, 106
   production, 47, 75, 89
   transshipment, 28
   transport, 35, 77ff, 89, 99ff, 138, 150,
     159, 177
   variable, 65, 97ff, 136, 150

Dantzig, G. B., 197n
Dasgupta, P. S., 197n
Deakin, B. M., 77, 161
Dean, R. M., 197n
Deaton, A., 75
Decentralised planning, 39, 172
Delivered price, 165
Demand,
   cement, 80, 146
   curve, 165ff
   elastic, 164, 165
   final product, 33
   growth and location, 154
   inelastic, 27, 98, 129, 144, 201n

and location, 89, 93, 110, 112ff, 120,
   121, 129, 175
Diseconomies,
   of concentration, 95ff, 154, 176
   of scale, 50, 52, 184
Diwan, R. K., 197n
Doig, A. G., 59
Dorfman, R., 197n
Dunford, M., 81

Eaton, B. C., 12, 201n
Economies of scale, 25, 40ff, 56ff, 132,
   147, 172, 198n
   definition, 42
   external, 5
   industrial location and, 6, 13ff, 25,
     88ff, 154
   internal, 5
   to production, 14, 50, 66, 106ff
   sources, 45ff, 135
Edge effects, 134, 139ff, 147
Elasticity
   arc, 95
   of cost function, 43ff, 89ff, 100, 129
   of demand, 165, 166, 177
   of employment with scale, 66, 198n
   point, 95
   of scale, 44, 69, 100, 173
   of sensitivity curve, 95ff, 109, 110
Ellman, M., 172
Elshafei, A. N., 197n
Entry
   free, 157
   sequential, 159
Exclusiveness, degree of, 62
Existing capacity *see also* green-field
     sites, 132, 138, 151

Farrell, M. J., 56
Fieldhouse, M., 56
Fixed costs, 136ff
Freight absorption, 165

Gass, S. I., 197n
Gee, J. M. A., 16, 158

Getis, A., 10
Gomory, R. E., 53
Graph
    branches in, 20, 27 ff, 130
    market area as, 20, 27 ff, 78 ff, 130
    nodes in, 20, 27, 78 ff
    theory, 196 n
Green-field sites, 19, 40, 127, 129, 134,
    159
Greenhut, J., 165
Greenhut, M. L., 13, 165
Griliches, Z., 44, 69
Guigou, J.-L., 196 n

Haldi, J., 197 n
Hadley, G., 196 n, 197 n
Heal, G. M., 172, 196 n, 197 n
Hoover, E. M., 6, 164
Hotelling, H., 11, 157

Imputed values see also shadow prices,
    37 ff, 53
Increasing returns see economies of scale
Industrial location
    comparison, actual and optimal, 23 ff,
        118 ff
    competitive, 7, 164
    and demand, 14, 89 ff, 166, 174
    degree of response, 24, 94 ff
    optimal, 88, 103 ff, 153, 162 ff
    rate of response, 23, 122, 123
    and time, 16, 25, 125, 176
    and transport costs, 38, 99 ff, 177
Infinite horizon, 140 ff
Integer constraints, 39, 52, 55, 58, 133
Intriligator, M. D., 37
Isard, W., 6, 13, 195 n
Isodapanes, 4
Isotims, 3

Johnston, J., 184
Joint production, 54 ff

Kendrick, D. A., 139, 142
Koopmans, T. C., 31, 39, 196 n
Kornai, J., 172
Kuhn-Tucker theorem, 37

Labour see also costs, 30, 32
    in cement production, 60 ff
Land, A. H., 59
Lea, A. C., 6
Linear programme, 36 ff, 90
Linear spline, 47, 75 ff, 97, 98, 115, 132,
    146
Lipsey, R., 12, 201 n
Location theory see also industrial location
    central place, 7 ff
    competitive, 157
    interdependence, 11 ff
    least cost, 2 ff, 157
Losch, A., 7 ff, 157

Manne, A. S., 14, 196 n, 197 n
Market area see also graph
    cement study, 78 ff, 145, 160
    as a lattice, 158
Materials index, 4, 195 n
Mill pricing, 201 n
Minimum efficient scale, 69, 89, 147
    and competition, 177
    and time, 155, 176
Mixed integer programme, 53, 59 ff, 90,
    110, 112, 127 ff
MPCODE, 59

Net output, 32, 34, 182
Network see graph
Nijkamp, P., 196 n, 198 n
Nodes see graph
Norman, G., 165, 201 n

Oligopoly see also location theory
    spatial, 12 ff

Paelinck, J. H., 198n
Parr, J. B., 196n
Planning,
    horizon, 137, 139ff, 144, 152
    models, 21ff, 172
Powell, S., 59
Pratten, C. F., 69, 73, 89, 172, 197n
Pricing policy see spatial pricing policy
Production
    sites, 85ff, 128, 158
    unit, 41ff
Profit
    maximisation, 159
    minimum, 160, 162
    supernormal, 160, 201n
Programming model, 36ff

Quasi production activity, 48, 77, 90, 93ff,
    158

Robinson, E. A. G., 197n
Rothschild, R., 12, 158
Ringstad, V., 44, 69

Samuelson, P., 197n
Scale see also economies of scale
    dimensions, 42, 134, 142
    factor, 44
    of production unit, 42
Scherer, F. M., 6, 13, 177, 197n
Sensitivity analysis, 24, 94ff, 101ff, 110ff,
    174
Seward, T., 77
Shadow prices see also imputed values, 172
Silberston, A., 42, 44

Simplex method, 58
Singer, H. W., 164
Smithies, A. F., 11ff
Solow, R. M., 197n
Spatial pricing policy, 159, 164ff
Specialisation, degree of, 62
Stability, 160
Starrett, D. A., 11
Storage, 129, 130, 138
Sub-market, 112, 127, 145

Technology see also cement, 19, 40
    matrices, 32
Tonne miles, 94ff
Towns, 29, 79ff
Transshipment, 28
Transport see also costs
    constraints, 34
    cost minimisation, 2ff, 93, 177
    mode, 28, 114
    network, 79, 112

Uniform pricing, 201n

Value added, 182
Vietorisz, T., 14, 196n, 197n
Vintage of capital, 131, 134ff, 141

Wage rate, 68, 149
Waste see also commodity, 31
Weber, A., 2ff, 175
White, C. H., 59
Witcomb, D., 197n